The PUMA

The PUMA
Legendary Lion of the Americas

Jim Bob Tinsley

Texas
Western
Press

The University of Texas at El Paso

Jim Bob Tinsley is a hunter —
who
Knows when, where, how, and what
to do.
At tyin' knots in cougars'
tails,
His spizzerinctum never
fails.
An' if you are inclined to
doubt it,
Just ask the undersigned
about it...

S. Omar Barker and Elsa Barker,
former presidents of the
Western Writers of America.

The author with a 140-pound "blue" lion he killed in June
1964 in the Rocky Mountains north of Craig, Colorado.

Copyright © 1987
Texas Western Press
The University of Texas at El Paso
El Paso, Texas 79968-0633

First Edition
Library of Congress Catalog Card No. 86-051648
ISBN 0-87404-203-8

To the memory of Aunt Oam, Zane Grey, Ernest Thompson Seton, and Theodore Roosevelt, who planted the seed, and to Dottie, who nourished its growth.

This is believed to be the largest and last catamount killed in Vermont, near Barnard, 24 November 1881 by Alexander Crowell. It weighed 182 pounds and the overall length was 7 feet 6 inches. (Reprinted, by permission, from John Spargo, The Catamount in Vermont, *1950)*

*White puma (*Weisse puma*) acquired by the Cologne Zoo in 1964. The animal died of tuberculosis in 1967. (Courtesy Werner Strangenberg)*

U.S. Commemorative stamp in the American Wildlife Series, 1987

Contents

Puma on the banks of the Rupununi River in southern Guyana. The three-year-old specimen shows slight retention of youth-like spots. (Courtesy Stanley E. Brock)

Foreword

by
David M. Newell,
former editor-in-chief,
Field & Stream
(1898-1986)

The woods have always been full of "outdoor authorities," and in these days of tremendously increased interest in the outdoors and its wild creatures, there is an authority behind every tree, or so it seems. Unfortunately, many of these writers are men of limited experience and careless observation — the sort whom Theodore Roosevelt would have designated as "nature fakers."

It is, therefore, a source of real pleasure and satisfaction to find an author who has taken the time and effort to know whereof he speaks — through painstaking research into the experience of others and the actual experiencing himself. In doing this book on the most widely distributed, yet least understood of our American cats, the mountain lion, puma, cougar, panther, or whatever you prefer to call him, Jim Bob Tinsley has shown tremendous interest in his subject. This is understandable when we recognize the fact that here is the most mysterious of our wild creatures — an animal about which there are more myths and superstitions than we can name.

Nobody can know all there is to know about any subject, especially the life cycle and habits of a wild animal. But Tinsley comes close. This is a book I would be proud to have written about an animal I have hunted and studied for forty years — from Vancouver Island to the *pantanal* of Matto Grosso. I admire the author and I recommend this book.

Ben V. Lilly, master lion hunter, on a hunt in the Big Thicket of Texas in December 1906. (Reprinted, by permission, from Dobie, The Ben Lilly Legend, *1950)*

Introduction

The first panther story I ever heard was told to me by "Aunt Oam" Harkins, when I was a youngster in the mountains of western North Carolina. Aunt Oam was born Naomi Osteen on the headwaters of Davidson River below Johns Rock in 1845, a daughter of pioneer Luke Osteen.

Aunt Oam recalled that when she was a small girl, a panther was attracted to their home by the cries of her baby sister. The panther ascended to the roof of the house and moved back and forth for a long time, occasionally emitting its own cry.

Aunt Oam was a hardy mountain woman who lived to be ninety-nine years old. If a car came along the dirt road by her small home at Catheys Creek during her later life, she would throw rocks or clods of dirt at it.

As a young man, I also was enthralled by the writings of Zane Grey, Ernest Thompson Seton, and Theodore Roosevelt.

It has been forty years since the first printing of *The Puma: Mysterious American Cat,* by Stanley P. Young and Edward A. Goldman, the only definitive book on the animal. Much relevant material has been written and important research projects have been done since then.

Since the Young and Goldman book in 1946, two new existing and one extinct subspecies have been named, i.e., *F.c. punensis* from northern Chile, *F.c. hudsoni* from the Argentine pampas, and *F.c. schorgeri* from the upper Mississippi River valley.

I have included in this study many colorful legends about the animal as opposed to the completely scientific study by Young and Goldman. Differences in fact and fiction are pointed out in this volume when they conflict with one another.

The present volume contains a chapter on the black puma, one of the rarest cats in the world. I saw a photograph of a specimen reproduced in *Revista Conservadora* in 1963. Four years later, through the American Embassy

Mountain lion looking over a deer herd in the San Luis Valley, Colorado, in 1965. (Courtesy Homer Brown)

staffs in both Managua, Nicaragua, and San Jose, Costa Rica, I was able to obtain a photograph of the rare animal. To my knowledge, it is the only one ever reproduced in the United States.

The mysterious onza of northern Mexico is the subject of another story. Although not confirmed at present by scientists, it would be hard to convince Mexicans who coexist that the animal is not real.

No story of the puma would be complete without recognizing the fact that it can and does kill humans on occasion. Most writings on the animal overlook this, either intentionally or by design, or else the observers are unsure that it happens. Conservation measures are better promoted by bearing useful facts and giving plausible reasons.

It is not possible for me to acknowledge all the people who helped me over the last thirty or thirty-five years in gathering material on the puma. I thank them all nevertheless. Unfortunately, two of my longtime friends, S. Omar Barker and Dave Newell, died while the manuscript was in its final stages. Both of these former "cougar chasers" added to this volume with their introductory remarks as well as their counsel.

1
A New Lease on Life

An enigma of the American wilderness is that the puma exists today at all. In spite of a reckless extermination policy against it as an unwanted varmint, the alteration of its habitats, a depletion of its natural foods, and a widespread hunting pressure for sport, this magnificent animal has miraculously survived over three centuries throughout the Americas. But its struggle to exist has been long, even in the United States where it has only recently begun to benefit from favorable public sentiment and the inauguration of laws that offer full or partial protection. At last, the puma is becoming recognized as a desirable part of the American wildlife scene.

Suggesting that ancient American Indians may have used some type of predator control directed at the puma is a rock inscription some ten miles below the mouth of Rio la Plata on the San Juan River in northwestern New Mexico. Etched in the rocks is a procession of animals, possibly intended to chronicle a migration of an ancient tribe with its herds and flocks. Depicted in the inscription are two long-tailed cats that resemble pumas in the act of entering traps.[1]

Pit-trapping along game trails was used in early America to capture undesirable predators including the puma. Large pitfalls were dug and covered with brush and litter, leaving a dirt column in the center where a live bait was secured. Generally, a lamb or other small domestic animal was used for bait and was made uncomfortable so that it would cry intermittently. As the predator lunged for the bait, its weight caused the pit covering to cave in, trapping the animal in the deep pit.

In Guyana box traps were used by early British settlers to capture the puma. In the mid-1840s, twenty to thirty pumas and jaguars were taken yearly by this method.[2]

The bounty system is old in the United States as well as in other parts of the Americas. Jesuit priests offered a bounty of one bull for each puma that was killed in Lower California in the late 1500s.[3]

◄ *Portrait of a New Mexico mountain lion. (Courtesy New Mexico Department of Game and Fish)*

As early as 1694, Connecticut offered a bounty of twenty shillings apiece for the killing of "cattamounts," the local name for the puma in the colony.[4]

In the early statutes of South Carolina is a 1695 law that requires any Indian, who was able to kill a deer, to kill a wolf, tiger [puma], bear, or two wildcats yearly. Those Indians in noncompliance suffered the humiliation of a public whipping as dictated in the following wording of the law:

> And if any Indian as aforesaid shall not bring into the receiver, one woolfes skinn, or one tigers skinn, or one beare skinn, or two catt skinns, as aforesaid, the casique or cheife of every nation, together with the assistance of his capitanes and those men which have before delivered to the receiver as before by this Act appoynted, is hereby required and impowered the Indian or Indians soe neglecting to bring to Charlestowne some tyme before the Twenty-fifth day of December, one thousand six hundred and ninety six, and so yearely forever, and the same there upon his bare back severely whipp in sight of the inhabittants of the saide towne, which whipping shall be instead of that skinn which otherwise the saide Indian ought to have given to the receiver aforesaid.

The unjust law was repealed in 1700, forbidding the punishment and providing a five shillings payment to Indians as an "incouragement" to kill beasts of prey.[5]

Massachusetts offered a reward of forty shillings for the animal in 1742 and increased the sum to four pounds in 1753. The payment of bounties continued to spread throughout the years until every state in the union except one eventually had a price on the head of the puma.[6]

Following a persistent plea from stockmen and sportsmen in the western United States, Congress appropriated money for predator control in 1915, and put the U.S. Biological Survey, now the U.S. Fish and Wildlife Service, in charge of exterminating undesirable animals. Professional hunters became salaried employees, thus eliminating some of the defects of the bounty system. Some of these hunters were already famous houndsmen. Others gained the

The author examines a cougar scratch beside an old logging road on Vancouver Island (1968).

reputation rapidly. Ben V. Lilly, Charles Jesse ("Buffalo") Jones, J.T. ("Uncle Jimmy") Owens, and their hounds were so skillful and untiring in their efforts that they are credited with killing upwards of one thousand pumas each.

State-employed hunters in California received a bounty in addition to their salaries at one time. Some counties and stockman associations increased the sum until hunters could receive as much as $629 for each lion.

In addition to hunting with hounds, some of the professionals became highly skilled in capturing pumas in steel traps. The animals were attracted with various animal scents or with oil of catnip diluted with pure petrolatum; the traps were placed near kills, scent stations, or on regular travel routes of the puma.

Poisons have been used mainly in the control of coyotes but have taken their toll of pumas. Earliest poisons included strychnine, but the more recent Compound 1080, or sodium fluoroacetate, has been more effective.

In 1899 the puma was hunted in the Yellowstone National Park by scouts of the federal government for fear that the predator would kill all of the mountain sheep in a very short time. Commenting on the regulation of predators in the park, artist Frederic Remington offered a frontier solution that shifted part of the blame and named another predator: "The *broncho* white man of the adjacent regions is the worst of all. If it were possible to have him killed it would be a good thing for the rest of the population of the United States. The panther, the bear, and the coyote can be excused, but the white man is a selfish brute who knows he is doing wrong."[7]

In the early 1900s, elk in the Yellowstone were "protected" from the puma by a campaign to eliminate the predator completely. By 1914 elk herds had increased in numbers far in excess of the carrying capacity of their range. A massive die-off occurred in 1919-20. Still suffering from the absence of natural predators, nearly five thousand elk had to be shot during the winter of 1961-62.[8]

In 1908 Uncle Jimmy Owens was sent to the Kaibab Forest game preserve on the North Rim of the Grand Canyon as a predator animal hunter. Uncle Jimmy had been a buffalo hunter, ranch foreman for Charles Goodnight in the Texas Panhandle, game keeper, and a warden in the Yellowstone. He chased the puma from rim to riffle in the Grand Canyon, and his job of killing the predator was so thorough that by 1919 deer had increased until they were beginning to consume more forage than the range could produce. In one meadow, seventeen hundred deer were counted in 1924. During the winters they died by the thousands due to disease and starvation. Finally the area was opened to hunters, and by 1930 the deer population had been greatly reduced. The complex problem was traced to the puma-deer relationship and is remembered today as one of the type cases of game mismanagement in which the value of one animal was stressed at the expense of another.[9]

In Santa Clara County, California, twenty-two pumas were once killed in a two-year span of time. Deer multiplied until their range was depleted with a resulting disease outbreak that caused a 60 percent loss of the herd.[10]

The major discussion at the annual conference of the Western Association of State Game and Fish Commissioners in 1951 was the need to make the puma bounty system more uniform from state to state. Representatives from ten of the westernmost states agreed that the animal indeed did sufficient damage to wildlife to warrant such a bounty system. Only one voted against it. Three states had no method of marking hides that were bountied. Two used ink and tattooing. Three required portions of the hide or skeleton. Three states perforated or cut the hide. It was discussed at the meeting that unscrupulous bounty hunters could cross state lines and collect more than one bounty for a single kill unless a uniform marking method was adopted. After the discussion, however, no action was taken on the matter.[11]

Within the next decade, the need for any bounty laws at all was being questioned. Evidence began to show that the bounty system was an ineffective way to control predation. Too often there had not been concentrated efforts against individual offenders but rather a wholesale destruction of the species. Efforts were made in accessible areas while outlying remote areas were often shunned. The bounty

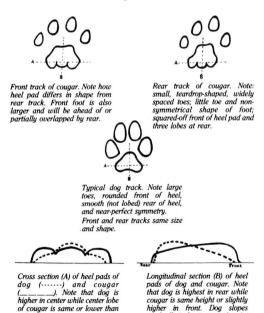

Front track of cougar. Note how heel pad differs in shape from rear track. Front foot is also larger and will be ahead of or partially overlapped by rear.

Rear track of cougar. Note: small, teardrop-shaped, widely spaced toes; little toe and non-symmetrical shape of foot; squared-off front of heel pad and three lobes at rear.

Typical dog track. Note large toes, rounded front of heel, smooth (not lobed) rear of heel, and near-perfect symmetry. Front and rear tracks same size and shape.

Cross section (A) of heel pads of dog (-------) and cougar (_____). Note that dog is higher in center while center lobe of cougar is same or lower than side lobes.

Longitudinal section (B) of heel pads of dog and cougar. Note that dog is highest in rear while cougar is same height or slightly higher in front. Dog slopes gradually in front; cougar's print is squared off.

(Reprinted, by permission, from Robert L. Downing and Virginia L. Fifield, "Differences between tracks of dogs and cougars," 1978)

system was abused by the bootlegging of skins or scalps from states that had no bounty into those that did. Another fraud was the releasing of captured females to maintain a breeding stock. The bounty system was expensive because it paid on animals killed accidentally or incidentally, and it placed the financial burden on the people who benefitted the least. Finally, the harvest of game animals in some states had been found to be about the same after bounties were discontinued as it was during the payment periods.

With the exception of Florida, the only political units in the United States and Canada that have recognized puma populations are the twelve far western states and the Canadian provinces of British Columbia and Alberta. The term "cougar states," used in a 1983 population estimate, are Washington, Oregon, Idaho, Montana, Wyoming, California, Nevada, Utah, Colorado, Arizona, New Mexico, and Texas.[12]

The bounty on the puma was discontinued in British Columbia in 1958 and in Alberta in 1963. Game animal status was granted to the animal by the latter province in 1969 and British Columbia did the same in 1970. It is now protected by game laws and regulations in both provinces.

Nevada is the only far western state that has never had a bounty on the puma, although a state control program was begun in the 1930s and expanded in 1949 when a full-time hunter was hired to help reduce predation on domestic livestock and deer.

New Mexico discontinued the bounty in 1923 and Wyoming followed in 1941, but the puma continued to be an unprotected predator in both states. In the remaining nine states and the two Canadian provinces, bounties were still being paid on the puma as late as 1958. It did not attain game status in any of the twelve states until 1965. Since then, a steady rise in the strictness of game regulations affecting the animal has occurred. Bounty laws in all of the states except one had been repealed by 1972.

State funds for the bounty on the puma in Arizona ended in 1970 and the animal was classified as a "big game" species a year later. An intense pressure on the puma population remains because of a provision in Arizona Re-

Cougar tracks, 5 1/2 inches across the pad, in Alberta, Canada. The 165-pound, 8-foot, 11-inch specimen was killed in February 1951 one mile from these tracks. Note the hind foot is placed partly on the print of the front foot. (Courtesy Ed Burton)

vised Statute 17-302 that allows livestock operators to pay bounties on the animal to avoid stock losses. This discretionary clause is often abused.

Texas is the only state with a viable puma population that has not either conferred game status to the animal or given it full protection. Officially, it is recognized as an unregulated predator. Large-scale predator control was dropped in 1955, and state control agents and private trappers have been used since then only on a limited basis. However, farmers and ranchers are allowed to destroy the animal when they believe its presence is not compatible with the raising of livestock. County judges also have the authority to establish bounties in their respective counties whenever the need for such action is deemed necessary.

Ironically, in the last twenty years the puma appears to be increasing in Texas, according to Floyd E. Potter, Jr., a wildlife biologist with the Texas Parks and Wildlife Department. Several estimates place the number statewide in the neighborhood of one thousand animals. Approximately seventy to eighty are taken annually by sportsmen, and others are destroyed as nuisance animals throughout the year.[13]

The puma now has full legal protection east of the Mississippi River, based on the Endangered Species Act of 1973, which supersedes all state statutes and regulations.[14]

Two subspecies of the puma once inhabited the eastern part of the United States. The Eastern cougar was distributed as far north as Maine, extended into southern Ontario and Quebec, and integrated southward with the Florida panther near the southern border of the two Carolinas. The latter subspecies may have ranged at one time to eastern Texas or western Louisiana, over the Lower Mississippi Valley, and east throughout Alabama, Georgia, and Florida.

In the fall of 1966, the Congress of the United States passed the Endangered Species Protection Act acknowledging a national responsibility to protect wildlife threatened with extinction. This first law directed the secretary of the Interior to publish a list of endangered native species and prohibited the killing or possessing of any of the rare animals, birds, and fishes on federal lands or waters.[15]

The Florida panther (*Felis concolor coryi*) was included in the first endangered list published in the *Federal Register* on 11 March 1967. Listed among extinct mammals that were once a part of eastern America was the Eastern cougar (*Felis concolor couguar*).[16]

In the amended list of rare and endangered wildlife, published after the Endangered Species Conservation Act of 1969, is the belief that the Eastern cougar may have been reestablished from Canadian relicts.[17]

The present operative statute is the expanded Endangered Species Act of 1973 which strengthened all previous laws and also provided federal funds for endangered species programs administered by states. For the first time it became unlawful to take endangered wildlife anywhere within the United States or its territorial waters. Take was defined as "pursue, hunt, shoot, capture, collect, kill, or attempt to pursue, hunt, shoot, capture, collect or kill."[18]

Formerly regarded as extinct, the Eastern cougar was placed on the endangered species list in 1973.[19]

Endangered status was recommended in 1976 for the Costa Rican puma (*Felis concolor costaricensis*), which inhabits Nicaragua, Costa Rica, and Panama.[20]

Florida, the first known habitat of the puma in North America, was the first state to grant it the right to live. Partial protection was given in 1950, wherein it could be hunted only during the open season for deer.[21] On 2 July 1958, the puma was removed from the native-game animal list and declared protected throughout the state.[22] Governor Bob Graham signed a bill on 19 March 1982, designating the Florida panther the official state animal after school children of the state had overwhelmingly voted it their first choice over the alligator and the manatee.[23]

In spite of its full legal protection in Florida, the state animal has a high mortality rate. High-speed highways, oil developments, and unrestricted use of panther habitats are continued threats to its existence. During an eighteen-month period in the early 1980s, three panthers, one of which was a female carrying four fetuses, were killed when hit by motor vehicles. Other such kills no doubt go undetected or unreported.[24]

To correct past environmental mistakes and hopefully reduce the carnage of the rare Florida panther on Alligator Alley, a fast-lane, cross-state highway in southern Florida, construction began in 1986 on a 76-mile, $383 million project that includes the building of 23 new underpasses and the modification of 13 existing bridges to allow the endangered animal to make safe crossings from one part of its bisected environment to another. Plans also call for the grading of land to correct the waterflow problem caused by the existing highway, once again permitting in this unique ecosystem its vital flow of shallow water southward from Lake Okeechobee to the Florida Everglades.

Joe Peebles, cattleman and former Florida state legislator from Glades County, recognizes the ecological value of the puma and is happy to coexist with the animal. Dr. O. Earle Frye, then director of the Florida Game and Fresh Water Fish Commission, appreciated the verbal reaction of the cattleman, who told him that a panther killed a calf on his ranch: "He said there weren't too many panthers left, he liked to see them around, the cat had a right to make a living too, and that he didn't care if it got a calf once in a while."[25]

The puma has aesthetic and ecological values that far exceed the damage it does. It deserves to be looking ahead to a secure future instead of forever looking back to find something dogging its tracks. Up to now, it has almost been hounded to death.

2
Still a Puma by Any Name

Felis concolor, the puma, or lion of the Americas, is unique for its multiplicity of English names, probably having more than any other native animal. One researcher lists forty-two English names for the animal that have come to his attention.[1] Nineteen are recorded by another writer for the one animal, which he says would lead persons to believe that America once teemed with creatures now extinct.[2] It is entered in dictionaries under more names than any other animal in the United States, and the five or six commonly used names are believed by many to represent different animals.

The earliest Portuguese, Spanish, French, Dutch, and English plunged into the American wilderness, bent on exploring, claiming, sometimes pillaging, and finally settling. The names of animals, hitherto unknown to the outside world, as recorded in the writings of these explorers and travelers, were misapplications, corruptions, or barbarizations. Pioneer semantics followed the same pattern of transferring or giving wider currency to provincial names, leading to the faulty naming of such animals in America as the buffalo, jack rabbit, prairie dog, antelope, elk, and mountain goat. And indeed, the people encountered in the new land were erroneously called Indians.

Columbus applied the name "lion" to the large, unicolored American cat in 1502, because it resembled a young lioness of the Old World in shape and tint.[3] No other name appeared in literature until 1609, when Garcilasso de la Vega, the Inca, recorded the name *puma* for the beast. He identified it, however, as a "lion."[4] From earliest times in America the animal has been called *león* or *león americano* by the Spanish, and is so called by them almost universally to this day.

Some early explorers in America assumed that the lions they encountered were females because of an absence of mane and tufted tail and that the maned males were too elusive to be seen. Based on information from Indians, an early resident of the Dutch colony wrote that lions were found far to the southwest of New

◄*Closeup of an angry young Vancouver Island cougar.*

Colorado mountain lion. (Courtesy Don Domenick, Colorado Game, Fish, and Parks Department)

Netherlands in very high mountains and that the males were too active and fierce to be taken, although he had seen the skins of what he called female lions.[5]

French naturalist Georges Frédéric Cuvier is quoted in the Griffin synopsis: "The name by which it is most generally known is that of the American lion; so called from a distant similarity it bears to the Lion of the old world, in the uniformity of colour."[6] Although improperly applied, the name leaves little doubt as to the identity of the animal anywhere. The solid color and unadornment of mane and tufted tail explains a later reference to the animal as the "plain lion."[7]

In the southwestern United States and in the Rocky Mountain region, the American lion is widely known simply as the lion or mountain lion. It has been called the California lion and Mexican lion in obvious areas. Members of the 1540 Coronado expedition in the Southwest re-

ferred to it as the "gray lion."[8] The name "silver lion" was recorded in 1876 and is still used in Brazil.[9] Another writer later stated: "Carnivora are not rare in the Sertão (backlands); above all, the 'Silver Lion' or Puma, the Brazilian onça or ounce."[10] The Portuguese in Brazil call the animal *leao* ["lion"], *onça vermelha* ["red ounce"],[11] and *onça parda* ["brown ounce"].[12] It is the *leon bayo* ["bay lion"] in Venezuela and Colombia because of its reddish-brown coat. The same coloration is responsible for the name "red lion" from Guatemala and Belize.[13]

American zoologist William T. Hornaday added still another appellative: "Let me give him one more name, and call him the Story Lion! Owing to his size, agility, alleged fierceness, and very wide geographical distribution, he is the story-teller's animal *par excellence*."[14]

William Byrd, Virginia planter and surveyor, wrote that the Spanish complimented the puma

8

with the name leopard.[15] More recently, an American sportsman says, "In many localities in Mexico until quite recently, the puma was known as *leopardo* (leopard)."[16]

Many early travelers indiscriminately ascribed the name tiger to all spotted felines. French naturalist Comte de Buffon says the error began in Europe and was transported to America where it was doubly augmented.[17] In time the name has been falsely applied to all native American wild cats. The jaguar is still called the *tigre* by Spanish Americans, and the name still survives, sometimes in a modified form, to denominate the American lion in widely scattered areas.

The name *tyger* was used for the American lion in the Carolinas as early as 1680.[18] *Tigre* was common for the animal in the vast Louisiana country. One traveler, describing a trip into the inland parts of South America, wrote in 1747: "The *tygers* I have seen in *America*, and which are very common in all the hot woody countries, have not seem'd to fall short, either in size or beauty, of those of Africa: There is one sort of them, whose skin is only brown, without being spotted."[19] This probably led to the brown tiger of Thomas Pennant,[20] "the father of British natural history," and later writers. The antiquated spelling is retained in the Tyger River system of the South Carolina upcountry, where local tradition perpetuates the story that a "tyger" was victorious in an encounter with a bear on the banks of the river in early days.[21]

Different color phases were important in early identification of the American lion and led to a number of book names. The "gray tiger" was recorded in 1744 from the Iroquois country where the writer found "tigers of a grayish colour, but not spotted. They have a long tail, and hunt the porcupine."[22] It is still called the "red tiger" (*tigre rouge*) in parts of South America owing to its uniform redness of color. The "black tiger" of Pennant was for a different color phase or a different animal altogether.[23] Another writer explains the name "deer tiger," used in Guyana, which surprisingly enough does not signify predator activity, but rather "On account of its resemblance to the deer in colour, the puma frequently passes locally under the name Deer Tiger, just as the black variety of jaguar is known as the Maipuri Tiger."[24] Indians of Guyana say that the deer tiger imitates the bleating of the forest deer so well that men as well as deer are deceived by it, thereby another possible reason for the name.

In 1771 "les Tigres & les Lions Americains" were less numerous than those of Africa and Asia, and a species of tiger in Canada, i.e., *Cougouar*, was given the name *Tigre poltron* ["poltroon tiger"] with propriety, because it was known to live as peacefully as a dog with a keeper of wild beasts.[25]

"The Deserted Village," an Oliver Goldsmith poem published in 1770, sang of the wild beauty of the Altamaha River in southeast Georgia "Where crouching tigers wait their hapless prey."[26] The zoogeographical knowledge of Goldsmith was not as faulty as some critics have supposed because the animal was almost invariably spoken of as the "tiger" in the Okefenokee Swamp region lying astride the Georgia-Florida line.[27] The beast was also known by the same name in Florida during the Seminole Wars.[28] A number of old-timers in Florida still call a tiger what most Floridians today know as the panther. "Mountain tiger" was recorded in 1838 for the animal in the early Ohio country.[29]

The name cougar is derived from the Guaraní language. German geographer Georg Marcgrave briefly described the American lion from Brazil in 1648 under the name *Cuguacuarana*.[30] Ten years later, the name was shortened to *Cuguacuara*.[31] The present form of the ancient name, however, is the modification of one man. Comte de Buffon recognized that the lion of the Americas should not be confounded with the genuine lions of Africa and Asia, differing in stature, color, form of head, length of tail, want of mane, and in manner and disposition. He gave it the name *Couguar* with the following explanation: "The couguar, which we have contracted from the Brazilian name *caguacu ara*, pronounced *cougouacouare*, is called the *red tiger* in Guiana." He added that the beast in no way resembled the true tiger and differed greatly from the panther because of a red color devoid of spots.[32]

The meaning of the word *cuguacuarana* is uncertain, but it has been related to *sassúaràna* ("false deer"), the Tupi name for the same animal of the lower Amazon basin, so called because of the deceptive color superficially resembling the forest deer. Marcgrave was said to have incorrectly transcribed *sassúaràna* to *cuguacuarana;* hence the name *cougouar* employed by French zoologists.[33]

American ornithologist Elliott Coues wrote that the original form of the name cougar was thought to have been bestowed because of a fanciful resemblance of the word to a common cry of the animal.[34] Another writer says the mournful note of the animal resounding throughout the solitudes of the Arizona desert sounded appropriate to the native name cougar as pronounced in Spanish.[35]

Cougar is a recognized name almost anywhere and is most commonly used in Canada and the Pacific Northwest. Theodore Roosevelt, in his role as a naturalist, offered the following discourse on its adoption: "No American beast has been the subject of so much loose writing or of such wild fables as the cougar. Even its name is unsettled. In the Eastern States it is usually called panther or painter; in the Western States, mountain lion, or toward the South, Mexican lion. The Spanish-speaking people call it simply lion. It is, however, sometimes called cougar in the West and Southwest of our country, and in South America, puma. As it is desirable where possible not to use a name that is misleading and is already appropriated to some entirely different animal, it is best to call it cougar."[36]

Panther, derived from the Greek *panthēr,* was originally another name for the leopard, the largest spotted cat of the Old World. Today it is still used in that reference, but more generally applied to the black leopard, which is not a distinct species but a conspicuous example of melanism that is quite common in certain areas or climates. Panther is also used as a general name for any wild feline with a uniform color. A few modern zoologists prefer *Panthera* over *Felis* as the generic name for all cats that roar. The Anglicized panther was extended to the original English colonies in America by early settlers and assigned to the American lion,

where the animal quickly became the source of storied fables and tales the same as its namesake. Some recognized the faultiness of the transfer and modified the name. One early French traveler called it the "red panther."[37] James Copen ("Grizzly") Adams, hunter extraordinary, spoke of the famous "purple panther" of the Pacific Northwest.[38] "Florida panther" is firmly established as the common name in the peninsula state.

William Penn listed the panther among the natural creatures of Penn's woods that could be used for skin or fur profit.[39] One Pennsylvania writer questioned the use of the name for the animal: "William Penn called it panther — why, cannot be imagined; it is colored very differently from the *panthere* of Northern Africa which he probably had in mind. The backwoodsmen called it *painter.*" The writer added that Germans in Pennsylvania at one time called it the "Bender."[40]

In 1705 the panther was recorded in Virginia by Robert Beverly, a colonist.[41] John Lawson described the panther from Carolina in 1709, where he said it was known as the "tyger."[42] The early American naturalist, William Bartram, whose travels carried him throughout most of the Eastern Seaboard, said this about the local names for the animal: "This creature is called in Pennsylvania and the northern states, panther; but in Carolina and the southern states, is called tyger."[43]

Panther usually became "painter" in the phraseology of the Anglo-American hunters, fur traders, and cowboys. Novels, stories, and poems of American frontier life have given permanence to the substandard variant. American novelist James Fenimore Cooper called the animal a panther in his tales of Leatherstocking and the Allegheny frontier. But in the backwoods dialect that Cooper knew firsthand, the less formal corruption was typical. A part of one dialogue reads: "I say, Mister Oliver, we'd like to have had a bad job of that panther, or painter's work — some calls it one, and some calls it t'other — but I know little of the beast, seeing that it is not of British growth."[44] In a setting among the poor whites of the mountains of the central South, a James Whitcomb Riley verse warned that cattle should be watched during the darkest nights because of "*painters* prowlin' 'bout."[45]

Perhaps more colloquial than illiterate is the "painther" of the Balsam Range of North Carolina mountains as recorded by William Gilmore Simms, writer of Southern border romances.[46]

In addition to panther and the debased painter or panter, Yankee hunters called this greatly feared animal a catamount, as well as *carcajou* or *quinquajou*. The latter two were applied by French traveler Pierre Francois Xavier de Charlevoix in 1744,[47] but both are mistakes in identity, for they are French-Canadian for the wolverine. Catamount remains the popular name in New England for the American lion, although there and elsewhere it has been applied to various other members of the cat family. The statement made in 1794 by Samuel Williams, the first historian of Vermont, however, leaves little doubt as to the identity of the animal he had in mind: "The CATAMOUNT, seems to be the same animal which the ancients called Lynx, and which is known in Siberia, by the name of Ounce. In the form of its body, it most resembles the common cat, but is of a much larger size. It is generally of a yellowish grey colour, bordering upon a red or sandy; and is larger than our largest dogs."[48] The catamount has become a symbol of the state of Vermont and prominent in its folklore, despite the apparent rarity of the animal at any time throughout the history of the state.

The name catamount is an acronym for cat-of-the-mountain and is synonymous with the Spanish *gato-monte* or *catus montainus*. "Cattermount" has been transcribed in the Yankee diction of the time.[49] The name catamount will survive probably, if only in New England and in American literature. Evidence of this is the following passage from a song written by Oliver Wendell Holmes for the centennial celebration at Harvard College in 1836:

When the Puritans came over
  Our hills and swamps to clear
The woods were full of catamounts,
  And Indians red as deer.[50]

Catawampus, an alternate of catamount, was quite common with frontier folks when they spoke of the fierce animal or in reference to any wild imaginary beast. Old-time cowboys had their own mythical animal of similar ancestry which they called the "wouser." This dreaded folktale villain was accorded any physical appearance or predator habit suitable to the conversation or whims of the talebearer. It usually had hydrophobia and was made a subspecies of the bear or the mountain lion.[51]

In early references the American lion was often called simply a cat, wild cat, big cat, or the less conventional king-cat. In certain parts of South America, it is still called the pampas cat. A villainous assortment of regionalisms arose due to the criminal instincts of the animal, expressed as horse thief, deer killer, varmint, mountain devil, mountain demon, and mountain screamer. Folk names in Florida include swamp devil, swamp screamer, night screamer, white lion, swamp lion, southern panther, southern lion, tall grass creeper, slough walker, night crier, and swamp crier.[52] In the Canadian Northwest, the alias sneak-cat is recurrent. Ghost walker is said to be an apt name for the animal in the Selkirk Mountains of British Columbia.[53]

In Eastern Canada, backwoods settlers referred to the dangerous American lion as the Indian devil.[54] From this came the dialectal Injun devil. The name may be derived from the Penobscot *lunxus*, recorded from Maine by Henry David Thoreau.[55] A probable variant is the name used by William Williamson, early Maine historian, who said that the Indian name in Maine for the "Cattamount" was *lunkson*, or "evil devil."[56]

Converseley, the so-called gentle disposition of the animal toward man in Argentina inspired the gauchos of the pampas to give it the appellative *amigo del cristiano* ["friend of the Christians"]. Justifications were based on the passivity of the animal in the presence of man, its curious habit of following man, and the almost uncanny anecdotes of its protectiveness of man on occasion.[57]

The lion of the Americas was a hunter god of the Zuñi Indians of New Mexico and Arizona. They called it Long Tail. Other prey gods of theirs were known by equally descriptive names. The bear was known as Clumsy Foot;

the badger, Black Mark Face; the wolf, Hang Tail; and the eagle, White Cap.[58]

The Mandan tribe, a division of the Sioux nation almost completely destroyed by smallpox in 1837, called the American lion *shunta-haschka*, literally the "long tail."[59] The *pi-tawl* of the Malecite Indians of the St. Johns River in New Brunswick also means "the long-tailed one."[60] Aptly applied to the bearer of the longest cat tail in America, the name Long Tail has been popular with a number of writers in the southwesten part of the United States because it is fitting, poetic, and helps to avoid repetition. New Mexico hunter-writer Elliott Barker subtitled his authoritative book on hunting experiences *A Year on the Trail of the Longtails*.[61]

The related name of an Indian tribe in Pennsylvania has an interesting derivation: "The Erie tribe who were blotted out by the Iroquois in 1656 were called the Yenresh, or 'the long tailed,' which was Gallicised into 'Eri,' hence Erie, 'the place of the panther.' The French called the Erie, 'Nation du Chat,' or Cat Nation, which was simply a translation of Yenresh, the name of the panther."[62]

In research on the panther among the Indians of the southeastern United States, is the following on their names for the animal: "He was Klandaghi, lord of the forest [to the Cherokees]. . . . To the Creeks he was Katalgar, greatest of wild hunters, and Creek boys slept on panther skins to absorb his unrivaled skill in woodcraft. Koe-Ishto, or Ko-Icto, the Cat of God, the brave and warlike Chickasaws called him."[63]

Indian names for the puma in the United States include:

Muskogee	*catsa*
Miccosukee	*coo-ot-cha-bee*
Cherokee	*tlv-da-tsi*
Ojibwa	*mischipischu,* *mischipichin,* or *mishi-biji*
Dakota and Ogallala Sioux	*inmu-tanka* or *igmu-tank-a*
Mandan	*shunta-han-ska,* *schunta-haschka,* or *schunta-haschla*
Gosiute	*toyaduko*
Hidatsa	*itupa-ichtia*
Minnetaree	*ihtupah-aehati* or *ihtuphu-achati*
Arikara	*wachtas*
Taos	*tham-mena* or *tham-menka*
Pueblo Indians of New Mexico	*K'eres*
Klamath	*dos-lotch*
Chinook	*le-lu*
Nisqualli	*swo-wah*
Piute	*to-qua-to-hoo-oo*
Osage	*ingronga*
Omaha	*ingronga-sinda*
Santee Sioux	*mnaza*
Pinal Apache	*uto-itcho, ntu-itchu, ndu-tchu,* or *nto-i-tcho*
Apache	*yutin*
Shoshone	*loupang* and *tokvitc*

Indians in the Mackenzie District of northern Canada seldom saw the cougar around the end of the nineteenth century but occasionally observed their tracks. Those that visited Fort Liard called the animal *e-wed-sie*.[64]

In Southern California, the Cahuilla Indians of the Coachella Valley and the San Jacinto and Santa Rosa mountains call the mountain lion *tu'kwit*, or the synonym *iswit*. Older members of the tribe say the terms refer also to the wolf, or in fact any strange animal.[65] In Arizona and New Mexico, Zuñi Indians carried fetishes of the mountain lion as a part of their curious prey-god theogony and were said to refer to the animal as the Father of Game.[66]

Francois Javier Clavijero, a Mexican historian and missionary, recorded the California lion of the Cochimí Indians of Lower California as *chimbiká* in 1789: "The *Chimbiká* is as large as a fat mastiff, and is protected by very strong claws; it has the same color as the African lion but is without a mane."[67]

Zoologist Hans Gadow wrote in 1908: "The Axtec name of the puma, the *Felis concolor*, is 'miztli' = the killer."[68] Professor C.S. Rafinesque states that the name is originally from the language of the Miztecas, or Mixtecas, a fierce nation of the central plateau of Mexico who were never subdued by the Aztecs. His interesting note on the derivation of the name of the tribe sheds some light on the origin of *miztli*: "Their name has been spelt Mixtecas, Mictec, Mixos, Migues, &c. All these names, leaving off the *tecas* which means people, imply Lion or rather Cauguar, an animal of the tiger genus, which was an emblem or progenitor of the nation (*Miz* tiger genus in Azteca)."[69]

The Mayan name *ah coh* has been registered for the animal from Guatemala and Honduras.[70] The spelling has also been written as *cabcoh* and interpreted as having reference to the red coloration of the beast.

Deer tiger, the colonists' name for the puma in Guyana, has been taken from a number of Indian names for the animal. Missionary W.H. Brett recorded the Arawak name *kwiarra-aruá-te* [deer tiger], stating that all cats, except the domestic variety, were "tigers" in the patois of the river people.[71] The Indians of Guyana recognized two species of the puma: *wawula arowa* [deer tiger] of the Arawaks and *saosoaranna*, a variety restricted to the open savannahs of the Orinoco River.[72] The Wapishana Indians of southern Guyana also distinguish between the two pumas by giving them separate names. The red variety is *crushara-din* [deer cat], owing to its similarity in color to the red brocket deer (*crush-ara*) of the forests. The fawn phase is called *aaro-din* because of a likeness in color to the whitetail deer (*aaro*) of the open savannahs.[73]

The ancient name *güazúará* was used by the Guaraní Indians of Paraguay and applied to both the puma and the jaguar. Others called the puma *yagüá-pitá* [red jaguar] and *yagüatí* [white jaguar].[74] The first two names were later transcribed as *guasuara* and *yaguá-pithá*.[75] According to another source, *yagua* originally signified a dog, or big dog.[76] The early Creoles in Paraguay called the yellow-red puma *yagua-pyta* [red dog].[77]

The tall Tehuelche Indians of Patagonia, noted for their hunting prowess, refer to the puma as the *gol* or *góol*. The name *haina* is used by the Puelche, a people of the Argentine pampas.[78] Based on correspondence with Angel Cabrera, of the Museo de la Plata in Argentina, one puma researcher wrote that the Puelche also used *goolen* and *chaur* for the adult puma and *cechine* for the kitten. Cabrera also supplied the name *essavagash*, used for the puma by the Mocovi of the Mato Grosso.[79] The native name for the animal in the Argentine province of Salta is *aracho*.[80]

Pagi and *trapial* are Araucanian, the language of a tribe of central Chile. *Pagi* was first recorded in 1782.[81] Variants are *paggi*, *paghi*, *pagui*, and *pangui*. In recent times, however, *puma* has become generally used throughout Chile, as indeed it has in all parts of South America.

The name puma is Aymaran and Quechuan, according to R.P. Rafael Housse of the Academia Chilena de Ciencias Naturales.[82] Attempts have been made to standardize it as the common name and some zoologists accept *Puma* as the scientific name for the genus or subgenus. This first recorded native American name in its original form is widely accepted throughout the world, although it is seldom used in North America other than by naturalists. A more general adoption seems to be the name cougar. Both puma and cougar are unmistakable, with the former unaltered from the native pronunciation and original Spanish spelling. However, because of the wide distribution and scarcity of the legendary animal, many local common names have become deeply ingrained in the folklore and traditions of cultures throughout the Western Hemisphere, making a basic name with general consent improbable. Regional names are the only known ones in many areas. Most nontechnical writers today use a variety of names interchangeably for the animal. No doubt it is destined to remain the cat of many names.

3
Description

The puma is the only large, unspotted, native American cat, the second largest plain-colored cat in the world, and the fourth largest of all cats. In America it is second in size only to the jaguar, but its longer legs, proportionately smaller head, and longer tail sometimes give it the appearance of being larger. The puma is easily distinguished from other American cats by its large size and a coloration that has little marking, except in the very young.

Although the puma is widely known as the American lion, it resembles its Old World namesake mainly in color only. In shape it is much more like the Afro-Asian leopard, which it slightly exceeds in size. In the sophisticated humor of Ogden Nash is the simile:

The panther is like a leopard,
Except it hasn't been peppered.[1]

The puma had already assumed a legendary role in American folklore by 1741, when the *Boston Weekly News-Letter* described it under the name "Cattamount" as a mixture of everything that was fierce and savage: "It has a Tail like a Lyon, its Legs are like a Bears, its Claws like an Eagle, it's Eyes like a Tyger."[2] Little wonder the early settlers feared the beast as the living embodiment of terror.

Linnaeus gave the puma its scientific name in 1771, with a brief note on its distinctive differences from the other members of the cat family: "Concolor FELIS tail long, body solid tawny. Cat reddish yellow, chin and under belly white."[3]

The maximum size of adult pumas has been discussed and debated since colonial times. Reports of specimens up to twelve feet in length and weighing as much as five hundred pounds have not been accompanied by documented evidence. Tales of these huge animals have grown, as have the subjects, from one story teller to another. The early Eastern press only added to the legends of oversized pumas. In 1874 the *Illustrated Police News, Law Courts & Weekly Record* of Boston, Massachusetts, re-

◄ *Head of the young mountain lion showing the vertical stripes over the eyes. (© Walt Disney Productions, reprinted by permission)*

ported that exceedingly vigorous panthers thirteen feet long offered sport for hunters in Texas.[4]

Although the North American hunting records on the size of pumas, kept by the Boone and Crockett Club, are based on a mathematical formula of skull measurements, the record applications do contain length and weight data. The North American record therefore would not necessarily be the longest or the heaviest. The longest "cougar" to date in the Boone and Crockett Club files is a male, killed in Alberta, Canada, in 1935, that measured 112 inches, or 9 feet 4 inches in total length.

The heaviest documented North American specimen is one from Arizona, killed in 1917, that was certified to the U.S. Biological Survey in Phoenix, at 276 pounds with intestines removed. The animal was taken by government predator hunter J.R. Patterson near Kirkland and is not a part of the records of the Boone and Crockett Club. Longer and heavier pumas are said to have been taken in certain parts of South America, but unfortunately most of the records are unverified or nonextant.

A writer for the American News Company, using the pen name "Rambler," records the largest Florida puma known. The animal was killed near the town of Eau Gallie in December 1873. It weighed over 240 pounds and was 9 feet 4 inches from end of snout to tip of tail. A rug made from the hide graced the parlor of the Argonauta Rowing Club for many years.[5]

Adult pumas will average 6 to 8 feet in length and weigh 100 to 200 pounds, with few reaching these maximum figures. The male is larger and more muscular than the female. She is slenderer in the neck and foreparts.

The fourteen pumas killed in Colorado by Theodore Roosevelt and party in 1901 had a length range from 4 feet 11 inches to 8 feet, and weights ranging from 47 pounds to 227 pounds. All but three of the kills were females and were the smallest taken. Females trapped in Arizona during 1941 and 1942 had weights in pounds that almost numerically equaled their lengths in inches. One specimen, showing signs of rearing, weighed 70 pounds and was 73 inches in total length. Seven other females showed similar approximating weight-length ratios.[6]

Leon T. Mott took a giant puma in the Gran Chaco of Paraguay in 1958, whose size he recorded at 9 feet 8 inches in length and 375

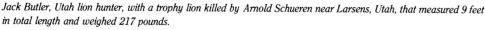

Jack Butler, Utah lion hunter, with a trophy lion killed by Arnold Schueren near Larsens, Utah, that measured 9 feet in total length and weighed 217 pounds.

16

pounds in weight.[7] Conversely, from the same frontier, Robert Eaton, an American rancher who owns vast estancias in the Gran Chaco and is an experienced hunter of many years, wrote to the author about a dwarf puma that inhabits parts of the country. "Out in the open grassland of the chaco, which usually has open forests, we find a type of small lion which lived pretty much on ostriches and small game. These seldom grow more than four feet from nose to the tip of the tail. I have killed lions of this size that had their tusks worn flat indicating great age. The coloring is the same as all American lions. I like to believe that this is a distinct species of the puma family that does not grow to any larger size. The suggestion that it is a case of undernourishment, which retards the growth, does not convince me."[8]

Some zoologists place all cats into two arbitrary groups, the Big Cats and the Small Cats. The so-called Big Cats are characterized by round pupils and a roaring voice as well as size. The Small Cats have in common the vertical oval pupils and the purr. The puma is undoubtedly a big cat by its size, but it has neither round pupils nor a roaring voice.

Other zoologists call all felines either the Great Cats, the Not-So-Great Cats, or the Lesser Cats. With reservation, Ivan T. Sanderson, American naturalist, placed the puma in the Not-So-Great Cats, those of an intermediate size and lacking the ability to roar, although he stated that those of the Andean region were known to make a pumping roar.[9] While zoologists disagree, hunters have little doubt that this fit and clever predator is a big cat.

Generally, the external appearance of all pumas is similar. Subspecies differ mainly in color or proportions in cranial structure.

The body of the puma is conspicuously thin and long with flat sides. Its massive hindquarters cause the body to stand an inch or two taller in the rear than at the shoulders. Shoulder height in the adult reaches up to two feet or over.

The long legs, long tail, and small body give the puma almost perfect muscular coordination and exceptional capabilities in running, jumping, and climbing. Its gait is smooth and flowing without the jerkiness of action associated with other quadrupeds. Stan Brock says "its agility, grace and poise are sheer poetry of motion."[10] Frank Dufresne, author-sportsman, says it is "as airy in its grace as a puff of campfire smoke."[11]

The loose skin of the puma is tough as leather. It has been compared to a coat of mail, the pliable armor of linked metal used by medieval knights for protection against the weapons of adversaries.[12] Theodore Roosevelt observed that during his hunting trips the dogs never did succeed in getting their teeth through the thick skins of the animals, and that when one was found to have battle scars it was generally accepted by experienced hunters that this was the result of fighting among themselves.[13]

The pelage of the puma is short, compact, and closely pressed to the skin except on the undersides. On the belly and the inner surfaces of the limbs, the hair is longer and has a tendency to be ruffled. The Florida variety has a distinctive whorl of hairs, similar to a cowlick, in the middorsal region of the back.

The plain color of the adult puma runs the spectrum of earthy colors from light to dark shades with a decided darkness running down the central line of the back and tail. Underparts are white or whitish. Individual hairs have somewhat darker tips that occasionally convey a deceptive hue. Forest dwellers, or those living in heavy cover, tend to have a darker color, while those of open country or canyon habitat are lighter. Early travelers used a multitude of adjectives to describe the colors of the puma: tawny, brown, red, rust, terra cotta, fallow, sallow, yellow, gold, gray, buff, cinnamon, russett, olive, chestnut, pink, orange, clay, hazel, white, silver, and black. Angel Cabrera used some forty-three color variations for the cats of Argentina.[14] Less technical observers are more general and tolerant of variations or intermediates. Two subspecies currently recognized in Argentina have a chief difference in the predominant color. One is commonly referred to as a reddish-fawn and the other a silver-gray. The same two color phases are common in the United States. Roosevelt described the general colors of his kills: "Some were slaty-gray as deer when in the so-called 'blue'; others, rufous, almost as bright as deer in the 'red'."[15] These two variations have led many to believe that the pelage varies with the season in the precise tint as that of the deer family, its favorite prey, hence, an aid to its predatory activity.

Extremely rare cases of albinism in pumas are reported to occur in South America and less rare melanistic phases, or black pumas.[16]

Aztec physicians in the sixteenth century prescribed certain parts of the "white lion" for medicinal purposes, as stated in the Badianus Manuscript.[17] A white panther was killed in 1881 in the Allegheny Mountains; its pelt was inspected by a Professor St. Clair. The animal was described as "the Phantom Cougar, white as snow" and the only albino specimen ever seen in the Alleghenies, according to the report.[18] A journal for sportsmen, *American Field*, reported in 1883 that their editors had received several reports of white mountain lions having been seen in New Mexico. Because the sizes of the animals differed with the several descriptions, they concluded that more than one white lion was seen, or that the nerves of the different observers were the cause of the various forms in which a single specimen was reportedly seen.[19]

Theodore Roosevelt questioned his 1913 Arizona hunting guide, Uncle Jimmy Owens, about "milk white" cougars, supposedly inhabiting the northern rim of the Grand Canyon. Uncle Jimmy had heard yarns about the animals but his answer was that he had never seen one and never expected to see one.[20]

Literature contains many references to the occurrences of black pumas in South America, but no documented specimens are known from North America. Several dark ones have been reported in the United States, but a black one has yet to be verified.

The young puma is not unpatterned like its parents. Its body is marked with blackish-brown bars or sooty spots and scattered marks on the sides, neck, and shoulders. The tail is ringed with like colors and is solidly dark at the tip. There is a well-defined vertical stripe above the inside corner of the eye and a slight horizontal bar extends from the outside corner of the eye. Dark blotches on the young usually

disappear at about six months of age. Markings on some individuals persist, however, until the animal is full grown, and in some cases may be faintly evident throughout life.

The spotted young led some early observers to believe that they were hybrids. Garcilasso de la Vega, in his commentaries on the Incas of Peru, first published in 1609, wrote: "A Spaniard, whom I knew killed a great lioness in the country of the Antis, near Cuzco. She had climbed into a high tree, and was killed by four thrusts of a lance. They found two whelps in her belly, which were the sons of a tiger [jaguar], for their skins were marked with the sire's spots."[21]

Charles Darwin believed that the feeble stripes and rows of spots on the young puma were vestiges of markings from a primogenitor that was striped.[22]

The head of the puma is one of its most distinctive features. It is small and rounded, showing a decided difference from the squareness of head associated with the true lion. Contrary to the writings of early chroniclers, it has no mane. The puma has short, rounded ears, evenly furred, without the tufts at the tips. Externally, they are dark colored with a whitish central area.

The muzzle, chin, and throat of the puma are white. There is a patch of black on either side at the base of the whiskers. The forward tip of the muzzle is white in a butterfly-shaped pattern. The whiskers are in a horizontal series and white in color, with a few black ones in the upper portions. Some chin whiskers are white.

Nostrils of the puma are flesh colored, in rare cases black. The eyes are prominent, rounded, and have yellow irises with a greenish or bluish tint. Ferris Weddle, who wrote extensively on the puma, calls the translucent quality a "gooseberry green." The green cast usually indicates that the animal is in a serious mood.[23]

The puma has heavy muscular flanks and proportionately large legs that are longer than those of the jaguar, giving the animal a rangy appearance. Except for the toe pads and the central pads, the paws are covered on the bottom with hair that enables the animal to walk noiselessly. The front feet are slightly larger than the rear ones. There are four toes on each

Profile of the mountain lion showing its comparatively small head. (© Walt Disney Productions, reprinted by permission)

hind foot and five on each fore foot. The extra digit on each front leg is a partially serviceable dewclaw located on the inside surface of the leg above the foot. It does not touch the ground as do the other toes; consequently, it is not a part of the track of the animal. The functional toes are elongated and form a hemicircle with distinct spacing in advance of the central foot pad.

The dewclaw is not subject to the normal wear of the other claws, remaining a formidable weapon capable of inflicting heavy damage to foe or prey. Many hunters refer to the curved, knife-sharp instrument as the "killing claw." Residents in Patagonia call the awesome appendage *uña cazador*, the hunter's claw, with the capacity to hook, slit, and rip into anything it grips.[24] All claws are retractile and are whitish in color.

The puma has a tail that is long enough to be a major identifying characteristic. It is cylindrical in shape and one-half the length of the

Killer claw of the mountain lion. (Courtesy Arnold C. Schueren)

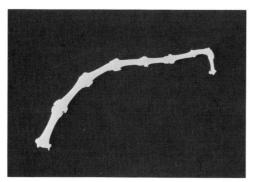

The distal end of the tail of the Florida puma F. concolor coryi. *Not all of the "crooked" tails look like this, but all appear to involve some skeletal modification of the last caudal vertebra. (Courtesy Florida State Museum)*

head and body together, or one-third of a total length that includes the tail. Ernest Thompson Seton says that the smallest puma has a finer tail than the biggest tiger. "It's grand, it's full of character, it is next in size to that of the Lion, or relatively far larger," he adds.[25] The long appendage is covered with thick fur and in color corresponds to the upper and under surfaces of the body. The tip is very dark and its somewhat longer hair gives the tail the appearance of having a slightly bushy end. It could not be regarded as a distinct tuft, however, as suggested by some early writers. A subspecies in Guyana has a tail that slightly exceeds the ratio in length of those found in North America.

In an examination of seven live Florida pumas, Chris Belden, Florida puma expert, found two consistent characteristics of the Florida variety not previously described by researchers. In addition to the cowlick in the middle of the back, there is a ninety-degree crook in the last vertebra of the tail that gives a distinct kink to the end of the appendage. Belden summarized by saying: "Although these characteristics occur randomly in individuals of other subspecies, only in the Florida panther do they occur in combination."[26]

Despite the fact that the puma lacks the decorative spots, rosettes, or stripes of other members of the cat family, its warm subtle hues and flowing form are most attractive. Facial features of the animal are richly accented against a background of soft body colors as if beauty aids were a part of its makeup. It has been chiseled in stone, etched, and duplicated in precious metals and stones, painted on pottery, and its image woven into fabrics since before recorded history in America. Poets and artists have praised the beauty and motion of the magnificent animal, and it has long been a favorite of ceramic artisans. Charles Livingstone Bull, American artist and writer on outdoor subjects, penned the following tribute: "Oh, the beautiful, splendid, supple, graceful, powerful, silent puma! I would rather watch and draw and dream about it than about any other living thing."[27]

Naturalist-writer-photographer Willis Peterson sat one moonlit night on the Mogollon Rim overlooking the Tonto Basin in Arizona and watched the silhouette of a puma below him as the animal leaped from one rampart to another and sat undisturbed on ledge after ledge. He wrote regarding the majesty of the beauty and movement of the beast: "It seemed that all the cats born during centuries past had willed some subtle characteristics to this creature. Sublimely, it epitomized all the felines I had ever seen."[28]

In one of the Walt Disney Productions books on the world of nature is the following statement about the puma: "He is one of the most beautiful creatures that ever lived."[29] No less could be said for the handsome animal.

Mountain lion in the Grand Canyon. (Scene from "Brighty of the Grand Canyon," © 1966 by Stephen F. Booth Productions, reprinted by permission)

4
Role
in Amerind
Cultures

The puma is prominent in American Indian mythology, with its cunning, ability, and strength respected and admired by many tribes. The animal figures in the magic and shamanism of nearly all ancients as their progenitor, protector, or as a source of power to ward off disease or to excel as a hunter. Others are awed by the animal and consider it an omen of disaster.

Little or nothing is known of the role of the puma in many aboriginal cultures, but evidence shows that its influence was widespread. Archeological sites have yielded figurines, effigies, and artifacts that indicate the animal was important, if not prominent, in the lives and spirits of all native Americans.

Petroglyphs or rock inscriptions of the puma exist in a number of areas in the southwestern United States. One large petroglyph "lion" was found in the Blue Mesa section of the Painted Desert in Arizona in the 1930s. There is no precise dating for the stone etching because it was not found in association with a datable site, but archeological evidence indicates that pueblo-type Indians with a culture similar to the Hopis and Zuñis left the region around the thirteenth century.[1]

Believed to have been carved in the same century are the sacred "Lions of Cochiti," two crouched pumas carved from huge boulders, located in the Bandelier National Monument in New Mexico. The date is fixed because of the community that was established in the area in the thirteenth century. The shrine is still visited by a few Indians from the Cochiti pueblo to give offerings, which supposedly bring good luck and hunting success.[2]

Effigy pipes and bones of the puma have been unearthed from mounds and village sites of ancient Indians near Portsmouth, Ohio.[3]

A statuette of a puma, or panther god, was found in 1895 in the ruins of ancient dwellers in Key Marco, on the southwesten coast of Florida. The six-inch idol had been carved from an exceedingly hard knot or gnarled block of fine wood and was in a remarkable state of

Large ancient Indian petroglyph of a mountain lion found in the Blue Mesa section of the Painted Desert in Arizona, now located outside the museum in Petrified Forest National Park. (Courtesy William Coxon)

The "Lions of Cochiti," an Indian shrine of two mountain lions in crouched position, carved from huge boulders, located in Bandelier National Monument, New Mexico. Vandals have damaged the figures. (Courtesy National Park Service)

preservation. The site of the remains is believed to have been occupied by Calusa Indians somewhere between A.D. 1400 and 1500.[4]

The puma was the emblem of the ancient Mixtec nation of Mexico and was considered the progenitor of the tribe. These Lion People ascribed their origin to the Lion Snake and the Tiger Snake.[5]

Ancient Peruvians gave the name puma to some of their most illustrious families. *Puma-caqua* was the Lord of the Brave Lion, and *colqui-puma* the Lord of the Silver Lion.[6] Vázquez de Espinosa, the Spanish priest who lived in Peru in the early 1600s, wrote that the puma was worshiped at Cuzco and was used as an insignia in solemn feasts. Lion skins were used for dress to represent bravery.[7]

Districts and wards of Incan cities bore the name of the puma. One province was called *puma-tampu*, literally a "deposit of lions," either originating from a den found there, or because more of the animals inhabited the area than elsewhere. In the kingdom of Quitu was the province of *puma-llacta*, the "land of lions." Here, they were more abundant than in neighboring districts and were worshiped as gods.[8]

Fierce pumas were kept by the Incas to punish their criminals. Parts of the city of Cuzco, where they were kept, were called *puma-curcu* and *puma-chupan*. The first ward contained the *curcu*, a large beam where captured pumas were fastened and kept until removed to a more permanent place. The latter ward was the "tail of the lion," so called because it ended at a point where two streams united at the very southernmost tip of the city.[9]

Near Machu Picchu, one of the great strongholds of the Incas, towers the Peruvian peak Pumasillo, the "puma's claw," one of their sacred mountains. A young British mountaineering team scaled the seemingly invincible 20,490-foot needle-sharp summit for the first time in 1957.[10]

The Cochimi Indians of Lower California had a superstitious fear of the puma before the introduction of Christianity and would not kill the animal. Established missions and presidios were hampered in their efforts to raise domestic animals because of the havoc spread by the predator. Jesuits offered bulls to the Indians as rewards for killing the puma, but the superstitious belief was overcome only by gradual education and the passage of time.[11]

Scavenger birds enabled the Cochimis to discover the remains of a puma kill so they could utilize the cached portions.[12]

The animal was also considered a friend and provider by the Cheyenne Indians who watched crows and buzzards to guide them to the remains of a puma feast for the same purpose. In the Cheyenne tradition is the story of a woman who strayed into the woods mourning the death of her baby. Finding a den of motherless panther kittens, she gently pressed one close to her breast and affectionately stroked the tiny animal. Apparently hungry, it began to suckle. The woman raised the kitten, and in time it repaid her by killing deer and bringing in meat to share. After that, other Cheyenne women raised puma kittens for the same purpose, according to their legends.[13]

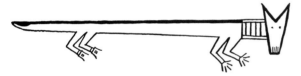

Puma symbol from a Navajo sand painting. (Reprinted, by permission, from Franc Johnson Newcomb, et al., "A study of Navajo symbolism," 1956)

The animal in Navajo sand paintings is usually depicted as a messenger or informer. Occasionally, pumas are shown bearing gifts of medicinal herbs.[14]

The wail of the puma was a death warning to the Apaches and Walapais of Arizona, and their medicine men dangled dried paws and claws of the animal over sick members of the tribes to ward off evil spirits. The Havasupais of the Grand Canyon used the gall of the animal for the treatment of weakness and pain to instill strength and fight in the victim.[15] Early Aztec healers also used portions of the animal for medicinal purposes. The sharpened bone of a light-colored lion was used to prick the breast of an ailing member of the tribe to defend against death.[16]

The mountain lion, *Hâ'k-ti tä'sh-a-na* ("tail long"), was the master of all Zuñi prey gods, as it was indeed of all terrestrial animals known to them. The guardian spirit protected all six regions surrounding the tribe: the north, east, south, west, earth, and sky. The North took precedence over all other ancient sacred places. The yellow lion became the master Prey Being or Hunter God of the North, but his younger brothers, the blue, the red, the white, the spotted, and the black mountain lions were recognized for the other regions.[17]

Fetish worship of the Zuñis reached its highest development in its relationship to the chase, and these small idols were carried on hunting trips. The original fetishes were carved from materials that represented the coloration of the regional lion gods.[18]

The fetish of the blue mountain lion of the skies was preferred by the deity society of the Priesthood of the Bow and was carried by Zuñi warriors in enemy country.[19]

Even though the puma was known to the Pacific Coast Indians of the northwestern United States and Canada, and was fairly common in some areas, it suprisingly does not figure in their legends to any extent. The animal is restricted in use as a crest or topic on their heraldic and storied totem, as is the deer which is even more abundant.

A tribal tale of the Yakimas and Lummis in the Puget Sound area regards the puma as a

Stone mountain lion fetish of the Zuñi Indians characterized by rounded ears and long tail laid lengthwise along the top of the body.

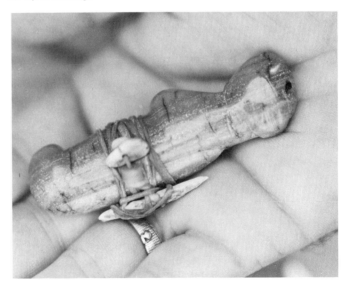

dreadful myth of the Pacific northwoods. In August of every year, according to legend, a large puma appears as the great Fire Cat, jumping from the Olympic mountains to the Selkirks, to Baker, to Rainier, and back to the Olympics, setting fires. It is said that many moons ago a chief of the Lummi Indians on the islands in Puget Sound acquired great wealth and stored it in a huge cave. He captured a large female puma and trained her to live in the cave and guard his treasures. The chief told his two sons that if misfortune should come to them after his death, they should go with fifty men to the cave and tie a fawn at the entrance to lure the big cat out. They then could slay the animal and recover the riches stored inside the cave.[20]

One of the sons grew greedy and gathered fifty warriors with him to steal the wealth. They followed the directions of the chief and killed the puma as it bounded out of the cave. In their greed and haste, they did not realize they had killed a kitten of the big female. While rejoicing over their kill, the great guardian cat charged from the depths of the cave and killed the son of the chief with one swipe of her massive paw

and then pursued the warriors into the timber, seeking them out one by one until she had killed them all. The beast was so enraged that she clawed the huge tree until the pitch burst into flames and the forests roared with fire. Since then, the great Fire Cat is supposed to return annually in all her fury to fire the mountains in August.[21]

In areas of America where the puma was found in numbers, early Indians recognized it as a master hunter of the animals they depended upon for food, shelter, and clothing. Attempts were made to exercise some form of control over the predator. Motifs in pre-Hispanic art in Central and South America suggest that the Indians frequently organized *chacos* to hunt the puma and that magic rites were sometimes practiced to appease it. In areas where the puma was less abundant, the red man respected and even copied the hunting art of the predator. Everywhere, the puma was rare enough to be the subject of fables and superstitions. Myths surrounding the animal did not originate entirely with the Indians, however. The white man added his share.

Drawings of mountain lions and other animals in the kiva, sacred ceremonial chamber, in Zuñi Pueblo, New Mexico, photographed in 1900. (Courtesy Smithsonian Office of Anthropology, Bureau of American Ethnology Collection)

Inca figures of the puma, used as a decorative motif on pottery and textiles from all parts of Peru. All antedate the conquest of 1532 under Pizarro. (Reprinted, by permission, from Charles W. Mead, "Conventional figures in ancient Peruvian art," 1916)

Fig. 1. Jaguar on poncho from the island of Titicaca.

Fig. 2. Puma on painted pottery vessel from Chimbote.

Fig. 3. Molded head on pottery vessel of the titi, or mountain cat, from Caudeville.

Figs. 4, 5. Common puma forms in tapestry with raised back characteristic.

Figs. 6-10. Puma designs used in weaving from coastal regions.

Fig. 11. Common puma design used on cloth, pottery, and metal objects.

Fig. 12. Pumas joined.

Fig. 13. Conventionalized puma heads joined by serpentine band.

Fig. 14. A form of the puma facial decoration on a vessel from Pachacamac. Puma head faces upward under the eye. Compare with Figs. 13, 15, 18, and 19.

Fig. 15. Puma heads on the extremeties of the belt on the central figure of the great monolithic gateway at Tiahuanaco.

Fig. 16. Joined puma heads on a painted pottery vessel from Pachacamac.

Fig. 17. Molded puma head on pottery from Tiahuanaco.

Figs. 18, 19. Two common forms of the puma head on pottery from Pachacamac.

5
Early Chroniclers

◄ Couguar. (From Georges Louis Leclerc comte de Buffon, Histoire naturelle, géńerale et particulière, 1761)

Perhaps it is only appropriate that the first person to record the American lion in the New World was Christopher Columbus (1451-1506). While on his fourth voyage in 1502, the discoverer sailed along the Atlantic coast of Central America from Honduras to Veragua in the western part of the Isthmus of Panama. Here he attempted a settlement and recorded some of the animals in a letter written from Jamaica the following year: "I saw some very large fowls (the feathers of which resemble wool), lions, stags, fallow-deer and birds."[1]

Conquistadors saw the American lion in an animal compound of Moctezuma during the conquest of Mexico by Hernán Cortés in 1520. One of them, Bernal Díaz del Castillo (1492?-?1581), wrote that the country had "tigers and two kinds of lions."[2] Bernardino de Sahagún (d.1590) went to Mexico in 1529. He recorded the ancient name *miztli* for the lion and said the country contained ruddy ones, yellow ones, blond ones, and white ones.[3]

Alvar Núñez Cabeza de Vaca (1490?-?1557), the intrepid Spanish explorer, landed on the west coast of Florida in the vicinity of Tampa Bay in 1528. Lured by tales of gold and vast treasures, Cabeza de Vaca moved northward into the country of the Apalachee Indians, in a part of Florida from the Aucilla River westward to the Perdido River. In describing the character of the country, he wrote: "In this province are many maize fields; and the houses are scattered as are those of the Gelves. There are deer of three kinds, rabbits, hares, bears, lions, and other wild beasts. Among them we saw an animal with a pocket on its belly."[4]

Hernando de Soto (1500?-1542) landed in Florida on Friday, 30 May 1539. The first published true relation of the expedition was written by a fellow voyager from the Portuguese town of Elvas who recorded: "There are many lions and bears in Florida, wolves, deer, jackals, cats, and rabbits."[5]

In the following year, far to the west of Florida, Francisco Vásquez de Coronado (1510-44) led his expedition in quest of the fabled Seven

Cities of Cíbola. Pedro de Castañeda, a private soldier in the army, wrote the narrative of the expedition. In the vicinity of Chichilticalli ["red house"], whose ruins are supposed to be in what is now Graham County, Arizona, "Gray lions and leopards [wildcats] were seen," the chronicler wrote. Continuing into the present New Mexico, Coronado's expedition reached the Zuñi pueblo of Hawikuh, one of seven villages. Hawikuh, or what they called "Granada," was located about fifteen miles southwest of the present Zuñi near the Zuñi River. "There are large numbers of bears in this province, and lions, wildcats, deer and otter," Castañeda recorded.[6]

René Goulaine de Laudonnière (fl.1562-82) wrote three long letters on the French expedition to Florida in 1562, 1564, and 1565. Here he found "a certain kind of beast that differs little from the lion of Africa."[7] The animal was also spoken of by Sir John Hawkins (1532-95), British sea dog and first English slave trader, who befriended the starving Laudonnière colony at Fort Caroline in Florida. Hawkins wrote: "Of beasts in this country besides deere, foxes, hares, polcats, conies, ownces, & leopards, I am not able certeinly to say: but it is thought that there are lions and tygers as well as unicorns; lions especially."[8]

Francisco Hernández (1514-78), Spanish naturalist, traveled in Mexico from 1570 to 1576 and wrote a short description of the American lion under the ancient Mexican name *Miztli*, stating that it was not related to "our lion which has a mane."[9]

Sent by Sir Walter Raleigh (1552?-1618) to Virginia in 1585 as a surveyor and historian to the first English colony in America was Thomas Hariot (1560-1621). Among twelve sorts of beasts discovered, Hariot wrote that "The inhabitants sometime kil the *Lyon* & eat him."[10] Hariot was picked up the following year by Sir Francis Drake at Roanoke Island, with his notes and two strange commodities of the new found land, tobacco and potatoes.

Raleigh himself explored Guyana in 1595 and wrote about its appeal to sportsmen:

"There is no countrey which yeeldeth more pleasure to the inhabitants, either for these common delights of hunting, hawking, fishing, fowling, and the rest, then *Guiana* doth. It hath so many plaines, cleare rivers, abundance of Phesants, Partridges, Quailes, Rayles̀, Cranes, Herons, and al other fowle: Deare of alsorts, Porkes, Hares, Lyons, Tygers, Leopards, and divers other sorts of beastes, eyther for Chace, or foode."[11]

John Brereton (fl. 1603), the English voyager, who, with twenty-four gentlemen and eight slaves, was the first to attempt to settle in the land since called New England, did not record the American lion, unless his statement that the party saw "Wilde-Cats, verie large and great," had reference to the beast.[12]

Garcilasso de la Vega (1539-1616), the Inca, was the first authority on the civilization of the Incas in Peru. This son of a Spanish conquistador and Incan princess was born in Cuzco. His royal commentaries contain many references to the maneless lion of South America and its importance to the culture of the ancient peoples of Peru. Introduced into literature by the Incan was the first permanent native American name for the animal: "Lions are met with, though they are not so large nor so fierce as those of Africa. The Indians call them *puma*."[13]

In 1571 José de Acosta (1539?-1600), a Spanish author, was sent to Peru as a missionary. His natural history of the country was published in Seville in 1590, and translated into six languages within fourteen years. In telling the world about the wild animals found in America, Acosta wrote: "There are in *America* and *Peru* many wilde beastes, as *Lyons*: (Although they may not be in greatness, fierceness, nor of the same colour, redde, to the reknowned Lyons of Affrica.) There also many Tygers [jaguars] very cruell, and more to the *Indians* than to the Spainiardes." Acosta described briefly the method of hunting the American lion used by the Indians.[14]

Antonio Vázques de Espinosa (*d.* 1630), a friar of the Carmelite Order, lived many years in Peru and New Spain in the late sixteenth and early seventeenth centuries. His writings are based almost entirely on personal inspection. Near the city of La Plata, "There are dark gray lions called in the Indian language poma," he wrote. He referred to the animal numerous times in his compendium on the Americas.[15]

A most important contributor to the history of the first English colony in Jamestown in 1609 was Henry Spelman (1595-1623), third son of Sir Henry Spelman, the antiquary. Writing about the country of Virginia, he mentioned some of the animals. "The cuntry is full of wood in some partes, and water they have plentiful, they have marish ground and smal-fields, for corne, and other grounds wher on ther Deare, goates and stages feadeth, ther be in this cuntry Lions, Beares, woulves, foxes, muskecatts, Hares, afleinge squirells and othr squirels being all graye like conyes, great store of foule only Peacockes and common hens wanting."[16]

Captain John Smith (1580-1631) did not mention the American lion in his general history of Virginia, but recorded the following observation: "An *Vtchunquoyes* is like a wilde Cat."[17]

William Wood (1580?-1639), Massachusetts colonist, whose prospect on the colony was first published in 1634, said that he had never seen the American lion but that others had. Colonists lost in the woods reported terrible roarings and reckoned that they had to be either Devils or Lions. "Plimouth men have traded for Lyon skinnes in former times. But sure it was that there be Lyons on that Continent, for the Viginiians saw an old Lyon in their plantation, who having lost his Iskal, which was wont to hunt his prey, was brought so poore that he could go no further," Wood wrote. He gave the lion foremost rank of importance in what is probably the first rhyme on American mammals. His ounce was described as a wild cat with a bobtail.

Pennsylvania cougar, the first drawing of a North American specimen. (From Georges Louis Leclerc comte de Buffon, Histoire naturelle, génerale et particulière, *1776)*

The kingly lyon, and the strong arm'd Beare,
The large lim'd Mooses, with the tripping Deare,
Quill-darting Porcupines and Rackcoones be,
Castell'd in the hollow of an aged tree;
The skipping Squerrell, Rabbes, purblinde Hare,
Immured in the selfe same Castle are,
Lest red eyd Ferrets, wily Foxes should
Them undermine, if rampired but with mould.
The grim fac't Ounce, and ravenous howling Woolfe,
Whose meagre paunch suckes like a swallowing gulpe.
Blacke glistering Otters, and rich coated Bever,
The Civet scented Musquash smelling ever.[18]

John Josselyn (fl.1675), the English author, made a systematical account of botanical specimens collected in New England in 1638-39 and listed the lion among other animal rarities discovered there. "The *Jaccal*," he wrote, "is a Creature that hunts the *Lions* prey, a shrew'd sign that there are Lions upon the Continent; there are those that are yet living in the Countrey that do constantly affirm, that about six or seven and thirty years since an Indian shot a young Lion, sleeping upon the body of an Oak blown up by the roots, with an Arrow, not far from Cape *Anne*, and sold the skin to the English."[19]

The first student of American natural history was the young German geographer Georg Marcgrave (1610-44) who visited Brazil in 1640. His brief description and crude drawing of the American lion was published posthumously under the native name *Cuguacuarana* and the Portuguese *Tigre*.[20] The same illustration was published ten years later with the name altered to *Cuguacuara*.[21]

Adriaen van der Donck (1620-55), colonist and lawyer, wrote the following about the distribution of the American lion in the Dutch colony between New France and Virginia: "Although the New-Netherlands lay in a fine climate, and although the country in winter seems rather cold, nevertheless lions are found there, but not by the Christians, who have traversed the land wide and broad and have not seen one."[22]

Spanish author Francisco Coreal (1648?-1708) claimed to have traveled over nearly all of Spanish and Portuguese America between 1666 and 1697. His writings about the remarkable things he saw during his stay are generally believed to be fictitious, however. He recorded the lion in Florida and the Isthmus of Darien. Later writers have commented that the *ocorome*, also recorded by Coreal, was probably the American lion on the basis of his description that read: "The ocorome of Peru is of the size of a large dog. His hair is red, his muzzle pointed, and his teeth very sharp."[23]

Three marches to discover a passage through the Blue Ridge and Appalachian mountains were made in 1669-70 by John Lederer (fl.1668-1671), a German explorer. He recorded the following observation on the lion of the Americas: "Small leopards [wildcat] I have seen in the woods, but never any Lions, though their skins are much worn by the Indians." That Lederer was looking for a creature with a mane and tufted tail is possible, for he witnessed a creature "somewhat bigger than our English fox, of a reddish grey colour, and in every way agreeing with an ordinary Cat" in the act of killing a doe. The Indian guide let fly an arrow and killed the beast. Because of its size and color, the cat may have been an American lion.[24]

"Lions there be some, but seen very rarely" in the plantation of New England, was recorded in 1670 by the clergyman and popular English writer Samuel Clarke (1599-1683).[25]

Father Zénobe Membré (1645-87), a companion of La Salle in the exploration of the Mississippi River in 1681 and 1682, wrote the narrative of the expedition. It has sometimes been attributed to La Salle himself. One of the animals of the Mississippi River valley, recorded under an Indian name by Father Membré, was the American lion:

There are no wild beasts, formidable to man. That which is called Michybichy never attacks man, although it devours the strongest beasts; its head is like that of a lynx, though much larger; the body long and larger like a deer's, but much more slender; the legs also shorter, the paws like those of a wildcat, but much larger, with longer and stronger claws, which it uses to kill the beasts it would devour. It eats a little, then carries off the

rest on its back, and hides it under some leaves, which ordinarily no other beast of prey touches it. Its skin and tail resemble those of a lion, to which it is inferior only in size.[26]

By the latter part of the seventeenth century, wild beasts of the forest had become somewhat of a menace to domestic animals in Carolina. Thomas Ash (fl.1682), a young gentleman clerk on board HMS *Richmond*, was one of those sent to Carolina in 1680 to inquire into the state of the country. The investigators found that the American lion, called "tyger" in the Carolina low country, was one of the causes of cattle and hog losses on plantations. Ash wrote: "Hogs find more than enough of Fruits in the *Summer*, and Roots and Nuts in the *Winter*; from the abundance of their feeding, great numbers forsake their own Plantations, running wild in the Woods, the *Tyger, Wolf*, and *Wild Cat*, by devouring them oftentimes goes Share with the Planter; but when the Stock encreases and grows strong, the older surround the younger, and boldly oppose, and oftentimes attack their Invaders."[27]

William Penn (1644-1718), proprietary and governor of Pennsylvania, wrote a letter in 1683 to a committee of traders in London lauding the mercantile potential of the new American colony. A portion reads: "The Creatures for Profit only by *Skin* or *Fur* and that are natural to these parts, are the *Wild-Cat, Panther, Otter, Fox, Fisher, Minx, Musk-Rat*."[28] By now, the Old World name panther had been applied to the lion of the Americas.

English naturalist John Ray (1626-1705), in his synopsis of quadrupeds published in 1693, copied almost word for word and under the same name the brief Marcgrave description of *Cuguacurana*, the lion of Brazil.[29]

By 1705, according to Robert Beverly (1673?-1722), a native and inhabitant of Virginia, vermine hunting was yielding pleasure and profit to the sportsman. "In this sort of Hunting, they also carry their great Dogs out with them, because Wolves, Bears, Panthers, Wild-Cats, and all other Beasts of Prey, are abroad in the Night," he wrote.[30]

An Englishman, John Lawson (d.1711), arrived in Charles Town in 1700, and explored eastern Carolina before being captured and killed by Tuscarora Indians. Of the American panther, he warned: "This beast is the greatest Enemy of the Planter, of any Vermine in *Carolina*."[31]

Dr. John Brickell (1710?-1745) arrived in North Carolina around 1729. He lived for two years at Edenton before returning to his native Ireland. His natural history of the colony was first published in 1737. He stated, as did Lawson before him, that the *Panther*, being a swift beast of prey, was very destructive to planters in North Carolina.[32]

Woodes Rogers (*d*.1732), the English privateer, wrote in 1708, "They have many Lions" in Tucumán and along the Rio La Plata in Argentina. Continuing his world voyage around the tip of South America, Rogers visited Chile in 1709. He commented further on the beast: "They have no poysonous or ravenous Creatures, except a small sort of Lions, which sometimes prey on the Flocks, but always fly from Men; nor are these Lions numerous, there being only a few of them in the Woods and Desarts."[33]

Antoine Simon Le Page du Pratz (1690?-?1775), French historical writer and adventurer, lived in Louisiana in the land of the Natchez Indians from 1720 to 1734. He called the American lion a tiger [*tigre*] and the wildcat was designated a cat-a-mount [*pichous*]. Writing about Louisiana mammals, he said: "As in all this country, and in all the height of the colony we find numbers of wolves, some tigers, Cat-a-mounts and carrion-crows, all of them carnivorous." Le Page du Pratz added that the tiger was rare and that he had only seen two near his settlement, and had reason to believe that it was the same beast he had seen both times.[34]

Pierre Barrère (1690-1755), of the Academy of Sciences of Paris, briefly described the American lion from French Guiana in 1741 under the names *Tigris fulvus* and *Tigre rouge*. He said that it was the most insatiable and rapacious of all American animals.[35]

Unfortunately, English artist-naturalist Mark Catesby (1679?-1749) did not include the Panther, or *La Panthère*, in the first published drawings of North American animals in 1743. He did, however, give the following description: "The Panther at its full Growth is three Feet high, of a redish Colour, like that of a Lyon, without the Spots of a Leopard, or the Stripes of a Tyger, the tail is very long." Catesby continued with a short summary of other characteristics.[36]

Charles Marie de La Condamine (1701-74) was sent as a scientific observer to Peru by the Academy of Sciences of Paris from 1735 to 1744. He recorded the puma from the province of Quito and stated that he had not seen one alive but had viewed a specimen stuffed with straw. On a return trip, La Condamine made the first scientific exploration of the Amazon River. Here he saw brown, unspotted "tygers," believing they were different animals from the puma.[37]

In 1756 Mathurin Jacques Brisson (1723-1806), a French natural philosopher, applied the name *Tigris fulva* to the "red tiger" of Guyana and Brazil.[38]

In 1761 French naturalist Georges Louis Leclerc Comte de Buffon (1707-88) presented an intelligent natural history with much previously isolated and disconnected American material. Buffon assembled for the first time the known facts about the lion of Brazil under the name *couguar*, a contraction of its native name.[39] In a supplement to his work, Buffon described the *couguar* of Pennsylvania. Although somewhat crude, his illustrations are the first recognizable likenesses of the beast.[40]

Major Robert Rogers (1731-95), famed leader of Rogers' Rangers, recorded the lion as a catamount during his adventuresome search for a northwest passage into the interior of North America in 1765. One observation in his writings reads: "The *Catamounts* and *Wild-Cats* are great enemies to the elk, and often make a prey of him. He has no other way to disengage himself from these, but by plunging into the water."[41]

Pre-Linnean observers did little to formally classify the lion of the Americas. This remained a task for the great Swedish botanist himself, Carolus Linnaeus (1707-78), who briefly described it, in 1771, as a wild American cat of but one color and called it *Felis concolor*, the scientific name retained to this day.[42]

6

Range and Population

Native only to the Western Hemisphere, the puma ranges over practically all of the Americas. No other wild land mammal in the world can equal its distribution of more than 100 degrees of latitude from the Yukon to southern Argentina and from the Atlantic Ocean westward to the Pacific Ocean. One writer calls it "the universal American, the most total American of all."[1]

In its vast range, the puma has adapted to an endless variety of natural conditions in wet or dry terrain and hot or cold climates from sea level to timberline. In Ecuador it is known to occur at altitudes of 12,000 feet.[2] Puma footprints have been found in the snow around camps at an elevation of 14,762 feet near the Espinosa Glacier in the same country.[3] One scientist followed puma tracks across a shoulder of Cerro Ichuasi in southern Peru at an altitude of about 17,000 feet and found the mandible of a young puma at 16,000 feet.[4]

In addition to its natural adaptations, the puma has been suprisingly successful in enduring the relentless pursuit of man, its greatest enemy. In eastern North America, the animal has been driven from many of its original haunts, but even there seems to have either survived or reinvaded some of the wilder portions of its former range. The fastness of the Florida Everglades provided the necessary protection for a population that now appears to be diminishing.

The puma is not abundant anywhere but occurs more frequently in some areas than in others, mainly where the inroads of civilization are less numerous and harassment is less constant.

Early records of the primeval American forests teeming or abounding with the puma are unfounded. It could never exist in numbers beyond the limits set by its available food supply, and any natural adjustments in its numbers must vary with the numbers of its prey, principally the deer family.

As well as having the widest distribution of any American terrestrial animal, the puma is probably the most widely renowned in legend.

◄ Florida panther. (Courtesy Jim Reed, Florida Game and Fresh Water Fish Commission)

Despite a general fear and sometimes hatred for the animal, outdoor romanticists would like to believe that the puma can still be found almost anywhere in suburban America. It is kept alive and close by in spirit, if not in reality, as a dominant link with the frontier past. Solely because of its own furtiveness, however, the puma does have a habit of showing up in places where it is long since believed to be extinct.

In a preliminary 1964 study on the distribution and numbers of the puma in North America, Victor H. Cahalane, of the New York State Museum, arrived at a total figure of 7,300 to 17,500 in the United States and Canada, based on estimates of local authorities consulted in the survey. Cahalane found that the range was expanding into southern Yukon. The 4,000 to 6,500 plus population estimates in the United States were said to be static or decreasing.[5]

In a 1976 puma survey conducted by Ronald Nowak, of the Office of Endangered Species, U.S. Fish and Wildlife Service, the findings are summarized in the following statement: "Although exploitation may be excessive in some local areas, many biologists and field personnel with first hand knowledge of the species suggest that within the last few years there has been moderate numerical increases in most western states."[6]

An *Outdoor Life* puma survey conducted in 1982 shows a conservative population in twelve western states and British Columbia and Alberta of twenty thousand to twenty-two thousand pumas. The numbers were said to be stable in every state and increasing in most because of partial protection of the animal since the mid-1960s.[7]

CANADA

British Columbia has three main areas of puma population: the southeastern portion from Christina Lake east to the Canadian Rockies, the south-central Cariboo from Kamloops to Quesnel both east and west of the Fraser River, and Vancouver Island. Northerly records include a report of one from the headwaters of the Ketchika River and the fifty-eighth parallel of north latitude and one specimen taken at Big Muddy River on the Alaska Highway. Fair populations are in the Okanagan and Similikameen watersheds in the British Columbia mainland.

On an area basis, it is likely that Vancouver Island has more pumas than any other place on the North American continent. They occur throughout the length and breadth of the island and are occasional on Saltspring Island and Quadra Island. The Nimpkish country southeastward to the Upper Campbell Lookout, the Forbidden Plateau, and the Ninaimo lakes area are some of the favorite ranges on the main island of Vancouver.

Alberta has had a number of record pumas in the Boone and Crockett competition, both in skull measurements and in overall lengths. The animal appears to be more plentiful on the western slope of the Rockies than on the east and the range seems to be extending northward. They are distributed to a lesser extent in the central and eastern parklands. Tracks are observed regularly in the Bow, Cascade, and Spray valleys of the Banff National Park.

Sporadic occurrences of the puma are reported across the northern portions of the southern provinces of Canada, skirting the plains and agricultural areas to scattered timberlands all the way to Cape Breton Island in the east. Remnants have increased in the Maritimes to the extent that Bruce O. Wright, of the Northeastern Wildlife Station, writes that they have received more than 240 reports of the animal in recent years from New Brunswick alone.[8]

UNITED STATES

In the United States, the puma population is spread over eleven or twelve western states, generally in concentrated areas associated with the Rocky Mountains and coastal ranges. Individuals appear from time to time in the southeastern states, and Florida has a permanent population that is singular in eastern North America.

Alaska may have an occasional puma, or cougar as it is known there. One resident believes that he and his wife saw one within twenty yards of them, sauntering along the Livengood Road some twenty-five miles northwest of Fairbanks. According to him, it was a big cat, nearly as tall as a malamute dog, "very dark brown in color and very long in body, with a long tail." He reported that Tanana Indians had earlier seen what they called a "long-tailed Lynx."[9] The Wildlife Branch of the U.S. Forest Service in Alaska has had reliable reports of sightings of the animal but none have been collected and identified as such.

Pumas are found in practically all forested areas of the state of Washington, with the bulk of the population in the Cascade and Olympia mountains. Based on annual yield figures of the bounty period that was discontinued in 1961, recent questional estimates place the number at up to two thousand animals. The Olympic Peninsula in the vicinity of the national park and the Forks area contains relatively large numbers.

In Oregon the puma ranges throughout the Cascade, Coast Range, and Blue Mountain areas and adjacent suitable habitats. Probably the largest numbers exist in the southwestern part of the state in the more remote areas of the Coast Range and in the Siskiyous. The southeastern one-fourth of the state is the one place they are least likely to be found.

Idaho has a relatively stable puma population. Heavier concentrations are in the Salmon River drainage, followed by the Clearwater and Kootenai drainages. They are scattered in the mountain ranges across southern Idaho and occasionally in the semidesert area of Cassia County.

The puma is not uncommon in the mountainous western one-third of Montana and the south-central portion of the state north of Yellowstone Park. It is occasionally found in the north-central portion, but is missing from the eastern one-third of the state. Areas of heavier concentrations are the Bitterroot range of mountains along the Idaho-Montana border, the Sapphire Mountains, the upper Sun River drainage, the Garnet Range, and Glacier National Park.

There is a relatively light or small population of pumas scattered widely throughout Wyoming, with only a small number killed each calendar year. The Medicine Bow Mountains and the Bighorn Mountains have resident pumas and they are known to occur southwest of Rock Springs in the Green River country.

Except for the deserts, the northeastern part of the state, and the Coast Range immediately north of San Francisco, the puma can be encountered in the mountains and brushlands all over California. The animals are sparse in the southeastern desert ranges. The total number in the state has been estimated at about 2,400. The mountains of Kern County and the Coast Range south of Monterey are their centers of population.

The puma can be found in limited numbers in almost all mountain ranges in Nevada. The overall population is believed to have increased slightly in the last few years. Heaviest concentrations are found in the northeastern two-thirds of the state. Northern Nye County, northern Lincoln County, White Pine County, Eureka County, southern Lander County, and the eastern two-thirds of Elko County make up this area.

The range of the puma is statewide in the mountains and desert highlands of Utah. The

Mountain lion taken near Snowmass, Colorado. (Courtesy U.S. Department of Interior, Fish and Wildlife Service)

main concentrations are in the southern and eastern wilds of the state, with the Book Cliffs of Unitah County and the dry mountains of Washington County especially noted as hunting areas.

Pumas are present in the canyon and mesa country of extreme western Colorado from Montrose County northward to the Wyoming line. Isolated ones are reported in the eastern slope foothills. Areas of greater concentration are the Book Cliffs from the town of Rifle to the Utah line, the Green and Yampa rivers including Brown's Park, and the Sangre de Cristo Range in south-central Colorado bordering on New Mexico.

The current population of pumas in Arizona has been estimated to be in the neighborhood of two thousand animals. This figure is based on a sustained kill of around two hundred annually. The animal occurs in almost all of the mountainous areas of the state including the big washes and low mountains of the Colorado River. Areas of heavy concentration are the bushy mountains just south of the Mogollon Rim in the Bloody Basin and Tonto Creek areas. In a Yavapai County area of roughly thirty square miles, forty-seven pumas were killed in 1942. They also occur north of the escarpment, around and on the San Francisco Peaks and in the ponderosa forests from Flagstaff east to the Little Colorado River, the White Mountains, and the Kaibab Plateau north of the Grand Canyon. Despite the hunting pressure in Arizona, it is believed that puma numbers are not receding. Bob Housholder, of Phoenix, who has written extensively on the animal in Arizona, gives four reasons: "First of all, government hunters don't kill lions unless there is a depredation problem; second, Arizona has a continual influx of lions from Mexico; third, we have an excellent food supply, deer, and where you find the lion you find the deer; fourth, the number of lions taken by professional guides is easily augmented by reproduction, let alone the 'wetback cats' from south of the border."[10]

Pumas are in all the rougher mountain areas throughout the state of New Mexico. Specific regions of interest to sport-lion hunters are the San Mateos south of Magdalena; the Apache National Forest and the Gila National Forest, with emphasis on the Gila Wilderness perimeter ranges such as the Mogollons, Pinos Altos, and Black Range; and the southwestern corner including the Peloncillo and Alamo Hueco mountains. The Datil Range and the Truth or Consequences-Winston-Hillsboro triangle also have pumas.

Pumas are not common in Texas. Verified reports establish the range in the southwest portion of the state. Webb, Duval, McMullen, and La Salle counties, where they share parts of the Nueces River and its tributaries, represent the least likely puma country, but contain the greatest numbers. Westward, they are found in the Big Bend area of the Trans-Pecos region. There are pumas in the mountains of Brewster and Presidio counties, extending into Culberson and Hudspeth near the Rio Grande.

Some pumas wander outside the mountain areas of the western United States and into adjacent states. Oklahoma has had verified reports in recent years, and occasionally migrant specimens are known to be in the Black Hills and the Badlands of South Dakota.

Ernest Lee and Dave Newell skin the fifth of eight panthers taken on a 1935 hunt in the Big Cypress Swamp in Florida.

38

The statewide puma population in Florida is officially estimated to be around thirty or forty animals. The southwestern part of the state is the only area of any concentration, but according to latest reports, the current range would include other parts of the state. Recent sightings in northeast and northwest Florida are fairly well substantiated. In the central part of the state, the Ocala National Forest is known to contain some. State game officials have seen them in the Avon Park and Fisheating Creek Wildlife Management Areas in south Florida. Pumas appear to be more common in the cypress swamps immediately north and west of the Everglades National Park. A number of sightings have been made in the mangroves around Coot Bay and West Lake within the sanctuary. A number live in the Hole-in-the-Donut. Northward, the Big Cypress Swamp, specifically Raccoon Point and Fakahatchee Strand, has the largest numbers in the state.

MEXICO

Pumas can be found in almost any part of Mexico where there is heavy brush, forest, or jungle, and in the mountainous areas that have trees. They are hunted successfully in the Sierra Madre Occidental of Chihuahua, the

forests of Tamaulipas, the jungles of the Yucatán, and in the Istmo de Tehuantepec. Ironically, the only state in the republic where the animal is relatively scarce is Nuevo León. The highest population appears to be in the pine-oak zone of northern Mexico, especially in the Rio Gavilán basin in northwestern Chihuahua and the Sierra del Carmen in northern Coahuila.

BELIZE

Throughout Belize, formerly British Honduras, the puma seems to be fairly numerous in all areas in which one finds the jaguar. It is an animal shot or hunted only when it is causing damage to farm stock, although it is considered by one or two professional hunters in the country to be equal in cunning and intelligence to the jaguar.

GUATEMALA

The puma is found in any and all unpopulated regions of Guatemala from pine country to rain forest vegetation, ranging from sea level to ten thousand feet. The northern third of the country, called the Petén, is a thick, virgin rainforest jungle. The puma of this vast region is an ochre color and is found near small, fast streams. The Guatemalan puma is the smallest of all subspecies. The type specimen was taken in the Petén.

HONDURAS

Christopher Columbus recorded the puma for the first time while exploring the coast of

This 180-pound mountain lion was killed in 1934 near Bavispe, Sonora, Mexico. Dale Lee is in the foreground with black hat, Ernest Lee third from left facing the fire, and Dave Newell holds a coati on the right.

A sixty-nine-pound male puma killed on the Monkeytail River in the Chiquibul Mountains of Belize in January 1966. (Courtesy Steve M. Matthes)

Honduras and Nicaragua in 1502.[11] At one time the animal was fairly common in the jungles of Honduras. In 1904 the puma, as well as the jaguar, ocelot, and the black tiger (*Felis discolor*) were not uncommon in Honduras.[12]

EL SALVADOR

The puma is extremely rare in El Salvador and may only be a transient. A skull and parts of a skelton from Lago Olomega were recorded in 1961.[13] Reports say that pumas are still occasionally found in the small, heavily populated country.

NICARAGUA

The puma lives in the plains, hills, and rocky mountains of Nicaragua. It is easy to encounter but difficult to kill due to its suspiciousness. A local sportsman, Miguel Ruiz Herrero, says the animal can be heard crying in the calm nights, but generally flees from man if located. It is attracted by imitating the moan of some small animal in distress, such as a small deer that has strayed and looks for its mother, or a rabbit that has fallen prey to a coyote.[14]

COSTA RICA

Laws now prohibit the exportation of puma hides in Costa Rica, and many hunters who once killed the animal for this purpose have lost interest. As a result, there is a fairly good population on the Atlantic side of Costa Rica. On the Pacific coast, pumas are less abundant due to the fact that most of the land is developed into cattle ranches and agriculture, and because the area lacks the jungles of the Atlantic side.

PANAMA

The Darien Jungle is the major habitat of the puma in Panama. Although it occurs throughout the republic, it is rarely seen. It is more abundant in regions where deer and peccary are found. There is a natural undisturbed puma population on Barro Colorado, a large island within the Canal Zone. Various estimates number up to sixteen individuals, although it is not improbable that they swim from island to island or to the mainland.

COLOMBIA

In the *planadas* and llanos of Colombia the puma is found in the greatest numbers. These are the regions of large cattle ranches where puma predation is an occasional problem. In the past, professional hunters concentrated on taking jaguars and ocelots because of their valuable furs. Pumas were not hunted commercially because the best time was considered to be at night when they were on the prowl for food and the pelt was not valuable as a product.

VENEZUELA

The puma is not plentiful in Venezuela. It is still found occasionally in the big plains of Apure State and in some intricate jungle areas. It was reported as early as 1912 that pumas were seldom seen and that good dogs were necessary to successfully hunt the animal. At the time of the writing, they were not uncommon in certain districts near Maracaibo.[15]

GUYANA

In the former British colony that is now Guyana, Stanley E. Brock, onetime manager of the huge Dadanawa Ranch on the Rupununi River, summed up the range and distribution of the puma in a letter to the author: "The puma is found throughout the forested areas of British Guiana, and also on the scrub savannahs, lying up in heavy cover during the day. Everywhere it appears to be more common than the jaguar. We have quite a bit of trouble from both, killing cattle. The males run to a maximum of 120 pounds, the females rarely more than eighty."[16]

SURINAM

The puma is widely distributed in Surinam. The animal is lacking only in the rather thickly populated coastal areas. To many inhabitants, there exists little knowledge concerning any of the large carnivores, and rather often they try to sell a puma kitten as a rare young jaguar.

FRENCH GUIANA

The puma exists in French Guiana where the inhabitants call it the *tigre rouge* ["red tiger"] as opposed to the jaguar, called locally the *tigre marqué* ["marked tiger"]. The puma is relatively rare on the coast of the colony where the damp and boggy condition of the swamps and human habitation afford less shelter than in the higher, drier, and less populated interior. Besides, the animal seems to prefer the medium-sized and large prey living in the forests and only unwillingly consumes fish and turtles as does the jaguar in the coastal regions.

BRAZIL

The puma is fairly common in the Matto Grosso of Brazil, preferring the open, drier portions of the highlands, particularly in the vicinity of the low, sandy, openly-wooded ridges. Elsewhere, it can be found in lesser degrees of population in all parts of the country from the Amazonian basin to the delta.[17]

ECUADOR

With the exception of the places where human population is dense, the puma may be found in practically the whole of the Ecuadorian territory. Pumas are found in the wet tropical forests as well as the open lands like the ones called *páramos*, and from sea level to fifteen thousand feet of altitude. Several valleys situated between the eastern and western branches of the Andes are heavily peopled and the puma seldom appears, but it is not rare to find it higher in the slopes of the cordillera that face the valleys. The puma of the greater altitudes is notably smaller than that found in the forests.

PERU

Peru is one of the oldest areas in the world to record the puma. Here it played a major role in the highly developed ancient cultures inhabiting the Andes. Today the animal exists in nearly all parts of Peru with the exception of the very densely populated areas. Nowhere are the animals abundant. The gray pumas live in the Andean area and the more reddish ones in the woodlands. The Museo de Historia Natural in Lima has found traces of pumas in Cerro Illescas at the northwest Peruvian coast, which is an isolated mountain with poor vegetation in the Sechura Desert very near the seashore. It is known to the natives west of Lake Titicaca but is seldom encountered.[18] On the altiplano of southern Peru, the animal is rare and stays in the more remote areas.

BOLIVIA

The puma is found in the drainage of the Rio Beni, a tributary of the Amazon, and in the subandino forest of the yungas, the mountain valleys and gorges of the Cordillera Real. Predator damage to cattle herds was reported in 1969 in the antiplano. On the slopes of Sajama, the puma has been observed up to heights of 15,420 feet.[19] In 1973 it was reported that the puma ascended to the borders of eternal snow in quest of the vicuña and deer when impelled by hunger.[20]

The subspecies of Bolivian pumas was described in 1929 from specimens collected in Buena Vista in the Department of Santa Cruz with a notation that they occurred in the mountains of central Bolivia and along the slopes of the Andes to the northwest.[21]

Famed Arizona puma hunter Dale Lee found pumas in the tropical forests of the Rio Yapacani north of Santa Cruz and southwest in the arid country near the Argentine border. Referring to the rough habitation, he says, "Everything down there has a sticker on it."

PARAGUAY

The puma is found from one end of Paraguay to the other, occurring in practically all of the territory of the two major areas, the Gran Chaco and the Región Oriental. It shares the same range as the jaguar in the Gran Chaco but not the same prey. It is believed that 80 percent of the total puma population occurs in this western half of the country in the very dry flatlands. The northwestern two-thirds of the chaco is covered with a dense dry-country jungle. Leon T. Mott, an American sportsman, killed an unusually large specimen west of Puerto Pinasco near Catorice in 1959.[22]

URUGUAY

Apparently the puma is no longer a resident of Uruguay. It was reported in 1894 that its range was very limited and the animal was disappearing from that country.[23] This it appeared to do about 1920, with the last habitats of the animal in the uplands along the Rio

Uruguay. It may still visit the country, however. Information from the Museo Nacional de Historia Natural in Montevideo reveals that a puma was seen in 1957 in the region of the Brazilian frontier.

CHILE

Pumas live in the mountains that parallel the Pacific coast and the central valley of Chile. They prefer the highlands in forested areas and the rough and rocky places in the meadows. A variety appears periodically in search of the llamas and alpacas of the Indians in the Tarapaca puna, a high, wind-swept plateau in extreme northern Chile. The dark-colored puma lives in the wet jungles of the Cordillera de Nahuelbuta and the Andean mountains of Valdivia and Llanquihue provinces. They are distributed throughout Malleco Province except in the flatlands of the central valley. Light-colored pumas range from Llanquihue to Magallanes.

ARGENTINA

Argentina probably has more pumas than any other South American country. They are present in all the llanos of northern Argentina and in the lowlands of the upper Rio Paraguay. The humid jungles of Salta, the zones of the forest and Andean lakes of southeast Neuquén, and the Chilean frontier contain goodly numbers. There is an extensive range in the high cordillera southward throughout the pampean district of the republic to the Straits of Magellan. Mountain rancher Andreas Madsen killed pumas in the high glaciers of extreme southwestern Patagonia west of Lago Viedma and Lago Argentino.[24]

Admiral John ("Foul-weather Jack") Byron, grandfather of the poet Lord Byron, was shipwrecked as a young man near the Straits of Magellan in 1741. While on Tierra del Fuego, Byron and his companions were disturbed numerous times at night by large animals. Afterwards, they found large tracks containing claw impressions made by the intruders. On this authority, some later authors erroneously referred to the possible existence of the puma in this southernmost extremity of South America, and others assumed that it was a part of the Fuegian fauna.[25] Naturalist Andrew Murray could find no trustworthy record in 1866 of the puma's inhabiting Tierra del Fuego, although he saw no reason that it could not because of its capability to swim the narrow intervening strait. He criticized the assumption that the tracks seen by Byron were made by the puma, and said that they were probably the tracks of a domestic dog, which are similar except for the claw marks.[26]

Adult female Surinam puma photographed with Perutz Pergrano film that reveals latent stripes and spots.
(Courtesy Dr. H.L. Blonk)

43

7
Life Story

MATING

Female pumas reach sexual maturity at two and one-half to three years of age and about eighty pounds in weight. Initial breeding may occur during the first estrus.

The wide-ranging male discloses to the female his principal route of travel with numerous scent stations in heaped leaves or ground litter. Once the marks are discovered, she remains in the vicinity, knowing that he will return in a few days on his regular circuit.

A female may have as many as three males or more competing for her attention. A hunter in Chile surprised three males around a single female in Cordillera de Nahuelbuta. When the pumas saw the hunter, they bared their fangs momentarily, then returned their attentions to the female without further concern for the intruder. Females in zoos have been observed selecting a mate from among several, presumably because his amorous advances included strong impositions and gruntings accompanied by occasional slaps.[1]

Males may fight to the death for the favors of the female. In January 1924, Jay Bruce, onetime state predator hunter of California, killed a male that showed scars of a desperate battle. Back-tracking the puma, he found the tracks of another male, which in turn led him to the carcass of a younger suitor that had won and ultimately lost in love. Signs showed that a female had lingered with the dead body of the young mate until the hounds of the hunter approached. Bruce ended the triangular dispute by tracking down the female puma and disposing of her.[2]

The duration of the love affair is about a half day for pumas confined in cages. Copulation is brief, taking less than one minute in most instances, and is preceded with sparring and snarling. Robert Baudy, owner of the Rare Feline Breeding Compound in Bevilles Corner, Florida, described the copulation of Florida pumas in 1978: "I located myself outside their cage and within six feet of both animals. The male penetrated the female which let out piercing screams but remained in a normal position, slightly elevating her rear quarters and positioning her tail out of the way to the left side. The male proceeded with ten thrusts and let out a very loud, single scream (much more powerful than the female's) at the termination of the copulation."[3]

The female is in heat from eight to ten days and the condition is accompanied by vocalizations in the form of yowling and caterwauling. A span of some two weeks marks the end of one period and the beginning of the next. An estrus period may begin almost immediately after young are born.

The gestation period of the puma is about three months, generally not less than eighty-two days nor more than ninety-seven. Early records on the period were kept by Devereaux Fuller, headkeeper of the Zoological Society of London. The female, according to his 1832 report, admitted a male on 28 December and on the night of 2 April gave birth to two young. The period from copulation to birth was ninety-six days.[4] The same period of gestation is recorded for captive pumas in Texas for two different litters of kittens of four each in both 1891 and 1892.[5]

To deliver, the female looks for a safe place and complete isolation. Usually the consort remains nearby.

DENS

Puma kittens are born in beds that offer protection and concealment in windfalls or shallow recesses below projecting cliffs if possible. The mother will avoid deep caves where her line of vision or escape would be limited or hindered. In different habitats the bed may be in the security of dense brush or under low-hanging foliage of evergreen cover.

John James Audubon located lairs in heavy thickets and canebrakes in the southeastern United States, with the beds composed of sticks, weeds, leaves, and grasses or mosses. Rain was shed at all seasons by long evergreen blades of canes arching over the beds.[6] In the jungles of Central and South America, a puma often uses the trunk of a hollow tree for its home. Puma beds found in Chile have been lined with dry grass, small green boughs,

feathers, and hair from the abdomen of the female.[7]

Jay Bruce was able to investigate the den of a puma in California by trailing a female from a kill with his hounds. The trail led up a mountain and circled around a bluff of rocks. On the upper side of the barrier, the trail seemed to end. Further investigation revealed that the puma had jumped a ledge and worked her way down the bluff to the lair. Bruce's hunting dogs could not find the trail by investigation, but after some time were able to locate the lair by its scent. Bruce killed the female and captured three kittens. He described the place of refuge:

"The lair was about 6 feet long and 2 feet wide. The nest was bedded with pine needles, probably carried in the den by wood-rats for their nests at some time. There was also a small opening, perhaps 8 inches in diameter, through which the sun would shine on the kittens in the nest."[8]

A newly abandoned puma lair in the Black Hills of South Dakota in 1902 was found to be fastidiously clean. "This retreat was not the typical 'panther's den' of tradition, but a bush-grown harborage under the edge of a rock, with just enough of shelf to keep off the rain," commented the hunter.[9]

Mountain lion kittens. (© Walt Disney Productions, reprinted by permission)

46

One puma den in the Rocky Mountains had three approaches leading to it. The particular Colorado den was observed for several years while it was occupied by the same female puma. She would enter her sanctuary from a forested canyon below, an approach from a treeless ridge at about the same level, or else above from high timberline peaks.[10]

Arizona puma hunter Giles Goswick invariably found that young pumas were born in a habitat of heavy thickets. On Walnut Creek near Prescott, Goswick took three kittens in an area where their main cover was brush and a large pine log. He found another litter of kittens in an oak thicket in the Mazatzal Mountains northeast of Phoenix.[11]

Free of family ties, the female abandons her lair and lives alone without residence, except for temporary quarters that offer protection in heavy weather. An old homestead cabin in Weber Canyon in Utah was used by four pumas. It contained the remains of three deer almost entirely eaten. An abandoned mine shaft in the Nevada National Forest near Ely was also found to be used periodically by some pumas.[12]

LITTERS

Puma kittens are born at all seasons, in every month of the year, and at almost any altitude of their range. The majority of females in the wild probably have young every other year. Ben Lilly, mountain man and puma hunter extraordinary, wrote that a female will often raise two sets of young in twelve to fifteen months, adding that in good years the mother will sometimes have five kittens in the same span of time.[13]

The litter is usually one to four in number with verified births of up to six kittens. In the files of the U.S. Fish and Wildlife Service is a record of one litter of six kittens born to a female while she was in a trap. The one male and five females were taken by a hunter in Avintaquin Canyon, Utah, in 1940. The legendary Grizzly Adams found one den that contained five kittens.[14] In May 1939, a hunter killed a female puma in Simmons Canyon, Utah, and when he opened her he discovered five unborn kittens.[15]

W.H. Switzer of Flagstaff, Arizona, was clerk for the Board of Supervisors for Coconino County in 1909-10 and paid out bounties at that time. According to him, plainsman Buffalo Jones killed a mother puma with nine unborn kittens. He was said to have skinned the whole family and collected ten bounty payments on them in Flagstaff.[16]

A favorable temperature probably is not a factor in the birth of young pumas. Kittens have been found during every month of the year in Arizona and at altitudes ranging from three to seven thousand feet.[17] Nursing kittens have been found in Colorado on 10 February, ordinarily one of the coldest times of the year in that state.[18]

YOUNG

The newly born puma kitten, sometimes called a cub and less frequently a pup, has a birth weight of about one pound and is eight to twelve inches in length. It is colored very differently from the adult, with brownish black spots and short streaks on the back, sides, and front part of the legs. The tail is ringed and there are numerous facial markings. An exception to the normal coloration is reported from British Columbia. Two young kittens, about two months of age, had no spots whatsoever, yet the writer knew of another individual kitten that still had visible spots at a year-and-a-half.[19]

The hair of the young puma is considerably longer than in the adult. Their deep-set eyes open at about nine or ten days, and they cut their first teeth in about twenty days.

Puma kittens are suckled for four or five weeks but will continue until half grown if not prevented. At about six weeks of age, they will partake of fresh meat.[20] A four-month-old pet kitten was observed in April 1928 trying repeatedly to reach a mounted deer head on the wall in the home of a friend. When the kitten first noticed the head, it jumped for an hour until almost exhausted. The persistent kitten even tried jumping from a settee but was only able to touch the head occasionally, as it was some seven feet above the floor.[21]

The young puma will grow fast and generally will shed the long fur and lose its spots and blotches when it is six to ten months old. One

A nine-month-old mountain lion on a quaking aspen felled by beavers in Colorado. (Courtesy Wilford L. Miller)

kitten, taken by a hunter, weighed eight pounds at an estimated age of eight weeks.[22] Jay Bruce stated that California pumas weigh thirty-five to fifty pounds at six months and sixty-five for females and eighty for males as yearlings.[23]

Young pumas have weak backs that are vulnerable to injuries that could cause permanent disfiguration. They play and gambol recklessly, using poor judgement in jumping and landing on top of each other. They often have difficulty in gauging distances and obstacles in their rough-and-tumble activities.

Puma kittens are not always playful with each other. A different aspect of their disposition was observed in 1896 at the Higbee Ranch near Santa Barbara, California. At the age of three months, three captured kittens engaged in a fight over a piece of meat. When blood was drawn from one, the other two pounced upon the bleeding kitten and tore it to pieces.[24]

PARENTS' ROLE

The female puma generally assumes the entire burden of caring for the young and protecting them from their fathers. Given the opportunity, the male will sometimes kill and eat his own offspring.

Puma kittens are nursed by the mother about two months and remain with her beyond the weaning time for a year or longer, or at least until they are run off by a new mate of the mother. Breeding frequency is sometimes influenced by how long the young remain with their mother.

The earliest means of travel for the young puma is being carried by the nape of the neck in the mouth of the mother in the same way a domestic cat does her kittens. She will not range far from the litter for the first few weeks, but after three or four months she will move them to a kill that she has made and covered

Mother puma and her two kittens. (Harvey Patterson)

with leaves or brush. She often makes as many as three kills a week to feed her young.

A theory advanced by Theodore Roosevelt is that the puma is normally a solitary beast and that the male remains with the female only a short period of time during the mating season. He tends to travel far and wide in search of temporary mates.[25]

Evidence has been offered that shows the male will sometimes stay with a family unit. While fishing on the Pilchuck River in the Cascades of Washington, a sportsman found a young puma in the woods. He wrapped it in his coat, only to find himself confronted by two adult pumas, challenging his right to the kitten. The man killed the mother but the male carried off the young one.[26]

A man attempted to capture two kittens in Idaho in 1884. Their cries were answered by an adult male and an adult female. Both animals attacked the man in defense of the young.[27]

A detailed observation of an undisturbed puma family in the Humboldt Mountains of Nevada was described by mountain man Grizzly

Adams for his biographer. The hunter and a companion located a vantage point in an area where they knew a den was located and awaited the appearance of a puma. Just at sundown two large pumas, a male and a female, emerged from a cleft in the rocks. They played, wrestled, and caressed each other. The hunters did not disturb them. In a few moments three kittens emerged from the cleft. They commenced to play, springing onto the backs of the adults and off again. Before darkness fell, Adams signaled to his companion. They fired their rifles, but both had taken a bead on the female. She fell dead. The male remained unscathed. Adams described the actions of the remaining adult: "He could not see us, however, and, being confounded by the unaccustomed sound, did not fly, but pranced about, jumping over the dead body of his consort, looking in every direction and screeching every few minutes."

Adams reloaded as quickly as possible and fired a second shot, striking the beast but failing to inflict a fatal wound. The male bounded over a cliff and into the bushes. Adams and his companion tried to capture the little ones but they scampered into the recesses of the den.[28]

Young pumas are trained in the deception of prey and other fine arts of hunting and survival by the mother who takes them on hunting forays. They often remain together for a few months after their abandonment and ordinarily hunt as a team.

SEX RATIOS

Sex ratios for 1,704 juvenile and adult pumas from Arizona, Utah, Colorado, New Mexico, and Texas shows sixty-eight more females than males. These records cover a ten-year period from 1931 to 1941.[29]

Records of the California Division of Fish and Game reveal the total bounty kill on pumas in that state for 1942 was 162. Of these, 85 were females and 77 were males.[30] Sex records for 649 mature pumas from Utah and Nevada, 1946-58, show a ratio of 100 females per 92 males.[31] Similar ratios of a slight excess of females over males are evident in the few available reports of postnatal young or kittens.

C. Hart Merriam, the famous American naturalist, did not believe that old males killed young males as commonly thought at one time, but rather that the females were greatly preponderate at birth. Of twenty-eight reported by him killed in the Adirondack Mountains of New York, only five were males.[32]

Roosevelt believed that the species was polygamous, with the females far outnumbering the males.[33]

By way of contrast, in a sample of 127 hunter-killed pumas taken in British Columbia, males outnumbered the females 80 to 47.[34]

VOCAL BEHAVIOR

A married couple described the sound of the puma kitten as a "high-pitched, screechy whistle." Expecting a meow from a kitten under observation, the writers added:

"There seemed to be an effort to express an ordinary cat call, but the throat contracted in some way, and at the end of the wheezy attempt came this shrill, penetrating noise. It was a call almost ventriloquistic at times, used for the purpose of reaching away into the distance."[35]

Three California hunters were puzzled over an evasive sound they believed to be from a yellowhammer. The birdlike sound never seemed to come from the same direction twice. After considerable searching, they located three puma kittens in thick underbrush. The mystery was solved when the sounds were determined not to be from a bird but were "the screeching of the kittens as they lay in their nests."[36]

Charles B. Cory, for whom the Florida puma is named, wrote that the young screeched like a parrot but often uttered a soft whistle.[37] Another writer observed a four-month-old kitten for a considerable period of time in April 1928. He says the young animal growled when angry, whistled in the tone of a hawk call when walking about, and purred like a housecat when fondled by a human.[38]

Under ordinary circumstances, the adult puma is silent in its natural habitat because its predatory existence depends largely upon the ability to surprise the wariest of animals. Any undue sounds could betray its presence to any likely prey.

Vocal behavior is varied. When confronted with danger, the puma will lay back its ears and hiss and spit with repelling growls and snarls. It purrs with contentment and will occasionally meow like a domestic cat. It is capable of emitting a throat sound of such high frequency that it could only be described as a whistle. A puma was observed in the Sierra Madre of Chihuahua State, Mexico, in the act of caterwauling. During the performance, the head of the animal moved from side to side and the walking pace was slowed down.[39] Another observer says that at pairing time in South America they "squall most abominably."[40]

One of the most controversial issues in outdoor America concerns the so-called scream or piercing cry of the puma. Some observers call it a wild shriek, while others are unable to describe or classify the sound. One writer admits that he cannot even depict the sound onomatopoetically.[41]

Many experienced outdoorsmen are familiar with the various puma sounds, but seldom have they heard or recognized the scream in the wild. Many are still skeptical about the elusive sound, but it has been heard too often from captive pumas at certain times to deny its deliverance.

In Guatemala the sound of the puma has been likened to the sound of a distant steamship horn. The puma of the Andean region is said to make a pumping roar similar to that of the true lion.[42]

Stan Brock describes a high-pitched squeak of a puma in Guyana. Confronted by an alligator, the animal uttered a sound similar to a roar that came from the stomach instead of the mouth.[43]

The unusual whistle of the puma was seldom associated with the animal in years past. There was little reason to believe that the sound came from anything other than a bird. In recent years, however, a number of naturalists have been able to identify the sound and relegate it to its true source.

British Columbia resident Dave Hancock kept a pet puma on Vancouver Island that he raised from a kitten. He says the animal whistled in anxiety and maintained contact with him by characteristic squeaks and whistles.[44] Another observer had pet pumas for seven years on the edge of the Idaho Primitive Area.

He says that their whistles to him meant "come over here."[45]

The whistle of an unrestrained pet female puma on the Dadanawa Ranch in Guyana was audible at three hundred yards, according to Stan Brock, who owned the animal. He adds:

"She invariably responded [to a call] with a high-pitched, cheeping, whistle. It was a very difficult sound to imitate, but if you spell the meeow of a cat with a *wh* instead of an *m* and try to whistle the sound instead of speaking it, you'll find that you can't . . . but a puma can, and that's its call sign of affection! I have never heard this sound coming from a wild puma in the forest, or from one in captivity, and I have since become convinced that it is a call only used between either a puma and its mate, or a mother and her cubs, certainly as a show of affection, and equally as certainly as a means of communication between each other while prowling through the forest."[46]

Dr. Maurice G. Hornocker, who conducted an extensive study of the puma in the Idaho Primitive Area from 1964 to 1969, was able to recognize the whistle in the wild. He raised two kittens from infancy that enlightened him on how the species communicates:

"They started using different whistle-like sounds to greet me or call each other. A warbling note was a greeting; a piercing one, an alarm; and short, intense tones meant 'Come here!'

"I am certain lions 'talk' in the wilds by means of these whistle-like sounds produced with their vocal chords. It had been a mystery to us how pairs or families, hunting together, could separate — one dropping into a basin, the other circling a ridge — and then join each other at some seemingly predetermined spot to continue the hunt."[47]

TRAVEL

The puma is an extensive traveler, confining most of its prowling activity to the darkness and lying up in the shade or sunshine during the day, depending upon the season. A wide area of up to one hundred miles is covered regularly over lengthy beats that follow the same route.

51

Walking stride of the panther, Everglades National Park, Florida. (Courtesy U.S. Department of the Interior, National Park Service)

Pumas often migrate after a shift in the population of prey, pressure from hunters, or the encroachment of civilization.

In mountainous country, puma paths generally zigzag along the tops of ridges and over low gaps. They may crisscross at intervals or completely encircle the perimeter. A desert area of thirty or forty miles between mountain ranges is often covered in one night by the wanderer. The length of time to make a circuit varies. The trapping of two pumas on separate occasions indicates time lapses of fifteen and eighteen days.[48]

Puma beats are easily detected because of scent posts or scrapes of piled litter that contain feces or urine. Scent from anal or other glands also serve to bring pumas together or enable them to maintain distance, depending upon their disposition at the time. Scratch piles the size of a saucer, are heaped up, possibly to five inches in height. Beside one travelway in Mexico, a pine tree was used as a rubbing post and had puma hair stuck in the bark. A trap was set nearby and the animal was caught the second night.[49]

Another scent marking of the puma is the claw raking of tree trunks or posts. This removes loose claw sheath and also leaves visual and possible olfactory traces that have social significance to other pumas.[50]

The puma "markers" described by J. Frank Dobie, Texas historian and folklorist, consisted of two parallel scrapes on the ground, about eight inches in length, made with hooked claws.[51] Darwin found scores of scratches made by a puma on the bare, hard soil of Patagonia.

He believed the object of the practice was to tear off ragged parts of the claws and not to sharpen them as gauchos thought.[52]

Additional puma sign in Arizona includes relatively rare mounds of four to five feet in diameter that resemble buried kills but contain no remains. The mounds of pine needles and other debris are apparently made by females and may be related to the birth or presence of young litters.[53]

HOME RANGE AND SOCIAL STRUCTURE

A home range for the puma is determined by the availability of food, water, and protective covering. Scent markings and vocalization enable the elusive animal to establish ranges and regulate reproductive activities.

Until recently, little was known about the home range or social organization of sizable resident populations of pumas in the wild. Beginning in 1964, Idaho biologist Maurice Hornocker and his associate Wilbur Wiles made a landmark five-year study on "territories" to which unmolested pumas attach themselves in a two hundred-square-mile tract in the middle of the Idaho Primitive Area. The field work covered the winter and spring months between 1964 and 1968. Pumas were treed with trained hounds, immobilized with drugs, and marked with numbered ear tags and collars. Information on the territoriality of individuals was obtained through the capture of ten resident adults a total of fifty-nine times. Twenty-seven of the other thirty-six pumas studied by Hornocker were kittens and nine were transients. The home range of adult pumas varied from fifteen to thirty square miles and a smaller five to twenty-five square miles for females.[54]

Another team of researchers that included Hornocker conducted around-the-year field work on the social organization of pumas in what they referred to as the same "home areas" in the Idaho Primitive Area between 1968 and 1972. During the investigation, captured pumas were equipped with radio collars so they could be located and their day-to-day movement charted from ground units as well as light aircraft. A total of 669 days was spent on the project with 37 radio transmitters attached to 15 different pumas. It was found that males had firmly established ranges and maintained rigid boundaries with other males.

Home ranges of male pumas rarely extended into those of other males but often overlapped portions of more than one female range. The social tolerance of males was exhibited only during brief mating periods, and a social bond between females and their young lasted only during a period of juvenile dependency on the mother.[55]

A later study by Hornocker of harassed puma populations in less primitive localities disclosed that territorialism did not operate because of continued hunting pressure which prevented them from establishing social systems. Males traveled indiscriminately and frequently fought with others in a continual search for sole rights to an area. Fighting as a means of protecting areas had not been documented in earlier studies by Hornocker.[56]

SPEED

The puma has amazing speed for a few hundred yards but it tires quickly. One hunter wrote that even the pronghorn could not escape the sudden dash of the puma.[57] Presumably the element of surprise would be necessary to accomplish such a feat. Professor J. Evan Armstrong of the University of California at Berkeley observed a puma in the Nevada Mountains of California overtake and kill several jackrabbits in a chase through chaparral, leaping over boulders, cacti, and yucca clumps until it picked off all the fleet-footed animals one by one, then returned to the first victim and settled down to a feast.[58]

Roosevelt says the speed of the puma is astonishing; he cites one leaving the dogs more than a hundred yards behind on a downhill run of more than a quarter mile in Colorado.[59]

An Idaho hunter says the long, lithe beast travels in unbelievably long leaps in its bursting speed. He believes that no other creature on earth has as great a speed as the puma for short distances.[60]

The powerful hind legs of the puma act in unison at top speed, resulting in a half bound. It can easily outrun a pack of dogs for a few hundred yards, but its small lungs limit the distance it can cover at full stride. When out of breath, it must seek the temporary shelter of a tree or some other natural protection.

SWIMMING

The puma is a good swimmer and will take to the water when the need arises. Numbers were observed during the early colonization of French Guiana swimming from the mainland to the island of Cayenne where they devoured the flocks of the settlers.[61]

Two instances are recorded of pumas being killed while swimming the Fraser River in British Columbia in places where the river was nearly a mile wide.[62] An unsuccessful attack on a puma was launched with only a four-foot plank by a hunter from his open boat as the animal swam the open water between Vancouver Island and the mainland of British Columbia.[63] Other insular occurrences would tend to indicate that the animal undertakes fairly long swims.

From Vancouver Island, Dave Hancock described the swimming of his pet puma. He wrote that while cruising by boat to a smaller island nearby with his wife and the animal, the puma was so anxious to get to land that it jumped overboard before they neared shore.

"When his head broke the surface, he flattened his ears and with his three-foot tail trailing, struck out for the shore at a speed to be envied by an Olympic swimmer," Hancock wrote.

"I was interested to note that he was almost dry by the time he reached shore. It is commonly held that cats don't like water. But as a wildlife biologist, I knew that cougars often swim in the salt waters off the B.C. coast to change territory from island to island. Now I saw that the outer hair would take the water while the under hair stayed dry and provided insulation against the cold."[64]

In the neighborhood of the Parguaza Hills between Ciudad Bolívar and Ayacucho, Venezuela, a puma was encountered swimming the mile-wide Orinoco River in February 1930. When intercepted by the launch and crew of the governor, the puma became confused and tried to climb aboard. A number of shots were

Brazilian puma at full speed. (Courtesy Ditha Holesch)

fired at the beast from a distance of only a few feet but none took effect. Because of the scattered settlements along this part of the Orinoco, it was believed that the puma had not been cornered and driven into the stream.[65]

Although some authors have claimed that the puma once inhabited the Florida Keys, earliest writers did not mention it as a part of the fauna. Somewhat special is the kill of one on Key Largo, one of the closest of the chain of islands to the Florida mainland and the nearby Everglades.[66]

Merritt Island, along the central east coast of Florida, once had a steady population of pumas and several were killed by pioneer citrus growers. A local news item in the *Florida Star* states

Puma climbing a coconut palm in southern Guyana. (Courtesy Stanley E. Brock)

that while sailing through Banana Creek on 15 December 1883, Titusville resident Sam Norton killed a puma as it swam from shore to shore.[67] Banana Creek acts as a strait in separating islands in the Cape Canaveral area.

CLIMBING

American naturalist William Hornaday asserts that the puma is by far the best climber of all large cats of the world.[68] When pressed by hounds, it often jumps directly to the lowest limb of a tree, but it can scale the long, barren trunk of a tall pine with equal dexterity. Many observers have witnessed the puma spring from the earth and land twelve to fifteen feet above in a tree, and in dense jungles it may jump from tree to tree. In Paraguay it has been known to chase monkeys from bough to bough among trees in the density of entangled forests.[69]

As late as 1880, however, American sportsmen were still debating whether or not the mysterious animal could even climb trees. In that year, the outdoor journal *Forest & Stream* published numerous letters to the editor with supporting testimonies that it did.[70]

Without breaking its stride, the puma is capable of springing into the boughs of piñon, juniper, or other bushy trees so quickly and easily that it does not even resort to climbing.

If wounded, the puma sometimes ascends to the very top of the towering firs, hemlocks, and cedars in the coastal ranges of the Pacific Northwest. Frequently, these trees are three hundred feet high with their lowest limbs one hundred feet from the ground. Gamboling kittens bound up and down the tree trunks during play as if they were game props, tearing off bark and leaving claw marks far up the trees.

Stanley Brock, for many years the manager of the three thousand-square-mile Dadanawa Ranch in southern Guyana, had a pet female puma that had complete freedom of movement around the vast ranch, enabling Brock to observe many habits of the animal in its natural role.

Concerning the climbing ability of the puma, Brock states: "The leopard is a marvellous climber, far better than the jaguar, but the antics and agility of a puma in the treetops must be seen to be believed."[71]

Mountain lion jumping. (© Walt Disney Productions, reprinted by permission)

Brock believes that no cat in the world can match the puma as a climber and cites that it can easily climb a fifty-foot perpendicular coconut palm. Without hesitating, it leaves a tree in jumps. If not pressed, the big cat will slither down the trunk hind feet first, showing a reluctance to descend head first. Brock watched his puma decide against a twenty-foot drop from the canopy of a Brazil nut tree, running instead to the end of a limb where its weight bent the limb downward to within ten feet of the ground. Then with a twist, it turned tail first, still retaining a hold on the foliage at the tip of the limb. Swinging downward, the animal descended until its back feet were within inches of the ground, then dropped.[72]

AGILITY

For agility and maneuverability the puma has few equals. One authority says it is the most wonderful gymnast in all nature.[73]

Near the McCloud River in northern California, Livingston Stone followed the trail of a puma up the side of Mount Persephone to a blank wall of limestone cliffs where the tracks continued up to the very base. From here the beast sprang an amazing vertical leap of twenty feet up to the perpendicular precipice to a seemingly inaccessible retreat.[74] Another naturalist cites a measured horizontal leap in the snow of nearly forty feet.[75]

Idaho hunter Charles Lisle recorded the leap of the smaller of two pumas during a hunt:

56

"Some of the leaps were 30 feet, as we measured them; one, downhill was fully 40 feet from the take-off to where it ended."[76]

J. Frank Dobie, hunting in western New Mexico, describes the awesome leap of a puma that tried to escape the pursuit of hounds in Little Bear Canyon. Reaching the canyon rim, the puma never slackened its speed, but spread itself flat and leaped over into the abyss. Dobie estimated the first bench at 125 or 150 feet below, with numerous rocky spires jutting skyward. The outstretched paws of the puma caught one jagged upright and scraped a second one before the animal landed down in the canyon. It continued its flight until bayed and slain. All the claws on the left paw had been pulled out by the clasps at the rocks, but the animal had no broken bones as a result of its desperate leap.[77]

Alertness and quickness may be the reasons that the puma can and does defend itself successfully against the jaguar. An unusual incident that happened at the Hogle Zoological Garden in Salt Lake City dramatizes the agility of the puma confronted with what many persons would consider overhelming odds. One accidentally got into the cage of an African lion and a vicious battle resulted. Before the two were separated by attendants, the caretaker observed that the puma would strike the lion four or five times before the king of beasts could strike once. The caretaker felt that the puma was much the faster of the two.[78]

STALKING

Taking advantage of the shadows of the night, the puma will wander for miles in search of wild or domestic prey. It will make a kill in the daylight but generally prefers the stillness of dawn or twilight. A man watched a puma stalk nine deer for over an hour at midday in California. He first observed the animal standing motionless in the open over three hundred yards from the herd, alternately walking a short distance then stopping for a few minutes, constantly gazing at the deer. At times the herd watched the puma intently but showed no alarm. The puma maintained a steady pace of about two steps per second while stalking and carried its head and tail low. Frequently it sat erect and raised its head high. The puma seemed only mildly interested in the deer and never did make a final attack but disappeared instead into the brush.[79]

Deer will not always run from the scent or sight of a puma and will many times watch one as it looks over the herd.

The stalk is silent and stealthy. The big cat will take advantage of trees, bushes, and rocks for cover. It stalks to within striking distance of forty to fifty feet, and with two or three jumps that cover twenty to twenty-five feet each, the puma makes its final charge. Sometimes the prey is struck down by the sheer force of the onslaught. The puma is not always successful in catching its prey on the first leap but will make another trial approach or two before the attack is abandoned.

Profesor J.H. Allen of the University of Alberta witnessed a kill by a puma west of Banff. The geologist and his wife stopped their automobile and watched four Rocky Mountain goats ascending a game trail in single file. To the amazement of the couple, a puma paralleled the course of the goats a short distance from them. The lead goat became aware of the predator and bolted. The second goat in line followed but the third and fourth continued on course. The puma made a semicircular move and stopped in the trail at the top of the ridge ahead of the two remaining goats. It allowed the goat in front to pass but landed squarely on the head of the last one. Later, the park superintendent found the remains of the goat.[80]

Two methods are used in Chile by the puma to outwit its prey in open rangeland. It will expose itself to a flock of sheep at a distance and allow them to become accustomed to its presence. Edging always closer, it will amuse the flock like a mountebank to attract their attention. It throws itself to the ground, wallows, lies on its back and moves its legs, and runs in circles trying to catch its own tail in its teeth. Moved by curiosity, the sheep get closer. The puma continues its clownish acts. At last, with the sheep in extremely close quarters, the puma chooses its victim and launches the sudden attack of death.[81]

Another trick is employed by the puma in Chile to outwit colts, whose vicious kicks it must avoid. In full view, it begins a wide run completely encircling the colts. Sometimes closer, the perimeter is varied, causing the colts to become overconfident. At the opportune moment, the puma springs onto the back of a bewildered colt and slays it.[82]

Despite arguments to the contrary, the puma will sometimes lie in ambush and leap upon its prey from an elevated position. Early stories of this method of capture have been labeled as fabricated yarns, but it does happen on occasion. Near game trails and watering places in the jungles of Central and South America, the puma will hide among the grasses or on a low branch of a tree and pounce suddenly upon an unsuspecting victim. Edward J. Connolly, Jr., who wrote a thesis at the University of Utah on the food habits and life history of the animal, found evidence in the snow that a puma had employed this method of attack in Utah. It waited on a ledge until a young buck came within range and then jumped from its vantage point onto the back of the deer and rode "piggyback" down a hill for sixty feet before pulling the prey to the ground and killing it.[83]

THE KILL

The puma usually lands fully on the back of its victim holding on with its front feet, raking the sides and flanks with its hind feet, and sinking its fangs into the neck vertebrae behind the ears. The neck is almost always broken by one paw pulling the head to one side while biting. Death results from the impact, bite, strain, or a combination of any or all. If the wounds do not prove fatal, a series of bites in the jugular region or tearing open the large veins and arteries with the powerful claws will cause the desired effect. This is not usually necessary, however. Smaller and slower prey may be killed by a smashing blow to the head.

The puma occasionally displays a sadistic nature in the reenactment of a kill or a mock battle with the dead victim.

Stan Brock saw a puma in Guyana topple running sheep at full speed on a number of occasions. During the chase, the cat would hold one front paw up and maintain the fast pace on three while abreast the hind quarters of the sheep. At the precise moment in the gait of the quarry, the puma would trip the sheep with a swipe to the back leg. Brock also saw the puma kill quail on the wing by springing into the air and running along on its back legs. With lightning action, the animal swatted down birds as they flushed.[84]

Before feeding, the puma will disembowel its victim and pile the entrails aside and cover them. Believed to be a sanitary measure of removing distasteful portions, it also serves to preserve the meat from spoilage. The puma habitually drags its kill under a tree if available, gorges itself, and beds down for a nap.

The first meal will usually be the liver, heart, and lungs, removed through an opening in the rib cage. The puma will then dine on the loins and hams.

Presumably the puma has no preference for crippled animals, although it has been known to rob trap lines. Connolly found one that had passed up a bull elk with a broken front leg to make a kill two miles away on a deer. This was the second time Connolly had tracked individuals that had passed up wounded animals to make kills on animals in better physical condition.[85] Up until 1942, a puma held the record for the largest buck deer killed in the Kaibab area of northern Arizona. The antler spread of 46 11/16 inches was the greatest ever recorded from the area.[86]

MISFORTUNES

Damage to teeth and injuries to the head of the puma may result from falls or struggles with its prey. Several accidental fatalities have been recorded as a result of their hazardous method of obtaining food. Pumas have been killed by cows protecting their calves, and a bull will occasionally kill one. Horses and burros take a minor toll. In Chile the burro will not move when it sees a puma other than to lower its head and wait for an attack. As soon as the puma jumps on its back, the burro falls to the ground and wallows vigorously, repelling and sometimes killing the attacker.[87] The hooves of the burro are especially damaging. In the Lago Viedma region of southern Argentina ranchers keep a eunuch ass to ward off pumas from their stud harems.[88] Rocky Mountain naturalist Enos

Mills watched a mare successfully defend her colt against attack and drive away the puma.[89]

On the afternoon of 12 April 1949, a "bunged up" bull elk appeared at the door of the post office in Forney, Idaho, looking as if it had tangled with a wire fence. John O'Connor, postmaster, and Ray Westcott backtracked the animal out of town the next day and discovered a battle arena where a large puma lay dead. Checking the evidence, the men decided the big cat had attacked the elk and was astride it when the two crashed into a large ponderosa pine. The elk had evidently regained consciousness first and killed its adversary with its sharp forefeet. Several ribs of the puma had been broken and a large section of skin had been torn from its back. Meanwhile, back in town, the elk had taken refuge in the local garage and showed no inclination to leave.[90]

In the Glacier National Park in Montana, a doe mule deer was observed returning the attack of a puma. She leaped several times and landed with all four feet on the prostrate cat. It jumped into a tree at its first opportunity.[91] Several cases of deer and elk causing the deaths of pumas have been cited but the prey animals were unsuccesful in saving their own lives in the process.[92]

In killing the porcupine, the puma frequently gets the tormenting quills embedded in its lips, mouth, tongue, and paws. Those that are swallowed will pass through the intestinal tract with no apparent ill effects.

FOOD

Although the puma has been known to kill and eat almost anything from grasshoppers to moose, fresh deer meat forms its main diet, when and where available. It will kill domestic animals when it has the appetite.

One study, conducted in the southwestern United States, found that the puma would frequently pass by easily procurable cattle or horses for more difficult deer. From more than three thousand records of stomach analyses and dung specimens containing hair of the kill, the percentage of food items was overhelmingly deer. The Rocky Mountain mule deer was represented by 54 percent, with the Sonora whitetail deer and the Arizona whitetail deer another

28 percent. Next was the porcupine with 5.8 percent. The remaining food included the cottontail rabbit, jack rabbit, badger, skunk, fox, coyote, beaver, and prairie dog. Domestic cattle formed only 0.5 percent of the diet. A minor percentage represented various grasses and seeds. One puma on Mingus Mountain in Arizona lived almost entirely on porcupine in an area where deer were plentiful.[93]

A similar study of puma stomachs, intestinal tracts, and scats, conducted in Utah and eastern Nevada, also revealed that deer furnished the puma more food than all other prey species combined. Next in order of importance were the porcupine and domestic sheep, with lesser percentages of cottontail, hare, marmot, packrat, skunk, horse, domestic cow, dog, goat, bobcat, and unidentified bird, ground squirrel, coyote, pocket mouse, elk, and grasses. When necessary, the puma will eat various birds, snails, and lizards.[94]

Preliminary investigations into the prey of pumas in a wilderness environment were conducted in the Idaho Primitive Area in 1964-65. More wapiti, or elk, kills were found than deer kills. It was also found that pumas were killing deer of all ages, but they were selecting young and old elk alike.[95]

Stomach contents were kept of thirty-nine pumas killed in the fall and winter over a seven-year period in the Cariboo district of British Columbia and were reported in 1967. Rabbits made up the biggest share of prey at 26 percent. Next in order were deer at 23; carrion, 13; moose, domestic sheep, and porcupine, each 8 percent. Two cases indicated cannibalism. On Vancouver Island, the animal lives mainly on venison, blue grouse, and an occasional beaver.[96]

Arthur Wooley of Drain, Oregon, found bear meat and bear fur in the stomach contents of a puma.[97] Another record of the same food from the same state exists.[98]

The puma is especially fond of burro meat in Arizona, but finds the beast a formidable foe in combat. In the same state a heavy toll of wild turkeys is taken by pumas.

A good many bighorns are killed by the puma on the east face of the Sierra San Pedro Mártir in Baja California.[99] A U.S. Forest Service officer found portions of a desert bighorn killed and partly eaten by a puma in the San Bernardino National Forest in Southern California in 1947.[100]

In Florida, raccoons and free ranging hogs form a large part of the diet of the puma. A former director of the Florida Game and Fresh Water Fish Commission, Dr. O. Earle Frye, and coauthors itemize the remaining menu of the Florida variety: "Panthers will undoubtedly eat most any kind of wild animal of suitable size, or medium sized birds, rabbits, turtles, alligators, or snakes. Two trappers in the Everglades reported finding the remains of a six foot alligator killed by the panther."[101]

The puma in Florida will occasionally probe the ocean beaches for turtle eggs.

In tropical America, the puma feeds on all small mammals including the spotted cavy, armadillo, coati, deer, monkey, tapir, hare, agouti, capybara, porcupine, and peccary. In the Argentine pampas, it preys on the guanaco, huemul, and rhea. The hare, viscacha, rat, weasel, and fox have been listed from Chile.[102] In the high mountains of the Andes, llamas and vicuñas are a part of the diet. When the female puma in South America has young to feed, she becomes more fearless and invades the yards and corrals of human dwellings for hens, turkeys, and geese.

American naturalist Enos Mills observed a puma for half an hour while it chased, captured, and ate grasshoppers.[103] Subject to predation on the other extremity are the moose and bison. Timothy Flint, first biographer of Daniel Boone, knew the old scout personally and taught his grandson in school. He wrote that Boone killed a puma on the back of a buffalo in Kentucky as it was endeavoring to kill the huge animal.[104]

The availability of prey appears to be the main concern of the puma. Type, size, and defensive disposition seem to be relatively unimportant. Only infrequently does the bill of fare include carrion.

CANNIBALISM

Cannibalism is not rare with pumas. The male will eat its own young when given the opportunity and several records exist of the prac-

tice among adults. On record is an instance near Tucson, Arizona, in 1945, in which a puma robbed a trap of a meal of its own kind.[105]

In the Huachuca Mountains of Arizona, two pumas came mewing at the cabin door of a miner. One was shot and the skinned carcass was discarded a short distance from the dwelling. During the night, the other animal returned and ate nearly all of its dead companion. On the following day, it returned again uttering a peculiar cry. It was wounded by the miner but escaped into thick brush.[106]

A hunter in the San Isabel National Forest west of Pueblo, Colorado, killed a female puma that showed signs of nursing kittens. From additional signs in the immediate area, the hunter believed that a male was in the vicinity as well as the young. Returning a few days later, he found the den of the female and remnants of two kittens that had been partly devoured. Subsequently, tracks of the male were trailed in the snow back to the den several times. The hunter baited traps around the den carefully with catnip oil diluted with petrolatum. Ten days later the male was trapped. All indications and sign left no doubt to the hunter that the male had eaten the young when the female was not present to guard them.[107]

John Lesowski of the Fish and Game Branch, Williams Lake, British Columbia, killed and skinned a male puma near the town of Horsefly. Seven days later, he killed a mature female that had fed on the carcass of the former for four or five days. Deer and moose were plentiful in the area. On another occasion, Lesowski killed a large male 150 yards from a younger male that it had killed and partially eaten. The larger puma had sustained a three-inch gash on the chest during the fight.[108]

In a three-year study of food habits of pumas in the Boulder-Escalante mountains and adjacent canyonlands of south-central Utah, three cases of cannibalism were found. A young puma was killed, partly eaten, and buried by another. The kittens of two radio-tagged females were also eaten by other pumas.[109]

FOOD REQUIREMENTS

Because the puma is a fresh meat eater, it must kill in large numbers to survive. Occasionally, individuals will apparently kill for lust, rampaging through domestic stock, leaving large numbers of animals dead without feeding on any portions of them. Seldom does the puma eat anything other than its own kills.

Until recently, most estimates on the food requirements of the puma have been pieced together from observations covering long periods of time without concentrated study. Because the deer is the most important food item in the diet, it has been the basis of most estimates. These range up to one hundred deer per year killed by a single puma, with an average of one per week.

One study from Utah and Nevada is summarized as follows: "Some rough computations based on daily food requirements of cougars, the amount of meat consumed from the average deer, and the proportions of the diet consisting of deer indicate that a cougar kills a deer every four to ten days for an average of one weekly during cool winter months (November-April). There is some reason to believe the kill might be greater during summer."[110] Cache spoilage could justify the latter belief. Other studies and estimates substantiate the one kill per week average.

Once in a while a puma appears to have an insatiable desire to kill well beyond the limits of its food requirements. It may leave a fresh kill after one feeding and make a twenty-five- or thirty-mile trip around its beat in search of another victim. Jay Bruce found the carcasses of twelve deer killed in as many days by a male puma near the junction of Panther Creek and North Fork of the Mokelumne River in California. Trailing the beast for twelve miles, Bruce found another fresh kill before he finally killed the puma.[111] Stanley Calgrove of Brookings, Oregon, tracked a puma in the snow and found five civet cats, one raccoon, and two deer slain by the animal without stopping to eat any part of the kills.[112]

It is among domestic animals that the puma has been known to spread devastation with its wild forays. Destruction upon flocks of sheep in Patagonia in the early days of settlement was immense. One animal killed upwards of one hundred head from a single flock, with a total of fourteen for one night.[113]

The remains of 275 sheep that had been killed in two nights by a puma in the vicinity of Strawberry Reservoir, in Wasatch County, Utah, were viewed by W.O. Nelson, supervisor for the Predator and Rodent Division of the U.S. Fish and Wildlife Service in Utah. On another occasion, Nelson counted forty-eight sheep killed in a single foray by another puma. These were by far the heaviest stock losses Nelson knew about in his thirty years of predator work.[114] Near Glades Park, Colorado, a single puma entered a flock of bedding ewes in the early 1920s and killed 192.[115]

In the Gran Chaco frontier of Paraguay, ranchers are compelled to hunt the puma because of damages to their herds and flocks. Robert Eaton, a rancher in the western half of the country, had 150 sheep killed by one puma at an outlying camp over a six-month period. The sheep pen was moved up alongside the house, but still the lion made about two visits a week, killing from two to ten sheep a night. Herdsmen lay out at night alongside the corral and shot at the beast on several occasions. More than once the puma returned after being shot at. When finally killed, the animal turned out to be a small male only a little over five feet in total length.[116]

On Vancouver Island, a puma mangled 146 New Hampshire reds in three nights, leaving some of the chickens dead and others dying.[117]

In a study on puma depredations in Nevada between 1977 and 1981, it was found that ranchers suffered an annual average loss of 375 ewes, lambs, calves, and colts. By far the most losses were among the sheep producers. With an estimated total of 130,000 sheep in Nevada, this represented an average loss of 0.29 percent. If spread evenly over all producers in the state, this would not be excessive, but of the ninety major producers only an average of fifteen had problems and only five had serious problems. In the study, it was found that if a puma killed a large number of animals the first time it killed, it was likely to continue the trait. One such puma killed fifty-nine sheep in a single incident in the summer of 1980 near Ely, Nevada. When the puma was finally destroyed, it had 112 confirmed stock kills to its credit.[118]

On a statewide basis in Colorado, the puma is on the bottom of the list of sheep predators which include the coyote, bear, bobcat, dog, and eagle. The puma accounted for only 0.8 percent animal kills from 1962 to 1965.[119]

Studies in California from 1971 through 1977 reveal that 42 percent of puma depredations involve sheep, 22 percent goats, 16 percent cattle, 5 percent poultry, 4 percent horses, and 3 percent pigs. In 1976 there were only twenty-nine verified incidents of puma predation for all livestock species.[120]

The present trend in control policies calls for the removal of offending pumas based on depredation complaints, while at the same time presenting the removal of nontarget pumas.

STORING FOOD

During the La Salle explorations of the Mississippi River in 1681 and 1682, Father Zenobus Membré made an early recording of an unusual habit of the puma with its surplus food. He wrote: "It eats a little, then carries off the rest on its back, and hides it under some leaves, where ordinarily no other beast or prey touches it."[121]

Azara reported from Paraguay in 1802 on the same storage habit of the animal, stating that a captive pet he knew about would not refuse any food offered to it. If not hungry, the animal was said to bury the meat in the sand and dig it up when so inclined and wash it in a watering trough before eating.[122]

A cougar buries a mule deer doe that it killed in the Canadian Rockies of Alberta. (Courtesy Ed Cesar)

After feasting on a large kill, the puma makes a somewhat futile attempt to cache the uneaten portions by removing the carcass to a secluded spot and covering it with leaves, sticks, dirt, snow, stones, or other convenient residue. The animal may never return to eat from the remains, but if the cache is undisturbed and the puma does not make another fresh kill, it may come back several times over a span of one day or more.

Numerous instances are recorded in which wayfarers, compelled to sleep in the woods, have been covered with ground litter by pumas, presumably for feeding purposes later. In some cases, adult pumas have made hasty returns with their hungry young.

In the late 1700s, Pennsylvania wilderness hunter Jonathan Wheaton lay down to rest on Capouse Mountain in what is now Lackawanna County, and dropped off to sleep. He awakened to find himself covered with sticks and leaves. Knowing the habits of the puma, Wheaton decided that a female had reserved him for her offspring and would soon return. He climbed a nearby tree and shot the mother when she came back with her two young.[123]

Bill Long, called the Pennsylvania "King of Hunters," helped to bring about his own similar predicament. When he was a young man in the early 1800s, he killed a deer on the North Fork of the Allegheny River. Forced to spend the night in the woods, he covered himself with the pelt of the deer and lay down to sleep. Around midnight he awoke with forest debris all over him. Upon the return of a puma he lit a torch of pitch pine and scared the animal away.[124]

Henry Utt supplied meat for Nathaniel Massie and his surveying party from 1791 to 1801 in the Virginia Military District in Ohio. Night overtook Utt on one occasion while he was hunting on McCulloch Creek. The hunter wrapped himself in his blanket and lay down by a log to spend the night. Upon waking the next morning, he discovered that sometime during the night he had been covered with leaves. In a very short time a puma and her litter appeared on the scene. Utt killed the female.[125]

J. Frank Dobie relates a story of two pumas covering a man with leaves, told to him by Mrs. Ada Payne of Thalia, Texas. In 1824 her sixteen-year-old grandfather was a participant in the follow-up kill of one of the animals after the unusual happening in the "woods east of the Mississippi River," where settlers were clearing land for cabins and fields.[126]

A hunting companion of German wanderer Frederick Gerstächer in Arkansas told him about being covered with leaves by a puma back in Kentucky in earlier days.[127]

In July 1859 a similar incident happened to Corporal James Pike during an Indian campaign on the Clark Fork of the Brazos River in Texas.[128]

Alwin Frache of Waneta, British Columbia, had been hunting unsuccessfully from early morning to midafternoon. In a little glade in the forest, he stretched out in the dry leaves, pulled his hat over his eyes, and began a restful nap. About an hour later, his movements caused a rustling sound that aroused him. To sit upright, he had to emerge from a heaping of leaves with which he had been covered. Concluding that some animal had saved him as a future provision, Frache recreated the scene as best he could and shinned up a nearby tree to see the adventure through. He wrote:

"It was just as well that I awoke when I did, for I had been but a short time in the tree when a female cougar appeared, followed by two half grown kittens. Going straight to the pile of leaves, she circled it several times, crouching and apparently selecting a good place to spring from. When she made the leap she went through the air like a flash, scattering the leaves in a whirlwind and scratching and snarling. When she had cleared the ground without finding what she wanted, she did not stop to display disappointment. Instead she cast about, struck my scent and came direct to my tree.

"Seeing me sitting there, awake and gun in hand, her courage failed or perhaps her cunning taught her better. Feeling sure I had her, anyway, I waited to see what she would do. After a moment's pause she began climbing a tree a few yards from mine, evidently intending to get above me and bring me down with a flying leap. Whatever was her idea, I did not wait to see its development, but at the first chance put a bullet through her jaw and chest that stopped her climbing, for good."[129]

63

STRENGTH

The remarkable strength of the puma has been demonstrated time and again in its defensive actions, its attacks on formidable prey, and its removal of victims to places of concealment or retirement for feeding purposes. The powerful forepaws can overturn an assailant or disembowel one with a sweeping motion. Dogs are often dead before they hit the ground following a single blow to the head during the battle. The bite of the puma is bone crushing. Two Wyoming hunters saw a puma knock a full-grown buffalo cow to the ground in a smashing attack.[130]

The puma can drag or carry its fallen prey for a considerable distance and has been known to transport a deer carcass up a tree to feed in security.

A puma killed the mule of a plantation owner in Guyana and dragged it across a trench half filled with water. Naturalist Sir Robert Schomburgk, who recorded the incident in 1840, added: "So far as strength is concerned it is in no sense inferior to the jaguar."[131] Zadock Thompson, in his early natural history of Vermont, records that a puma killed a large calf and carried it to a retiring place with a leap of fifteen feet over a ledge of rocks.[132] In the Davis Mountains of Texas, a six-hundred-pound heifer was dragged out of a narrow spring-water hole and up the side of a mountain by a puma for safe keeping.[133]

M.E. Musgrave, of the U.S. Biological Survey in Arizona, was the head of a force of men that killed more than six hundred pumas in the course of their work. Based on field observations, Musgrave made the following report on the strength of the animal: "I have seen a horse weighing eight or nine hundred pounds which a mountain lion has dragged twenty-five or thirty feet, as proven by tracks in the snow. Even more surprising is the fact that it sometimes carries off what it has killed. I have seen both deer and big calves some distance from where the kill has been made, with no evidence of dragging. To do this the lion first turns the animal on its back, picks it up by the brisket, all four feet sticking up in the air, and walks off with its own head held high."[134]

ENEMIES

Man with his dogs and guns apparently is the only enemy that actually seeks the puma. With this one exception, it reigns supreme over a vast domain. Encounters with the grizzly bear are avoided whenever possible, but the puma has been known to perform admirably in a skirmish with the beast and in some instances has emerged the victor. Perhaps the worst enemies of the puma at one time were the wolf packs that roamed the countryside at will. Few, if any, wild animals could survive the relentless onslaught of these dreaded hordes.

Even the mighty jaguar is not fully the master of the puma. Naturalist W.H. Hudson asserts that where the two species inhabit the same district in South America, the puma is the persistent persecutor of the jaguar, following it and harassing it until an opportunity occurs for an attack.[135] The natives of Guatemala say that in a fight between the two the puma conquers the jaguar. Victor Gonzales K., a hunting guide in Guatemala, on seven or eight occasions had jaguars answering his calls and coming in angrily when a puma let its presence be known. In each instance, the jaguar stopped answering the call and did not come in for the rest of the night.[136] Many competent observers in Central and South America agree that the husky jaguar is more powerful than the puma, but the latter is lean, wiry, and more agile, accounting for the domination.

Major John C. Cremony was an interpreter with the U.S. Boundary Commission in the Southwest between 1849 and 1851. Along the Pecos River near Bosque Redondo in the present state of New Mexico, Cremony and his Apache guides killed a puma. They were about to return home when, hearing a terrible noise downstream, they dismounted and hastened to the place with caution. They came upon a deadly fight between another puma and a bear. The puma crouched in preparation for an attack with its long tail twisting like a wounded serpent. It leaped forward and engaged the bear, with both combatants rendering frightful cries. After about two minutes, the lion sprang from the arena. When both animals had licked their wounds for a short time, the lion resumed the offensive. In the second encounter, the lion tore open the back of the bear and ripped away at its vital organs until it died.[137]

Various fleas, ticks, and lice have been collected from the puma, but it is generally free of external parasites because of the absence of litter in the den and the short duration of attendance. Roundworms and tapeworms are known to infest the internal organs. One known disease in the wild is rabies. A puma, infested with rabies, attacked a woman and a young boy near Morgan Hill, Santa Clara County, California, in 1909, and was responsible for their subsequent deaths.[138]

An old forest puma killed on Vancouver Island was suffering from polynephritis. Although all normal kidney tissue had been destroyed by the disease, "the cat did not appear to be suffering, was approaching motherhood, and was carrying shot in its flesh."[139]

ATTACKING MAN

The puma is generally inoffensive toward man and has seldom been a menace, but it can easily kill a person if so inclined. Rarely does it attack humans, but scores of provoked and unprovoked cases are authenticated throughout American history with a few extraordinary instances of the puma devouring its victims.

D.J. Spaulding, a regional biologist with the Department of Recreation and Conservation in British Columbia, has kept records of the sex, age, and condition of pumas in twenty-three known attacks on humans in that province. He reveals that nineteen young, three adults, and one senile puma were involved in the attacks, with a tendency for females to predominate in the sample. Twelve of the attackers were listed as in poor condition as opposed to ten in good condition. Two of the attacks led to fatalities. Both victims were young boys.[140]

CURIOSITY AND FRIENDLINESS

Many so-called attacks on man are undoubtedly based on a fearful unawareness that the feline pursuer may be exhibiting a natural catlike curiosity. The puma is apparently fascinated by man and will sometimes follow him long distances in the wilds without launching an attack, although one might materialize

should the objective show signs of weakness or should the animal be crazed with hunger. Naturalist Einer Lönnberg says that in Ecuador the puma does not attack man as a rule, but that an intoxicated Indian is sometimes an exception. He believes that the puma is aware of feebleness in a faltering individual.[141]

A sawmill worker in Nahuelbuta, Chile, returned from lunch to find a puma sniffing around his sawmill engine. It sat down a few yards away from the man. The two watched each other for five minutes, the man keeping his eyes on both the puma and a nearby shelter should he suddenly need it. At last the puma stood up and very slowly strolled back into the woods.[142]

The Spanish in South America believe strongly in the friendliness of the puma toward Christians. They perpetuate the name *amigo del cristiano* and retell legends of human kindness displayed by the animal. Undoubtedly garnished with legend, but based on an actual happening, is the folktale of Maldonada, retold in slightly different versions for several centuries in Argentina.

Around 1537 Buenos Aires was a little colony besieged by Indians. The Spanish captain of the colony forbade anyone's leaving except for food; he threatened offenders with hanging. Plagued with hunger, a lovely young señorita named Maldonada slipped out into the wilds in search of something to eat. When darkness came, she happened upon a mother puma in the pains of birth and evidently needing help. Maldonada cleaned a newborn kitten with her dress and assisted with the birth of another. A strange friendship developed between the two, and Maldonada stayed for a time with the puma family, sharing food brought in by the mother.

Maldonada eventually wandered into an Indian village and was adopted by the tribe. A Spanish hunting party sometime later rescued her and the captain of the colony threatened to hang her for what he thought was desertion. However, on the insistence of citizens, he spared the girl from the usual public execution but decreed that she should be tied to a tree outside the colony where beasts could devour her. Courageous citizens visited the tree days later expecting to find her remains, but were surprised fo find her alive and unharmed. Beside her, as a protector and provider of raw meat, was a female puma.

Maldonada was spared. The colony moved up the river and founded the city of Asunción. Some colonists returned later and repopulated Buenos Aires. Across Rio de la Plata in Uruguay, another village was founded and named Maldonada, in memory of the lovely señorita with the strange adventure.

The story of Maldonada was written for the first time in 1612 by Rui Díaz Guzmán, who knew her personally. His history of Spanish colonization along the Rio de la Plata was first published in 1835.[143]

J. Frank Dobie says: "In Mexico and Central America there are innumerable stories of a lion's protecting a man against the attack of a jaguar." Dobie also says the Cheyenne Indians to some extent still consider the puma their friend and protector.[144]

According to naturalist Charles John Cornish, the puma actually seeks the society of man on occasion. He described an incident in which a puma spent the night beneath a hammock that contained a human occupant.[145]

Kittrell Mahon killed a man around 1905 at Clay Hammock, near the Kissimmee River in Florida. He fled to a hideout on a small bayhead on the east side of Lake Jack, now Lake Francis. Today his camp is known as Kit Bay.

Mountain lion carrying her kitten near Monte Vista, Colorado, in 1964. (Ernest Wilkinson)

One day Mahon killed a deer and carried it to his camp where he skinned it. He glanced around and a large puma was within a few feet of him. He mustered up enough courage to cut a piece of the flank meat and throw it on the ground near the big cat. Without taking her eyes off him, the puma ate the meat. He threw more meat, each time a little farther away. After the puma was satisfied with an ample hunk of meat, it moved back a few feet and lay down. Mahon noticed she was heavy with unborn kittens and decided not to kill her. A few minutes later she left. About a week later, while Mahon was sitting in his camp, the puma appeared again. This time however, she had two baby kittens. Kit had no fresh meat this time but did provide the mother with cooked food. She continued to return every few days for another meal.

After the trouble over killing a man had settled down, Mahon returned to his home near the community of Henscratch. The puma and her kittens followed him. She lay around the house for a few days but soon started killing chickens and turkeys. Mahon penned the big cat and her kittens and notified Ringling Brothers Circus and they came and took the animals away.[146]

In the wilds of the logging country of Skagit County, Washington, in the late 1880s, Charles Harmon was looking for lost oxen. A puma surprised the logger by trotting up to his side and displaying good will. Harmon headed for camp in a run with the animal in an easy swing stride behind him, frequently reaching up and licking the hand of the terrified logger. It followed into camp and crouched near the door of a cabin that the logger had safely reached, until it was shot. The bizarre incident dramatically illustrates what may be a strange affinity of the puma toward man on occasion.[147]

PLAYFULNESS

Cats are playful and the puma is no exception. Young ones play individually or together like small domestic cats. It is reported from South America that the puma is one of the most playful animals in existence, with the young spending large portions of the time in characteristic gambols. They delight in frolics,

66

hide-and-seek, lying in wait, mock battles, and practicing strategy in the capture of insects and small prey.[148] One writer on the puma described the antics of a grown specimen he observed on a sandbar of a creek in the Black Hills of Dakota Territory in 1882: "Its play was evidently made from the love of action and mimicry, and consisted in chasing mythical birds or small things, and pretending to catch and devour them. Its leaps, bounds, and shiftings of attitude were similar to those of a kitten in chasing and cuffing at an erratic and elusive butterfly. Some of its lithe, curving leaps were graceful in the extreme."[149]

Sometimes the puma will play with small prey before it satisfies its hunger. American artist Charles Livingston Bull watched a puma in the New York Zoological Park leap ten or twelve feet up the bars of its cage to catch sparrows and then play with each victim before devouring it.[150]

A most unusual incident happened in 1883 to Mary Campbell of York, British Columbia. Four miles from her home she was knocked from a pony into unconsciousness by a puma. When she revived, the animal was standing over her with one paw on her chest. She screamed and the puma jumped back. With her eyes on the big cat, she walked backwards toward her home as fast as she could go. Several times the puma grabbed parts of her dress, stopping to roll over, playfully clutching remnants of the garment. As the woman approached her home, the puma circled her and blocked the way. She reeled and fainted.

In the meantime a young boy had seen the antics of the puma and summoned the father of the woman. Before the animal could advance on the victim again, it was downed with a rifle ball. The woman was fully convinced that the puma meant to kill her, and that its action was a preliminary sport the way a house cat plays with a mouse.[151]

A number of cases are on record from frontier settlements of wild pumas playing with small children who did not understand the dangers involved.

An incident reported in 1948 describes how a puma near Lightning Creek in the Snake River region of Oregon seemingly tried to help a sheepman drive thirty-five sheep down a trail. Occasionally the puma would make a pass at one without hurting it in the manner of a sheep dog. The sheepman, however, did not appreciate the help. He withdrew into the forest and killed the puma as the strange procession passed by.[152]

Sometimes the adult puma can be quite gentle and perfectly harmless around humans. Dave Hancock described in 1968 the catnapping of his 150-pound pet puma after a day of romp and play on a small island adjacent to Vancouver Island. With Dave was his wife Lyn.

"We could hear that deep rumbling purr that seemed to shake the ground with cat-like contentment. Tom yawned and rolled over on his side until his nose was buried in a clump of vividly scarlet Indian Paint Brush plants. He opened his eyes and sniffed the perfume. Lethargically, he bit off a dainty flower. It dangled a moment between his teeth.

"'That's Tom,' said Lyn, 'our flower child.'"[153]

DOMESTICATION AND CAPTIVITY

Pumas show marked individuality within litters. Some are gentle and even affectionate, while others are vicious and never trustworthy. Docile kittens may become mean with maturity. Pets are generally playful with their owners, but with the right stimulus often resort instinctively to misdeeds. Many end up in zoos and parks. They adapt to confinement and will often reproduce in captivity.

The Spanish commissioner and commandant in Paraguay, Felix de Azara, recorded the domestication of a puma kitten in 1802 by a priest. The animal ran loose in the settlement for more than a year and was then presented to Azara. For four more months, the puma was kept as a pet, but it finally returned to the wild state of its own free will, simply jumping a fence to do so.[154]

A tame puma in Patagonia would fight with a pack of hounds during the day and then lie down with them to keep warm on a cold night.[155] Milt Holt, noted puma hunter of Gunlock, Utah, had a tame female puma that was raised from a kitten and slept with one of his hunting dogs. The two slept side by side and ate from the same feed bowl.[156]

LONGEVITY

Pumas may live up to twenty-five years. One lived in the Zoologischen Garten in Frankfurt, Germany, for seventeen years, one month, and nine days. It died of internal injuries received by accident.[157] Statistical data on the life span of twelve pumas, kept in confinement at the National Zoological Park in Washington, D.C., show that they lived an average of 7 1/2 years. One lived for seventeen years and eight months. Two of the specimens died prematurely because of pens located where persistent drafts occurred.[158]

Individual pumas in the wild state have been known to live up to eighteen years, based on track peculiarities in a defined locality.

In Santa Cruz County, Arizona, a male puma dubbed "Old Cross Toes" by local sportsmen, was known to have used a travelway periodically for ten years. When killed, it was estimated to be at least fifteen years old.[159]

"Old Tom" was known for twelve years in his habitat on the North Rim of the Grand Canyon, according to Zane Grey.[160]

Two renowned puma hunters, with broad experiences with the animal in its native haunts, believed that pumas lived to be quite old in the wild state. Jay Bruce, of California, put the average life at over fifteen years.[161] Uncle Jimmy Owens, of Grand Canyon hunting fame, placed the ordinary life of a puma from twenty to twenty-five years.[162]

ECONOMIC IMPORTANCE

The status of the puma to date has been an uneasy one. Intense efforts have been made to eliminate it completely for economic reasons, but there is a growing realization of late that the animal has a definite role in the balance of nature and that its destruction of domestic animals is not as great as it was once believed to be.

Peruvian Incas used the hide and skull of the puma for ceremonial purposes. At their feasts, puma pelts, with skulls intact, were drooped over individuals who took part in the ceremonials. The skin had gold ear pieces, and the teeth and claws had been replaced with gold.[163] The puma was also used for the punishment of treason and disobedience among the Incas.[164]

A mark of distinction among North American Indian tribes was a puma trophy of some kind worn as dress or ornament.

An early belief was that parts of the puma had medicinal value.

John Brickel, a "Dr. of Physick" who lived in North Carolina from 1729 to 1731, was an exponent of the humoral theory of the medical profession. His description of the "panther" of the Carolinas contains his own observations on the medicinal value of the animal:

The Fat is hot, dry, and cosmatick, and helps the *Vertigo, Palsie, Scabs, Ringworms*, and *Varices* (or swelling of the *Veins*.) The gall being drank, presently kills, for it burns the Humours by its violent heat, causing *Convulsions*, vomiting of *Green Cholor*, and Death. It is reported that some (Indians) Poyson the Arrows therewith, that they may kill the sooner.[165]

Early frontiersmen and trappers praised the value of puma meat as food, comparing it favorably with veal.

The pelt of the puma is not valuable. Luckily for the animal, the exportation of hides is prohibited by law in some Latin American countries. In others, commercial hunters consider the trade unprofitable.

Efforts are now being made to save the puma from extinction. It is an important game animal and could be working in favor of man and a more hardy deer population.

Mountain lion clawing a tree trunk. (Wide World)

BEADLE'S HALF DIME Library

Copyrighted in 1879 by BEADLE AND ADAMS.

Vol. IV.   Single Number.   BEADLE AND ADAMS, PUBLISHERS, No. 98 WILLIAM STREET, NEW YORK.   Price, 5 Cents.   No. 86.

DANDY ROCK, THE MAN FROM TEXAS.

A WILD ROMANCE OF THE LAND OF GOLD.

BY G. WALDO BROWNE.

Five, ten, fifteen minutes wore away, and still the cougar had not left his perch, neither had the gleaming eyes left for even a moment their prey.

8
Conflicting Accounts

OCCURRENCES

The sighting of a puma in areas of established distribution is rarely denied, but every time someone reports that he has seen one in certain areas of eastern North America he is subject to ridicule by many who discredit the claim. Others gain confidence in their belief that the animal has been there all along. Some observers of integrity are undoubtedly mistaken in their identification at times, simply because the mere thought of the animal truly excites the imagination. Yet, it is not impossible to see one in eastern woods and forests where they have long been believed to be extinct, and some of the reports must be dependable. One writer says: "A common sense view of the matter surely is that such reports are less 'fantastic' and 'incredible' than the unqualified denials of them."[1]

Hundreds of reports of the puma in former habitats are untrue. Something must have been seen, however, and there are explanations. Questionable occurrences in West Virginia, according to one writer, could be (1) wildcats crying on the mountain during mating time, (2) large dog tracks in the snow, (3) pranks, or (4) an excuse to get a permit to carry a gun in the woods out of hunting season. Rumors of the beast are popular for other reasons also. Weird sounds could be a fox, screech owl, or barn owl. Every town has its mighty nimrod who is a myth maker and elaborate hoaxes to gain publicity or notoriety have been exposed from time to time. At least one puma in West Virginia was found to have been imported from the southwest United States to be released and "hunted." Dogs and house cats roam the countryside at night also, becoming the subjects of occasional "sightings" by sleepy motorists.[2] Bill Walsh, writing in the *Pennsylvania Game News*, says that in that state "Some writers think that mountainfolk and other countryfolk spread the 'wild cat' rumors around berrying time in order to keep city folks from venturing out and competing for the crop."[3]

◄ *A typical adventure story of the nineteenth century that helped to popularize an unfounded reputation of assassin for the puma. (Courtesy Library of Congress)*

Sightings in the East are an electrifying shock to most residents and evoke responses from wild furor to mild hysteria. Early settlers believed that man and the marauder were incompatible and that the latter had to be eliminated. A strange howl ringing throughout the hills on the headwaters of the Missouri River once brought a posse of hunters who tracked down a steamboat.[4] Old timers in Malone, New York, grabbed their rifles at the cry of the panther and rushed out to meet the first locomotive coming into town.[5]

An assassin reputation has survived with the animal. Following a sighting in Watonwan County, Minnesota, in 1950, no less than the National Guard, the sheriff, coon hunters with hounds, and an airplane were used to hunt the beast with no luck.[6] Volunteer fire departments in the Southern Appalachians once offered their assistance in case they were needed to exterminate "panthers." It is a wonder that the animal would want to return to former haunts that offered receptions like these.

What is commonly called the Eastern panther is one of the rarest mammals in America. Its decline coincided with the loss of deer herds, vast burned-over areas, forest exploitation, the vanguards of civilization, and bounties. With the return of the deer to certain areas in abundance, their foe appears to have survived or returned also. Rumors of their presence persisted during the intervening years, however.

Officially, the last bounty paid on the panther in Pennsylvania was in 1886. Yet, from a compiled sixty-year collection of newspaper clippings, magazine articles, and written accounts, Henry W. Shoemaker of Altoona published a year-by-year list of sightings, hearings, and track observations with his belief that some survived in the state despite adverse living conditions. A more recent record was investigated and found to have been a huge, feral house cat.[7]

Few persons believed that a female puma and a large kitten wandered into the outskirts of Montreal, Canada, in March 1959, until the Redpath Museum of McGill University made a plaster cast of the tracks, confirming the occurrence.[8] Bruce S. Wright, of the Northeastern Wildlife Station in New Brunswick, has made

Puma killing an armadillo in Guyana. (Stanley E. Brock)

an extensive study to prove that the animal has returned to some of its former haunts in Eastern Canada.[9]

The fascinating controversy of panthers in New York has continued since the 1890s, when apparently the last one was killed in the Adirondacks. Eyewitness reports are published in newspapers practically every year, giving continued and ever wider publicity. Persistent reports in New Jersey tend to confirm that possibly one or two panthers may have been seen near the town of Lebanon in recent years.

It is claimed that a number of sightings and attacks on stock have been made by one or more of the big cats almost within sight of the Washington Monument and the U.S. Capitol in 1960 and 1961. Conservation officials believed that severe snowstorms were the cause of the animals' appearing in the populated communities of neighboring Maryland. The same report states that evidence indicates the coastal area of North Carolina may also have panthers.[10] From the mountainous western part of the state have also come a number of reliable reports on sightings.

Herbert Ravenel Sass, a Charlestown newspaperman who collected panther data, is as convincing as anyone could be, without offering absolute proof, that the panther prowls the

East again, especially in the South Carolina low country.[11]

Florida is the last definitive habitat of the sleek panther in the eastern United States. In spite of the removal of the animal from the hunting list and its complete protection by law, the animal is decreasing in numbers because of new highways through its habitats, housing developments, and the altering of panther environment through water management. The National Wildlife Federation released figures that seven Florida panthers were killed by highway vehicles in a twelve-year span between 1972 and 1984.[12]

It was once believed that the panther did not survive in Florida beyond the frontier days, but a group of professional hunters removed both doubt and uncertainty. Because of its retiring habits, the animal was able to exist without detection close to centers of heavy human population. In 1935 Dave Newell, a Florida sportsman and onetime professional predator hunter in Arizona, brought famed Arizona houndsmen Vince and Ernest Lee to the peninsula state to help confirm his belief that the animal could be found in numbers. In a five-week hunt the party killed a total of eight panthers in the tangled strands of the Big Cypress Swamp in Collier County alone. They got four of the big cats in the first three mornings of the hunt. With the aid of the expert Lee dogs, the hunters found numerous kills made by panthers in the fern heads of the swamp that would have eluded the attention of less experienced hunters and hounds.[13] Today the animal is found in limited numbers in the Everglades, Big Cypress Swamp, Green Swamp in the center of the state, and the Big Scrub east of Ocala.

The panther is apparently beginning a comeback in Alabama. One was killed in St. Clair County, on 16 March 1948, that weighed 109 pounds. Fully authenticated sightings occurred in the Bankhead National Forest in the 1940s and 1950s, preceding a widespread deer disease. No reports followed from the area, but since then a number of reports have originated from the Choccolocco Division of the Talladega National Forest. Other panther signs have been found in Washington County. In Dale County, a farmer trapped a young panther following the discovery of a cow that had been killed and partly covered with leaves and twigs. Several south Alabama newspapers carried a picture of the animal.[14]

Occurrences of the animal are reported regularly from the bottomlands of eastern Louisiana and from the central and western hills where reforestation and restocking of deer has occurred. A few could have survived from early days with the deep swamps and almost impenetrable canebrakes offering a refuge. A 116-pound specimen was killed on 30 November 1965 near the town of Keithville at a point less than ten miles south of Shreveport, a city of two hundred thousand. The total number of panthers in the state is believed to be no more than ten, according to a 1959 inventory of Louisiana wildlife. The number might be smaller because of the wide-ranging habit of the animal.[15]

Two pumas were reported to have been killed in Arkansas in late 1949. One, seven feet long and weighing 134 pounds, was shot in Montgomery County. Another specimen was trapped and killed in Warren County by a farmer who reported that tracks indicated three more at large in the vicinity.[16]

The mountain lion is once more a part of the fauna of Missouri and there is little doubt that it has returned to Minnesota.

In Nebraska, where the puma probably never did occur in numbers, sportsman Glenn Harris and a hunting companion are almost positive that they observed one through binoculars during the 1966 hunting season as it sneaked along through the timbers alongside the Little Blue River in the southeastern part of the state. He described it as a tan cat approximately four feet in length with a tail almost as long. The hunters had previously shrugged aside the reports of various farmers along the river of seeing and hearing a mountain lion.[17]

Pumas can survive surprisingly close to populated areas without detection. Hundreds of occurrences are unsupported by specimens taken, but one in the bush is worth two in the hand to game officials, conservationists, and sportsmen, or at least until public sentiment ceases to regard them as a parallel to the plague.

Vancouver Island cougar. (British Columbia Government Photograph)

SCREAM

Stories of the terrifying scream of the puma in the past have been widely publicized as an accepted fact and almost as widely criticized as wilderness mythology. Border romances and storybook tales of the frontier were generally embellished with the cry of the animal, designed to send a chill up the spine of the reader, and a typical yarn of the hardened woodsman had to contain a reference to the awesome scream to sound orthodox and authentic. The idea was established that the lonely wayfarer

had to survive the harrowing ordeal of listening to the squall if he were forced to spend a night in the woods. Doubtless the bloodcurdling and hair-raising cry will live in the marvels of tradition for all times to come, for as Theodore Roosevelt said: "Certainly no man could well listen to a stranger and wilder sound."[18]

Vernon Bailey, chief field naturalist with the U.S. Biological Survey during its early years, says there is confusion in the interpretation of the puma scream. He suggests that the wild sound of the animal could hardly be called a

74

scream, but rather a fair compromise between a caterwaul of a tomcat and the roar of a lion: "It is heavy and prolonged, slightly rising and falling and fairly well indicated by the letters o-o-W-O-U-H-u-u. On two occasions, in the woods, on dark nights the writer has heard this cry repeated several times at frequent intervals, and once from a cage in a zoological park."[19]

J.H. Batty, while on the Hayden Surveys in the West, also attempted to describe the sound. He wrote that the puma occasionally gave its dismal howl when hunger caused it to hang around the camps of hunters in Colorado: "He generally gives the prolonged howls, the first being the loudest, and the last one dying out and sounding as if he was at your side. His howls sound like o-o-o-Oh! O-o-o, repeated three times in succession."[20]

The following description of the puma cry is from the pen of Casper W. Whitney, editor of *Outing Magazine* from 1900 to 1909:

"Their cry is as terror-striking as it is varied. I have heard them wail as you would swear an infant had been left out in the cold by its mamma; I have heard them screech like a woman in distress; and again howl after the conventional manner attributed to the monarch of the forest."[21]

Near the present town of Blacksburg, South Carolina, is Whiticar Mountain, named in honor of Miss Sally Whiticar, who had an unusual experience on its slopes. The young Miss Whiticar imagined she heard the cry of a child one day as she strolled along the mountain. Her sympathies aroused, she hastened along until she came to a covert from which the cries came. Drawing aside the bushes, she came face to face with not a child, but a large American lion.[22]

From the Wind River and Gros Ventre country of Wyoming, William A. Baillie-Groham, British traveler and author, wrote about the sound: "The hoot of the owl is one of the most quaintly weird; but it is not like the unearthly wail of the puma, or mountain lion, demoniacal and ghoul-like as no other sound in the wide realm of nature."[23]

More recently from the scrub country around the Ocklawaha River in central Florida, the scream of the panther adds a new horror to the catalogue of evil, according to novelist Marjorie Kennan Rawlings, who heard the sound twice. "It is the shriek of a vampire woman, an insane shrill tremolo, half laughter and half moan," she wrote.[24]

In the proper setting, and if the listener were sufficiently imaginative, there is no limit to reactions the cry of the puma could arouse. One outdoor writer, who lived in the Montana Territory and wrote under the pen name "Ap-wa-cun-na," wrote that the noise made by the puma when wounded would cause the listener to lose his composure. He added: "They can *growl* fierce enough to cause a person to lose his hat, lock his snow shoes together, and fall over in entire disregard of a cocked rifle which, but a second before, he was pointing at the beast."[25]

Another writer said that the howl of the puma at night made a person more nervous than seeing the beast during the day.[26]

Early Kansas resident J.R. Mead wrote about the sound he heard in January 1868: "The unearthly scream of a panther close at hand will almost freeze the blood in one's veins, and for an instant paralyze almost any form of man or beast."[27]

For some observers in North America, the first half of the 1900s was an era of doubt or denial that the animal screamed at all. Chief among the exponents of this theory were many professional predator hunters of unquestionable reputation and competence. Their argument was based on the fact that they had never heard the scream. It could be that in some instances the fearful sound eluded them because they were almost always accompanied by noisy hounds; any vocalization on the part of the pursued would betray its presence or location. One observer wrote in 1902: "Everywhere that the animal has been found it has happened to the first settlers to listen to the unrestrained and natural voice of the cougar, and everywhere this discerning cat has stilled that voice at the bark of their dogs and the crack of their rifles."[28]

Some hunters believed that untrained adventurers in the outdoors were misinterpreting the weird cries of owls, wolves, coyotes, bobcats, lynx, and loons. Alarming vocalizations are uttered by a number of creatures in the wild and could certainly account for a goodly percentage of reported screams.

Most of the bounty hunters lived to realize the futility of further debate. It has been proven that the animal does emit a loud cry on occasion. Whether the eerie sound could properly be described as a scream, a yowl, a cry, a wail, or a call would depend upon the vocabulary of the listener. It could well be likened to the highly amplified sound of an ordinary housecat.

An unofficial decree of J.W. Aker, former court justice of Duncan, Arizona, is: "Mountain lions do scream. Many people have been hanged on far less and weaker evidence than the opposition has produced."[29]

As a youth, H.S. Garfield, M.D., taught in a backwoods school some thirty-five miles south of Olympia, Washington. He killed his first puma in 1877. One evening at dusk, one of the big cats approached a nearby barn that housed a mare and her young colt. The puma circled the barn, just within the timberline, "emitting at intervals the strange, half human cry of which he has been denied the possession." A pack of seven dogs ran the animal off but were unable to tree it. An hour before daylight the next morning, Garfield was aroused by an uproar near the barn. When he reached the building, the colt lay dead near the edge of the timber with a broken neck and slashed throat. The puma had entered the barn through an open gable in the loft and had taken the colt back over the same eight-foot barrier. The big cat was treed a half mile away and shot out of a large cedar just as dawn was breaking.

Dr. Garfield wrote that he could only speak of the puma in Washington, Oregon, and British Columbia, but that he never found anyone who disagreed that the animal frequently gave this distressful cry as well as a low whimper or whine. He admitted that the sounds were more prevalent when the animal suffered less molestation from hunters and their dogs. He then added:

"During the past twenty years I have not heard the puma give either of these sounds, though I have often, during that period, found their fresh 'sign' in my vicinity while hunting. I am unable to account for this silence, except upon the theory that long contact with the dangers of encroaching civilization has taught the puma the value of keeping his mouth shut."[30]

Walter Lee Davis, a resident of the Pacific Northwest, became disenchanted with the pros and cons of writers, old-timers, trappers, hunters, naturalists, and students who debated back and forth for years about the vocal powers of the puma. He divided them into three groups: those who still hold to the old belief that the animal screams, those who positively deny it, and those who just do not know.

Davis himself heard a puma scream and saw it when it did. Qualifying the validity of his argument, he wrote: "I am so sure of it that all the king's horses (and his asses too) can't disprove it.

"I spent a number of afternoons around the zoo in one of the city parks in Portland, Oregon. Looking at the two cages of cougars one afternoon I noticed that the single cougar in one cage was restless, and apparently lonesome, though the other cage, in plain sight of him, held four cougars. While he was back in his den and almost out of sight I heard him give a number of short, discontented mews much like a discontented housecat. Presently he walked out into the center of his cage, directly facing me and not more than ten feet from where I stood with a dozen other visitors. He seemed entirely unconcerned about our presence. After a few moments of aimless gazing at nothing in particular, he gave a concert of screams as terrifying as the most imaginative of hunters could have fancied. No experienced hunter could be fooled by that scream.

"The cougar's lips curled back along his jaws much farther than seemed natural. When the scream started, his conspicuously bare teeth were close together. As the sound continued they were opened a little, but never to their full limit. The scream itself started at a very high pitch and promised to be a long, shrill wail, but after a while the beast gave a series of explosive sounds, each of which momentarily sent the pitch higher still. On this afternoon the big cat screamed at least twenty times. On another occasion, he repeated the demonstration but screamed only three or four times."[31]

Stanley P. Young, co-author of the authoritative *The Puma: Mysterious American Cat,* summed up his argument with evidence of a different kind:

"It is believed that anyone who makes a critical study of the anatomy of the puma will come to the conclusion that the oft-repeated statement that it utters a 'scream' must be true, for there is only about an inch or an inch and a half between the glottis and the base of the tongue. It is evident to any person who observes the animal as it protrudes its tongue but an inch or slightly more that it would be impossible for it when in full voice to make any other utterance than a high, piercing shrill cry. The puma might rightly be called the lyric-soprano of the larger North American felines."[32]

Some observers believe that only the female emits the rare sound and only then during mating season.

Nyle Leatham, a photographer from Phoenix, Arizona, was forced to stop his convertible and raise the top during a rainstorm in the rim-rock country. He heard a scream "that sounded exactly as you would imagine a person might make." Leatham grabbed his pistol, plugged in a spotlight, and aimed it down the draw. Only about one hundred yards away were two pumas copulating. One was screaming, but Leatham could not determine which one.[33]

Robert Bean, formerly of the Chicago Zoological Park, has been quoted as saying that of the twenty to twenty-five females they had in their collection up to 1944, they never had one that did not scream. He also stated that he had never heard the cry from a male but had frequently heard them whistle.[34]

There are those who believe that the puma screams to startle its prey into movements that will betray their location. Deception may play a part of the strategy if one gives credence to folklore. A belief still exists in the Southern Appalachian Mountains of North Carolina that the panther, as it is called there, digs into the ground with its front paws and screams into the hole to deceive listeners into thinking it is farther away than it actually is.[35]

Pumas may scream from boredom or they may scream to announce their lordship of a wilderness domain. Some zoo keepers believe that they may scream when they are hungry. In 1911 a party of Colorado hunters killed the female of a pair and the male screamed periodically in an attempt to find his missing companion.[36]

Whatever the reason, the scream is rare but real.

A Philadelphia veterinarian, L.D. Rubin, has one last word for those who are not convinced that the animal screams. He suggests that the doubters try giving a captive puma an enema.[37]

COWARDICE

Probably somewhere between the extremes of ferociousness and cowardliness, both of which have been used to describe the puma, lies the true character of the beast. It is not a ghost-like marauder that prowls the reaches of the night ready to pounce upon unsuspecting humans, but it has killed man and is a death threat to prey and foe alike. Neither is it a craven coward that sheds tears and cries when cornered as it has been described, but rather a beast of stealth and rapine and quite reluctant to leave cover and expose itself without cause or reason.

In order to judge the conflicting testimony on the disposition of the puma, it is necessary to examine the writings of a few early naturalists from whom many later writers formulated theses. Unfortunately, some statements were taken out of context and not quoted in total for the sake of justifying a position.

Comte de Buffon in 1781 was one of the first to write about the disposition of the puma. He said: "Though weaker, he is equally ferocious, and, perhaps, more cruel than the jaguar." Later in his paper, he wrote of the two: "When gorged with prey, they are both equally indolent and cowardly."[38]

Don Félix de Azara, who spent twenty years in South America, said in 1802 that in Paraguay the puma was never known to hurt or threaten man or child, even when it found them sleeping.[39]

In 1823 Scottish naturalist T.D. Traill came to the defense of the puma and the jaguar by stating that most travelers and older naturalists ill-described the two with the favorite dogma of their inferiority in courage and ferocity to the animals of the Old World which they most nearly resembled. Traill said they equalled in both traits all felines of their size.[40]

It is evident that Dr. John Frost needed more knowledge than he had on the subject in 1853 when he wrote: "It has, for instance, been gravely said, that the Puma has been known to carry the body of a man that it has killed up into a tree. Now, in the first place, it has not been very satisfactorily ascertained that the puma is a climber of trees, even when it is not loaded; in the second place, if this were ascertained, it would be an argument against the killing of man, for the tree-cats are chiefly catchers of birds, squirrels, and monkeys; and in the third place, notwithstanding all the marvels that have been told of lions and tigers, there is no feat at all comparable with this told of either of them."[41]

John James Audubon wrote that the puma was "the most cowardly of any species of its size belonging to the genus," then proceeded to relate accounts of four attacks by the animal on human beings.[42]

Major S.W. Atkinson adopted the sobriquet "Oklahoma Bill" in the American West in the later 1800s. His generalizations on the fierceness of the puma sound like they are based on old wives' tales, hearsay, or haphazard gossip:

"The most dangerous animal in the west is the panther; you sometimes come right up to within ten or twelve feet of him, where he lays crouched like a huge dog, then the only way is to back off slowly, and at the same time keep your eye on him; when you are about twenty feet away you can raise your rifle and shoot, but should you wound him you must prepare for a fierce fight, for he will instantly spring on you, and once in his claws, you might as well say your prayers, but if you can get your hunting knife in his breast you are all right. Never turn your back to a panther, always walk off backwards, and very slowly too, so as not to excite him."[43]

In 1882 Dr. C. Hart Merriam, later to become the director of the U.S. Biological Survey, severely criticized the puma and its alleged fierceness and said that it was "one of the most cowardly of beasts and, never attacking man

unless wounded or cornered." Dr. Merriam admitted in the same paper that for most of his facts he was indebted to an experienced hunter and guide, E.L. Sheppard, who had killed or been instrumental in killing twenty-eight panthers in the Adirondacks.[44]

As a rebuttal to this widely quoted statement by Dr. Merriam, it is interesting to compare the words of an equally experienced puma hunter, Jay C. Bruce, the top California bounty hunter with 669 personal kills to his credit when he retired. In a letter to a puma researcher, he wrote: "The lion is game, and neither dogs nor man can keep one treed longer than he wants to stay there. At times he will jump, fighting, into the midst of dogs and men. He goes into the tree to rest, and not because of fear."[45]

William Henry Hudson, an English naturalist who was born in Argentina, was inconsistent in his appraisal of the Argentine puma. He stated that the animal had been singularly unfortunate in literature as always being spoken of as the most pusillanimous of the larger carnivores, "although to those personally acquainted with the habits of the lesser lion of the New World it is known to possess marvelous courage and daring." His condemnation of the animal was in its attitude toward man: "How strange that this most cunning, bold, and bloodthirsty of the Felidae, the persecutor of the jaguar and the scourge of the ruminants in the region it inhabits, able to kill its prey with the celerity of a rifle bullet, never attacks a human being!... Nor is this all: it will not as a rule, even defend itself against man, although in some rare instances it has been known to do so."[46]

In Argentine folklore, the friendliness of the puma toward man is a belief as firmly established as the opposite was at one time in North America. One writer on the puma says that Hudson let a group of vaqueros pull his leg and allowed him to start one of the most ridiculous puma fables of all times.[47]

Amadeo ("Chiché") Biló, puma hunter and outfitter of Río Negro, Argentina, wrote the following homage in defense of previous indictments of the animal in his country:

"He did not know you, without doubt, when he called you 'coward.' He never really succeeded in coming face to face with you. When he did, it was to kill you with bullets on the shore of the water where you went burdened with thirst.

"You did not tarnish your lineage, for he who pretends to hunt for you loyally, has to go after you often.

"Who in open contest, wants to succeed in conquering you, must sprinkle the earth with sweat, suffer sacrifices, weariness, and afflictions that give, definitely, the true magnitude of your image."[48]

The puma does display extreme caution in the presence of man and his dogs at times. Some observers consider this intelligence rather than cowardice. It may have learned to fear man with good reason, but the belief that the animal never attacks humans just is not so. It is true that sometimes a single dog can put one up a tree, but at other times a full pack cannot make one tree. Some will stand their ground and fight. One interesting theory is that in all wolf country the puma flees from dogs, yet in South America where there are no wolves the puma will attack any number of dogs "with an insatiate fury born of race animosity."[49]

There is a minimum of risk involved to the hunter with a treed or bayed puma, unless it is cornered, wounded, or protecting young. Without either handicap, it will generally attempt an escape when it rests and gets its wind back. If a hunter blocks the getaway route, some kind of defense arrangement should be considered. The author has grabbed the tail of a puma in a fight with hounds, but he certainly would not have considered the tactic had not the other end of the beast been busily engaged with snarling dogs.

The question of whether the puma is dangerous or not appears to be relative to both the individual animal and the person voicing the opinion. Some pumas display timidity at times, while others demonstrate considerable violence.

MAN KILLER

In the backwoods of North America, the puma was once a legendary terrorist. It retains the sinister character to this day in some areas mainly because of a misunderstanding of the animal, its formidable size, and its capacity to do harm. Typical of the tradition is the following portion of a dialogue from the Ozark Mountains of Arkansas: "Oncet, up on Wild Cat Slough," said Dee Sparks, "the people war at meetin' an' a painter war hid under a branch, an' when they all knelt down to pray the painter grabbed a baby outen a woman's arms an' run out the door, an' they never did ketch it nor find the baby."[50]

Some native Floridians still believe the puma is attracted to lonely dwellings in the backcountry by the cry of a baby, and that the big cat will actually ascend to the roof and wait for a chance to steal the child.

American novelist William Gilmore Simms made a trip into the wild mountains of western North Carolina in 1847 and camped with long hunters Jim Fisher and his part Choctaw son-in-law John Green near Hogback Mountain at the head of Toxaway River in the present Transylvania County. Simms kept notes in a journal for future use in his writings. One entry reads: "Fisher's story of the Panther, with himself & Green — Green's wife's story of the male panther — The appetite of the beast for women in pregnancy &c. — Horrid story of his eating one in this situation & of the discovery of her remains by her husband."[51]

Simms added a footnote to this entry in one of his border romances that the belief or faith that the panther has a special appetite for pregnant women "for which may or may not be good grounds," was the subject of many mountain narratives at the time of his travels.[52]

From the Big Scrub in Florida comes the story of another incident in which a panther was attracted to a pregnant woman. Raleigh Waldron told the story to his niece Davy Gnann Volkhardt about his aunt and her great aunt, Georgia Kingsley. The incident happened in the late 1890s at Bay Lake between Fort McCoy and Orange Springs.

Returning to her cabin home just before dark, after visiting her parents, the young pregnant woman heard a panther scream behind her. She knew that the animal would be intrigued by garments with human scent and would stop to investigate any article left along the trail. Each time Georgia would drop a piece of clothing, she would hear the panther snarl as it attacked the garment. By the time she got home, she had shed every stitch of clothing. The panther continued to circle the house until it heard the hoofbeats of the husband's horse when he returned home after dark.[53]

In South America, early inhabitants feared the animal also. One naturalist wrote in 1874: "The gaucho of the Pampas, the llanero of the Savannahs in the north, the herdsman on the slopes of the Cordilleras facing the Pacific, and the settlers on the eastern shore, dread the wide-ranging puma."[54]

Literature contains many accounts of fatal and non-fatal attacks on man in which it is impossible to separate fact from fancy. Doubtless many other attacks have never been recorded, especially from Central and South America. Roosevelt believed that in the days of American settlement the puma was an antagonist with the fury of the African or Indian leopard.[55] Ben V. Lilly, a master hunter during his lifetime, cites eight fatal attacks on man in the early days by the animal in Mississippi, Louisiana, and Texas, and says that at the time of the attacks in eastern and southern states the settlers were widely scattered and the animal had not yet learned to fear man.[56]

The puma is not instinctively a man killer. No records exist that confirm an individual as a rogue with a series of human kills for consumption, but individual variations in conduct and impelling circumstances do sometimes cause unprovoked attacks on humans. It is believed that the puma occasionally attacks man through mistaken identity. Cases exist where men have been jumped while sleeping in bedrolls and at other times when they were covered with ponchos. In most instances it is believed the pumas abandoned the attacks upon discovering the identity of the intended victims. Data kept in British Columbia by D.J. Spaulding indicate that humans are sometimes attacked by young pumas, frequently in good physical condition. Other attacks are sometimes caused by injuries to the animal, starvation, disease, or by individuals too old to hunt agile prey.[57]

The puma that attacked eleven-year-old Doreen Ashburnham and eight-year-old Anthony Farrar at Cowichan Lake, Vancouver Island, on 3 September 1916, was probably hungry as well as physically handicapped. Later killed, it was found to weigh only seventy-five pounds and had one eye afflicted with a cataract. The children fought the animal and finally drove it away with only a riding bridle. Anthony spent six weeks in the hospital at Duncan with forty-six stitches in his wounds. Both children were awarded the Albert Medal for gallantry by the king of England.[58]

An Apache Indian, Donner Clawson, and his wife were sleeping in the bed of their pickup truck at Cedar Creek west of Whitewater, Arizona, on the morning of 19 June 1963. Awakened by the barking of his dogs, Clawson jumped to the ground to investigate the cause. He was immediately knocked down from the rear by a puma that had been hiding beneath the truck. Sounds of the attack brought relatives of the Indian to his aid. They finally dragged Clawson away from the animal and noticed that it did not run away, but lay down after the fight. They reported that the lion looked, acted, and "smelled" sick to them. It was killed and its head sent to Phoenix where an examination revealed that the beast was rabid. Clawson suffered multiple cuts, severe puncture holes, and a compound fracture of his left arm where the strong jaws of the crazed animal had snapped the bones.[59]

Countless nonfatal attacks would have culminated in human fatalities except for intervening circumstances. Because man is not a common prey of the puma, the beast may not be as effective in its attacks as it is on deer and larger ungulates. On Vancouver Island, attacks are not as rare as elsewhere. It has been found here that known attacks have been centered on the shoulders and forearms rather than on more vulnerable parts of the human body. It could be that in aiming for the head, the attacker encounters the arms and shoulders of its victims as they try to shield their faces and heads.

Other than deer, natural prey for the puma is limited on Vancouver Island. During particularly hard winters, the puma forages the outskirts of towns and villages for dogs, cats, goats, and other domestic animals. Humans have not completely escaped the wrath of the starving animals either. Two or three recent attacks on man from the island and mainland of British Columbia reveal that the attackers were probably crazed with hunger. One was over six feet long, but weighed only seventy pounds. The other was five feet seven inches long and described as very thin.[60]

Elsewhere, particularly belligerent animals have been found to be gaunt and unable to hunt normal prey because of porcupine quills embedded in the lips and paws.

In the nonfictional literature on the puma, the author has found records of perhaps a hundred attacks on humans with fatalities represented by more than one-fourth this total figure. Many of the records are from competent sources, but others are questionable. Undoubtedly, many instances were never recorded. Typical of the suspect attacks is the following Arizona report from Flagstaff in 1884, as printed in the *Arizona Champion:* "A mountain lion was recently killed near Capt. Mike Gray's ranch (old Camp Rucker), in whose stomach was found a gold finger ring, and several pantaloon buttons."[61]

Records are scanty from certain parts of the hemisphere. Charles Darwin heard of two men and a woman killed by pumas when he was in Chile.[62] Dr. Rafael Housse records four homicides from the same country in more recent years:

(1) In 1913 near Rio Claro, a puma was found hiding portions of a partially eaten traveler under tree branches.

(2) A young peasant girl, in charge of a flock of sheep in Contulmo in 1913, noticed a puma carrying off one of the animals. She followed with a stick trying to scare the beast into abandoning its victim. Her body was found later totally mangled.

(3) The manager of a farm in the mountains east of Valdivia heard the bleating of sheep one night in 1928. He dressed and grabbed a candle to run out and inspect the fold. When he opened the door, a puma knocked him down and pulled out his throat.

(4) On 26 January 1936, in the range east of Parral, a puma jumped a young shepherd boy, partially ate him, and decapitated almost the whole flock.[63]

Colonel Henry W. Shoemaker wrote about nine Pennsylvanians believed to have been killed over the years.[64] He did not tell the famous story about Philip Tanner.

Tanner, mill owner and constable in Chester County, was supposedly killed by a panther on 6 May 1751, in a place called Betty's Patch. His tombstone is one of several interesting markers in a colonial burying ground in Lewisville, Pennsylvania, carved by an unknown folk artist whose handicraft depicts the final episode in the lives of the departed subjects.

Tanner owned a mill on Pigeon Creek, now Little Elk, in what was originally Nottingham Township. He first appears in county tax records in 1724. His original mill burned to the ground twenty years later, but was rebuilt. Area newspapers do not record his death, but a stonecutting craftsman left his own illustrated obituary for viewers to ponder over. A local newspaperman, Bill Hall, researched the story and said: "According to the story Tanner was killed by a panther, which animal supposedly lived in the area at that time. The tombstone artist carved the dastardly animal into the top of the stone over the grave of Tanner."[65]

Grave marker of Philip Tanner in Lewisville, Pennsylvania. The millwright was said to have been killed by a puma on 6 May 1751.

Another stone marker in the quaint cemetery, dated 13 July 1743, has the face of a fierce-looking Indian chiseled above the name of his unwary victim.

Among the many recorded human kills by pumas in North America, some are undeniable. The most recent documented instances have mostly occurred in the Pacific Northwest, where the animal is known as the lion or cougar, and all involve children.

On 30 March 1882, the *Clarke County Register* carried an article about a young boy killed by a cougar near the Columbia River in Washington Territory:

A most distressing accident occurred at Mount Vernon about six miles from Kalama, on the 21st inst. Gussie Graves, a five-year-old step-son of W.J. Magoon, was caught and terribly mangled by a cougar, from the effects of which he soon after died. The little fellow was several rods away from the house when he was heard to scream. Miss Baird, a neighbor who was there on a visit, first caught sight of the animal and her cries brought others to the spot. When he saw Miss Baird he dropped the boy and turned to attack her, but seeing others approaching, turned and seizing the boy again attempted to drag him over a fence. At this point Miss Graves struck him with a stick when he dropped the boy and walked away growling. Almost the entire scalp was torn off, the right ear torn loose from the skull, the right eye almost torn out, and the skull fractured in three places. Dr. Thornton, of Kalama, was summoned, but did not arrive until after the child died. Mr. Magoon was in Kalama when the accident happened.[66]

Arthur Dangle, eight-year-old son of Joseph and Margaret Dangle of Quartz Valley, Siskiyou County, California, was killed by two mountain lions on 21 June 1890. According to the *Siskiyou Telegraph*, the young lad had been picking flowers a short distance from his home. When he returned home, his mother praised him for the large bouquet he had gathered. He then told his parents he was going up a nearby gulch to gather oak balls. After an absence of two hours, the parents began to look for their son. Some 150 yards from the house they found signs of a struggle where the animals had pounced upon the child and dragged him off. Following the tracks of the lions, they came upon the mutilated body of their boy with his left arm and side entirely gone. One of the beasts was still feeding on the body of the victim. Hunting parties were enlisted to aid in the search for the animals but they could not be found. A calf was killed and sprinkled with strychine in an effort to lure the animals back to the scene. During the night, they both returned and dined heavily upon the calf. Dogs were put on the scent and the next morning the two lions were treed and killed.[67]

On 17 December 1924, Jimmy Fehlhaber, a thirteen-year-old boy, was killed and partly devoured by a cougar in a canyon near Brewster, Okanogan County, Washington. The mother of the slain boy had died in Spokane only two months before the tragedy and her son had secured employment at the ranch of Robert Nash near Brewster. On the fateful day, young Jimmy was headed to a nearby ranch to get a span of mules. Instead of taking the customary hill road, Jimmy followed a cutoff trail and was never seen alive again. He was killed in what the *Spokane Chronicle* termed "a fight to the death between a youth of civilization and a beast of the wild."[68]

The killer cougar was trapped and slain five weeks later about four miles from the scene of the tragedy. Stomach contents of the animal were sent to the Smithsonian Institution in Washington, D.C., and subsequently to the U.S. Biological Survey, where laboratory examinations disclosed human hair, remnants of clothing worn by the boy, and an empty cartridge case carried by him as a memento.[69]

Seven-year-old Norman Taylor wandered a few yards away from his parents during a Sunday picnic with fellow townspeople on 19 June 1949 at Walter's Bay near the Indian village of Kyuquot on the west side of Vancouver Island. Adults heard the child scream, looked up, and saw a cougar pounce upon the boy and drag him off into the brush. Men in the party ran to the rescue, causing the animal to drop the boy.

His face and throat were ripped open and one eye was gouged out. He died six hours later. Hunters killed the animal the following day. A news article in the *West Coast Advocate* for 23 June 1949 said that it was extremely rare and unusual for a cougar to kill a human. But a similar incident was recalled that happened "many years ago" near Cowichan in which an old cougar killed a youngster.[70]

On 2 January 1971 the three children of John Wells were playing on the CP mainline two hundred yards from their home in Lytton, British Columbia. For some strange reason, their dog would not enter a culvert in which they were playing. Just as twelve-year-old Lawrence Wells was climbing out of the drain, a cougar grabbed him from the rear. His two sisters, Bernadette, aged ten, and Valerie, aged seven, ran for their father. With the horrified family looking on, the animal killed the young boy and dragged him off. Wells shot the cougar three times as it was dragging away his son. It dropped its victim and ran. Royal Canadian Mounted Police tracked the animal into the brush, according to an article in the *Merritt Herald*, and found it lying on the ground. Just to make sure it was dead, they put two more bullets into the carcass.[71]

An emancipated fifty-pound mountain lion attacked and killed eight-year-old Kenneth Clark Nolan in the Arroyo Seco area near his trailer home five miles south of Espanola, New Mexico, on 20 January 1974. Kenneth and his half-brother, David Cordry, Jr., were resting on a ridge beneath a tree when the female lion attacked. David tried vainly to push the vicious animal from his companion and in return suffered scratches and the loss of a sleeve from his jacket. He then ran for help from his father, a member of the New Mexico State Police. When the two arrived at the scene, the lion was still mauling and biting the unfortunate lad. The officer emptied his service revolver, hitting the

animal at least twice and driving it off down the arroyo. Neighbors who had joined the hunt tracked the animal by bloodstains in patches of snow and found it licking its wounds under a ledge a quarter mile from the scene of the attack. Three 30-30 rifle slugs were required to finish off the growling animal. Two game officials said that the killer was young and the carcass revealed she had never given birth to young.[72]

A healthy male cougar between two and three years old mauled to death a seven-year-old girl, Matilda May Samuel of Port Alberni, Vancouver Island, as she walked along a gravel road picking berries eight miles west of Gold River on 14 July 1976. Two teenage boys were walking ahead of the victim when they heard some rustling behind them. Turning to look back, they saw the cougar jump the girl and pull her into some nearby bushes. The two youths ran down the road to get away. A few minutes later, they were able to flag an ambulance and relate the story. A telephone call was relayed by a worker at the Tahsia pulp mill to the Gold River Royal Canadian Mounted Police detachment who searched the area and found the body of the victim about two hours later. Before dark, the animal was treed and killed only forty yards from the site of the tragedy. The young girl had been visiting her aunt on the Mowachaht Indian Band Reserve when she was killed.[73] Only a short time before the fatal attack, the same cougar had chased a pulp mill worker while he was riding to work on his motorcycle.[74]

Incidents of fatal attacks on humans by the puma are atypical, yet the actions of the animal are unpredictable. It is a large, mysterious cat with all the common traits of the family and is known to be one of the most skillful killers in the animal kingdom. It has the capacity to kill man. Sometimes it has the will.

Plate CXX.

BLACK COUGUAR.

Black couguar. (Buffon, 1781)

FELIS NIGRA.

Felis nigra *or* Puma nigra, *the black puma of Paraguay. (From Sir William Jardine,* The natural history of the felinae, *1834)*

9
Black Panther Controversy

Originally, the name panther was applied only to the Afro-Asian leopard, with both names being used interchangeably for centuries. The occasional black-phase leopard was customarily referred to as a black panther. Today the term is loosely applied to all large black cats in the Americas, and especially to the rare melanistic puma that inherited the name "panther" in some areas regardless of color.

The black leopard is not a distinct species but a mutation, or color irregularity, that may occur within litters. Although appearing completely black, the animal has the normal spotted pattern faintly visible through the prevailing melanism. Black male and black female leopards are known to breed true. One such pair in the National Zoological Park in Washington, D.C., produced nothing but black kittens in numerous litters.

Large black cats were known by some of the earliest travelers in America and were mentioned under a variety of names. The *jaguarete* of Brazil was briefly described posthumously by Georg Marcgrave in 1648 as a shiny black cat mixed with shadows and variegated with black spots.[1] This became the *once* from Guyana, noted by chevalier Desmarchais in 1731,[2] and the *Felis nigra* or *Tigris nigra* in 1761.[3]

Étienne Renard Desmarchais, chevalier, was captain of the frigate *l'Expérience* in the service of the India Company. He sailed from Lorient in 1724 to Cayenne on the South American coast, returning in 1726. His memoirs were published posthumously by Jean Labat.

Thomas Pennant, British naturalist, figured and described the "Black Tiger" of Brazil and Guyana in 1771 as a scarce species the size of a year-old heifer and generally plain black in color with whitish or ashen underparts.[4] German naturalist Johann Christian Daniel Schreber figured the same animal in 1775 and described it three years later under the scientific name *Felis discolor*. He included the *jaguarete* in the new species, but stated that *Der schwarze Tiger* seen by Desmarchais and Pennant had no discernible black spots.[5]

British zoologist Robert Kerr attempted to systematize the type under the name *Felis discolor,* but included both the black jaguar and the black puma. He described the hair of the animal as short, very smooth, and of a brownish color. "The animal is mostly of a uniform colour, but is sometimes marked with spots of a full black colour," he added.[6]

The black variety of the jaguar, commonly known in South America as the *tigre negro* or *onça prieta,* occurs infrequently throughout its range. In Guyana it is known as the "Maipuri tiger." Although the color appears a uniform black, the typical dotted rosettes are discernible under certain light conditions.

The black puma is probably the rarest of all black cats. Comte de Buffon wrote that a variety, called the *black tiger,* inhabited America. He renamed it the *black couguar.* A wretched drawing in his book poorly represents the true beauty of the handsome beast. Buffon recognized the animal as different from the black jaguar with a smaller and thinner body, and said that it was very rare in the neighborhood of Cayenne. Regarding the name *jaguarete,* Buffon wrote: "The black couguar may be the same animal which Piso and Marcgrave call the *jaguarete,* or *jaguar with black hair.*"[7]

Scottish naturalist Sir William Jardine mentions the *chat nègre* or *el negro* of Paraguay as possible synonyms of his *black puma.* His accompanying illustration is much more detailed and recognizable than that of Buffon, and was drawn from three specimens taken to Greenock, Scotland, on a merchant vessel.[8]

In his economic geography of Nicaragua, Pablo Lévy applied the name *Felis concolor niger* Cuvier to "el Tigre Negro" of that country and said that it was ferocious but rare.[9]

A Canadian sportsman, William Thomson, killed a black puma in 1843, while he was on a 250-mile muleback journey from the province of Rio de Janeiro to the Carandaí River in Brazil. His account aptly describes the rare cat: "The whole head, back, and sides, and even the tail, were glossy black, while the throat, belly, and inner surfaces of the legs were shaded off to a stone-gray."[10]

British adventurer Frederick Boyle traveled unsettled jungle portions of Costa Rica in 1866

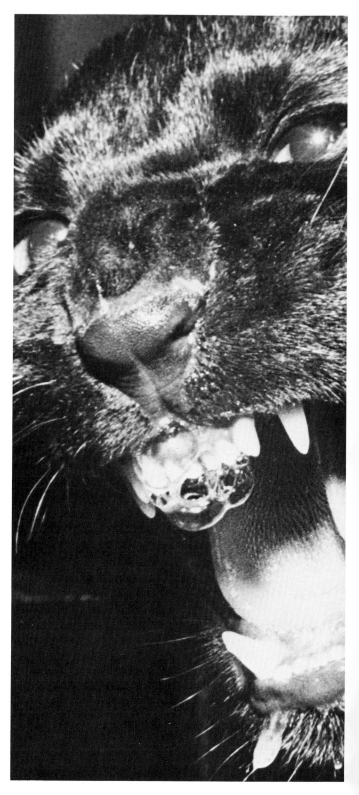

Black phase leopard, or black panther.

86

by floating numerous wilderness waterways. At the remote hacienda La Virgen on the Rio Sarapiquí, Boyle and a companion spent considerable time with an enterprising stockman who was extremely knowledgeable on the puma and jaguar, and who had made the dangerous hunting of the two marauders appealing to the natives by initiating his own bounty system. Following a lengthy discussion on the two animals, Boyle wrote about the black puma:

"We have diverged to the subject of black lions, an animal whose existence has been denied. The ranchero had nothing decisive to advance on this disputed question. He heard with astonishment and contempt that European savants doubted. Black pumas, he alleged, are as well authenticated as black jaguars. He had never killed one. Such skins as had come beneath his notice were very large truly. But he laughed scornfully at the idea that any woodsman could make a mistake."[11]

The black puma, or *pantera negra*, appear indistinctly in the zones of the Atlantic and Pacific in Nicaragua and Costa Rica, and is very difficult to hunt.[12] A California sportsman, Leon T. Mott, in personal correspondence with the author, wrote that he saw black pumas while he was riding a bobbing pipante down the Coco and Wawa rivers in Nicaragua in 1957. Knowing that the black variety of the puma has long been questionable, Mott added: "I examined some skins and it is my opinion that this Central American variety is, in fact, a black puma or panther — I could not discern any jaguar markings in or under the fur."[13]

Neal Griffith Smith, zoologist with the Smithsonian Tropical Research Institute in the Canal Zone, says the melanic forms of the puma are not infrequently shot in the Republic of Panama, and that in most cases the animals were hunting cattle.[14]

It has been reported that Indian warriors of the Argentine pampas were once baptized with the smoking blood of animals and given animal names. One such name was *Cadupani*, translated as "black lion."[15]

The black panther controversy in North America has been threefold mainly, with the general public misunderstanding the dual application of the name, denials that black pumas

Black puma, or pantera negra, *killed by Miguel Ruiz Herrero in 1959 in the province of Guanacaste along the north Pacific coast of Costa Rica. Ruiz's herdsman poses with the specimen that was estimated to weigh between 100 and 120 pounds.*

exist, and the diametrically opposing belief that they frequently occur in the United States. It is just another one of the many inconsistencies in the convictions of observers regarding the beast.

In an early history of the state of Maine, William D. Williamson wrote that three species of cats were found in the forests, identifying them as the catamount, wild-cat, and black cat. He was quite explicit in his description of the last named: "The *Black Cat* is much larger in size than the wild-cat, very ravenous and fierce,

Black jaguar. (Courtesy National Zoological Park)

has shorter legs and a long tail, and is of a black colour; called by the natives *Wooleneag*."[16]

Puma researcher Bruce Wright lists twenty specimens of black *Felis concolor* reported by observers in New Brunswick, Quebec, and Nova Scotia between 1 September 1951 and 2 August 1970. He states that although no North American specimen has ever been collected, he has no alternative but to accept the word of eye witnesses.[17]

A black puma has never been authentically recorded in North America despite reports and newspaper accounts to the contrary that tell of sightings year after year. Many persons believe that all American panthers must be black because of the widespread acceptance of the name panther in association with the color. Here is an exotic animal of mystery and intrigue that borders on the sensational and it is

the subject of fables and superstitions that befit any cat that is black.

Typical of the publicity and general confidence of the reality of wild black panthers in the United States is a headline from a Pennsylvania newspaper that minimizes the extremely rare possibility that an animal allegedly seen might have truly been black:

> That Black Panther Prowling
> in the South East Area Is
> in the "Spotlight" Again[18]

It is interesting to note that the attention of the newspaper reader is directed to "spotlight" rather than to the word black.

Florida has newspaper accounts of wild black panther sightings every year from all sections of the state where the ordinary tawny-colored panther draws little attention from the press. Game officials insist that no black ones exist in the state and that persons are seeing instead large feral house cats that increase in size through fright or excitement of observers, large dark-colored dogs that reverted to wildness, large otters temporarily blackish from dampness, or the least likely possibility of a black-phase leopard escaped from a carnival, zoo, or side show. Other alternatives are that people are inventing reports to gain publicity or that they are viewing normal-colored panthers in dim light or individuals with wet fur.

Naturalist Thomas Barbour notes the collecting of a young "black panther" skin from Matecumbe Key, Florida, by Alexander Sprunt, Jr., and states that other melanistic individuals have occurred on other islands in the chain.[19] Sprunt first saw the hide nailed to a barn door in the Florida Keys in 1927. He identified it as a black panther and communicated the information to E.D. Chamberlain of the Charleston Museum who purchased the skin and presented it to the institution in 1957. Wanting to obtain a positive identification of the specimen, E. Milby Burton, director of the Charleston Museum, sent the skin to the U.S. Museum the following year. In a letter dated 9 October 1958, Dr. David H. Johnson, curator, Division of Mammals, respectfully labeled the supposed black panther pelt as a greatly stretched skin of a large house cat beyond any doubt.[20]

All reports of blackish cat-like animals in Florida cannot be discounted, however. Some sightings of dark long-tailed cats slightly larger than the domestic variety strongly suggest the jaguarundi, an import from the Americas to the south. A few of these "panther-like" animals are known to have been released in the Hillsborough River State Park and in the Chiefland area around 1941.[21] Dr. Wilfred T. Neill, who directed a biological research project for the Ross Allen Reptile Institute at Silver Springs for over a decade, collected the first Florida jaguarundi specimen to reach a scientific collection from near Lake Placid in Highlands County. The young animal had been hit by a car and was found dead on the highway.[22]

Less likely is the remote possibility that instead of seeing black panthers, observers in Florida are seeing "black wildcats." According to John Paradiso, in 1973 only four melanistic bobcats had been recorded in literature and from nowhere else in North America except Florida. Paradiso examined a live black bobcat that had been captured in the town of Loughman in Polk County in the latter part of October 1970. He estimated the prime-condition specimen to be no more than two-and-a-half years old and gave a description of its coloration:

"At a distance of 2 1/2 feet or more, it does appear to be entirely black, but at closer range it can be seen that the belly and legs are actually mahogany in coloration. Also, at close range a few white hairs are visible, scattered over the entire body. When viewed at certain angles, a trace of spotting on the sides and banding on the legs is faintly evident."[23]

It has been noted earlier in a description of a melanistic specimen that the Florida bobcat was the darkest form of the genus, and also that a moist tropic or subtropic climate was probably an essential condition for melanism in them, as well as in all other members of the cat family.[24]

Bruce A. Hartman of West Jordan, Utah, killed what some writers have called a black cougar on 8 December 1912 near Cochetopa Creek south of Gunnison, Colorado. He told the author in a conversation that the animal was not pure black, but was the darkest he had ever seen.

A "black panther" seen by a Negro cook on a ranch in southern Arizona was probably a jaguar. The animal was tracked down and mortally wounded by ranch hands but was not found until nine days later in the advanced stages of decomposition. The cowboys were sure that the specimen had been a rare mutation of the Mexican jaguar that had drifted across the border.[25]

The black puma is real in certain parts of Central and South America, but if it occurs in North America, no qualified authority has seen one. Nor has anyone offered a dead specimen, pelt, or photograph as evidence of the numerous claims of a black North American puma. It is not impossible for them to have occurred, or to occur in the future, however. But until one is positively identified, the elusive creature must continue to blend with the obscure darkness of the unknown.

10
The Mysterious Onza

No one knows how long a strange and elusive wolf-jaguar-puma type animal has been said to exist in the Sierra Madre Occidental of Mexico. The Aztecs recognized it long before the conquest in 1520 by Hernán Cortés, and they had a name for the beast. In the royal menagerie of Moctezuma, the Aztec emperor, conquistadors saw lions of two different kinds. Bernal Díaz del Castillo, recorder for the expedition, wrote in the early 1600s that one of the two was built more like a wolf in the limbs and hindquarters than the other. The conquerors applied the name *adive* to the beast because of its jackal-like appearance.[1]

Bernardo de Sahagún closely followed the conquest with a general history of the new Spanish land in America. His work, first printed in 1829, mentioned an animal known by the Aztecs as the *cuitlamiztli*, that he identified as a "bastard lion."[2] The first Spanish naturalist in Mexico, Francisco Hernández, whose natural history was published posthumously in 1651, wrote: "The *CuitLamiztli* borrowed its name from the lion and the native wolf."[3]

Around the world voyager Woodes Rogers wrote about the animal from the west coast of Mexico where he visited in 1709: "There's also a strange Creature in those Woods, call'd by the *Spaniards* an Ounce, much of the Form and Size of a Woolf-dog, but it has Talons, and the Head is more like a Tyger: It kills Men and Beasts, which makes travelling through the Woods dangerous."[4]

In the 1794 writings of a Jesuit missionary, Ignaz Pfefferkorn, is a reference to the unusual beast from the province of Sonora. He said the Spanish called it *onza*, and in shape it was almost like a puma but longer in body and noticeably thinner and narrower in the rump. Pfefferkorn commented on its aggressiveness and unmercifulness with foe or prey.[5]

Mexican tradition holds that the onza is an offspring of a male jaguar and a female puma because of the small spots on the lower part of the legs and a wide dark stripe down the back.

Clell (left) and Dale Lee with a rare onza taken in 1938 in the Sierra Madre range of Sinaloa, Mexico.

The famed Lee brothers of Arizona, once regarded as the most reputable puma hunter-guides in all America, startled hunters and naturalists in 1938, when they collected a strangely different puma in the San Ignacio district of Sinaloa. The *Arizona Daily Star* for 1 October 1938 carried a description of the unusual specimen supplied by Ernest Lee, eldest of the hunting family:

"The Onca differs from any of the cat tribe I ever saw. It is, first hand, somewhat like a mountain lion, but its coloration is different. Its adobe-colored pelt has a broad black stripe running down the back like a gruya (grulla) mustang.

"It is the only member of the cat family I ever saw which does not entirely sheath its claws and which leaves a footprint which is not rounded, but pointed, with the claw marks showing. Its legs are thinner than the club-like leg of the lion, jaguar or *tigre* of the Mexican country, and its fur is more like that of the lynx than a lion."

In addition, the female specimen taken by the Lees was said to have a longer body than the conventional puma, slighter built in its hindquarters, and its ears were noticeably larger.[6]

The Lees had heard much native talk about the onza in Mexico throughout the years, but of over a thousand pumas taken by them, this specimen is the only one that vastly differed from all others. Speculation was that it must have been a new species or a hybrid.

Prompted by the Lee report and recurring folktales about the onza, Arizona sportsman Robert E. Marshall conducted a seven-year investigation to unravel the story of the phantom cat. His work culminated in 1961, in the only book written on the subject.

An onza trapped and shot by C.B. Ruggles in Sonora, Mexico, in 1926. The animal had just killed and eaten a forty-pound hunting dog while still in the trap.

In Arivaca, Arizona, Marshall found a former Indian agent, cowboy, trapper, and hunter, C.B. Ruggles, who had trapped and killed an onza southeast of the Yaqui River in Sonora, in the spring of 1926. Ruggles had written an account of the kill, but due to editorial skepticism and lack of reference material the story was rejected by magazine editors. Ruggles described his cat as a large off-colored, odd-shaped mountain lion with dark spots on the inside of the front and hind legs and skinny in the hindquarters. Indians with Ruggles did not hesitate to identify the beast as an onza.

In the Sierra de los Frailes of Sinaloa, Marshall talked to a number of natives that had killed furry onzas. One had sold a pelt the year before and thrown the carcass of the specimen into a ravine behind his camp. Marshall uncovered the skull of the beast, buried for nearly a year, and in a comparison with puma skulls from the same area, found noticeable differences. Marshall summed up his work with this statement: "So the fact that an onza was now well established, and that the onza was some kind of puma seemed equally certain. But of all the things that have to happen to make an onza, these remain unknown."[7]

Dr. A. Starker Leopold of the University of California wrote briefly of the persistent rumors of the onza in western Mexico in 1959. He summarized: "Such an animal has never come to the attention of taxonomic zoölogists, and until specimens are obtained and determined to be distinct from known species, the *onza* must remain in the status of a myth — admittedly, a very intriguing one."[8]

Perplexing is the thought that such a strangely different puma could exist in Mexico and be virtually unknown to zoologists. It can only add luster to the aura of mystery that already shrouds the legendary lion of the Americas. One thing is certain. Natives of the states of Sonora, Chihuahua, Durango, Nayarit, and Baja California are puzzled that outsiders are so skeptical about the existence of an animal that to them is so very real. But, as they would say, there is always mañana.

11
Hunting the American Lion

Nothing else in the hunting world is quite like the chase of the American lion. No other outdoor pursuit offers a similar challenge, action, and thrill.

"Lion hunters are nuts." So says Warren Page, one-time gun editor of *Field & Stream*, about those who chase the American lion. "At least that's the way it looks to me. You ride a horse day after day looking for tracks. When the horse gets tired or the country gets rough, you drag him. Maybe you even carry him a little bit. All of which takes a strong back and a weak mind. Then if you or the dogs do hit a fresh enough track, they run the hellangone out of the country and chase the cat up a tree."[1] Steve Trumbull, Miami newspaperman, who hunted the animal in the Florida Everglades, says it is a great pastime: "Just like hitting yourself in the head with a hammer. It feels so good when you stop."[2]

All this may be true enough. But few sports can equal the thrill-packed action and rugged adventure that comes with hellroaring trail hounds and hard brush-riding on horseback in spectacular wilderness country for one of the most elusive quarries in the animal kingdom.

The American lion, better known universally as the puma or cougar, is a challenging game animal. Sly and retiring, with keen senses of sight, smell, and hearing, it moves noiselessly on cushioned pads and has an uncanny ability to conceal itself. Without the aid of dogs, one is seldom seen by a hunter. Many sportsmen consider it the toughest North American trophy to bag. Dr. Frank Hibben, one-time head of the anthropology department at the University of New Mexico and a specialist on cougar lore, calls it the greatest game animal in North America and gives his list of standards: danger, difficulties, the speed and cunning of the animal, inaccessibility, endurance on the part of the hunter, and the use of hounds, all combining all the qualities of every other kind of sport hunting.[3] Famous oldtime hunters were high in their praise for the game qualities of the animal. Following a hand-to-paw encounter

Daniel Boone killing a panther on the back of a buffalo. (From Timothy Flint, Biographical Memoir of Daniel Boone, *1833)*

to the death, the mountain lion is more game than the black bear. He will fight with his last breath."[7]

Probably more dangerous to the hunter, however, are the accidents that can happen while riding horseback at breakneck speeds in rough terrain. Falls or slides by man and horse in country that sometimes seems to be straight up or straight down are likely possibilities. Injuries to the head from tree limbs and jutting boulders must be kept in mind. Knees and legs are often bruised. Horses know when they have just enough room to dart between trees, but the protruding legs of the rider are not a matter of consideration on their part. A dreaded thought of the hunter is that of being unseated with a foot left hanging in the stirrup. In most cases it is difficult for a rider to stop a horse in hot chase, but a dragging man frightens the animal and could result in disaster. S. Omar Barker, cowboy poet-author of New Mexico, comments: "What really makes mountain lion hunting a dangerous sport is that the chase is usually on horseback in steep, rocky-rough, crag-bound, cliffy, canyon-cut, loggy, timber thicketed, trailless country."[8]

with one on the banks of the Navasota River in Texas, David Crockett said: "I have had many fights with bears, but this was child's play; this was the first fight I ever had with a cougar, and I hope it may be the last."[4] Probably the greatest American lion hunter of all, Ben Lilly, wasted no words in his praise: "Anybody can kill a deer. It takes a man to kill a varmint."[5]

Hunting the American lion with hounds is typically American, with new action, excitement, and adventure in every hunt. No two are alike. "The only thing predictable about the sport is that something unpredictable will happen," wrote one writer.[6]

A hunt can be dangerous. A cornered or wounded lion is a potential killer of dogs and man alike. Although hunters are seldom attacked, the strong, powerful animal is a formidable foe to anything in its realm, including man. Take the words of Jay Bruce, who took a total of more than five hundred lions for the state of California before he retired: "In a fight

Jay C. Bruce, most famous of California lion hunters, with three mountain lions (male, male, female) obtained 26 January 1924 at Colony Mill, Marble Fork of Kaweah River, Sequoia National Park. (Courtesy Museum of Vertebrate Zoology, University of California at Berkeley)

96

The most reliable method to hunt the American lion is by trailing and treeing it with specially trained hounds. Herein lies a paradox. It is not uncommon for the animal to approach settlements in South America and carry away dogs. Yet there and elsewhere, a common trait of the animal is to flee from noisy dogs, no matter how small. It will kill and eat a large dog when hungry, while at other times a single cur will put it up a tree. Some observers believe that the animal is annoyed by the barking, or knows from experience that it signals the approach of man with a gun.

Lion dogs inspire the imagination. The long, drawn-out howl of a trail hound when it makes a strike is music to the ears of the hunter. Then comes a combined canine chorus as the pack works out a cold trail that may take hours of painstaking persistence to follow. When the long-tailed quarry is jumped, the baying changes to brisk, rapid yelps as the dogs accelerate their pace. At last comes the satisfying thrill as the eager vocalization suddenly changes to abrupt, sharp barks announcing that the lion has been treed or brought to bay. Here is a sport that combines the regal qualities of a fox hunt with the added thrill of chasing big game.

In all hunting areas where terrains allow for open trailing with hounds and horses, the chase of the American lion is practically the same. Dogs search for the scent or sight of the animal while the hunter looks for tracks and other signs. Once the presence or recency of the elusive cat is established, trailing and pursuit by the hunter follows on horseback over the countryside until the quarry is surrounded or forced to climb a tree.

Horses are not used in hunting the animal on Vancouver Island. Rushing streams, lengthy lakes, and dense forests of giant standing and downed timber limit the hunt to strenuous footwork. Sometimes a track can be picked up along coastal beaches, but in most cases the animal frequents the rugged uplands. Keeping up afoot with trail hounds is very difficult on the island terrain. Steep slopes have rotting conifers in wild disarray, and the deep woods are often carpeted with a deceptive latticework of matted mosses and ferns that give way under

Pup and Puse, straight-haired airdales, treed this male longtail in the rugged Sangre de Cristo mountains northwest of Las Vegas, New Mexico, for S. Omar Barker, cowboy poet-author, in January 1935. (Courtesy Elsa Barker)

Dave Williamson capturing a live adult cougar near Oyster River, Vancouver Island, in 1958. (Courtesy Charles Eatlin)

97

foot. Pursuit on horseback would be almost impossible. Otherwise, the general routine of hunting is the same as elsewhere.

One method of hunting the *león americano* in the dense jungles of Central America is through the use of a special call. Because of its nocturnal activity, the animal is lured almost exclusively at night. Moonlight is a prerequisite. Remote jungle hunting is generally near a waterway, for this is often the only route of travel for the hunter. He should be stationed in advance of the caller, near a moonlit opening or clearing in the jungle, in order to glimpse the approaching animal. Sometimes it will respond vocally to a call, becoming louder and louder as it nears. At other times, it will approach in deathly silence, testing the nerves of the hunter, who has probably realized by then that the hunter has become the hunted.

Two types of puma calls have been used successfully in Central America. One is a predator call that produces a squeal like that of a small wounded animal, causing the big cat to come in with a nasty disposition. The other is a modified jaguar call that imitates the sound of a puma. An animal called in with the latter instrument approaches without caution.

One type of jaguar call, that can be modified for the puma, is made from a hollow gourd, sealed with a taut deerskin on one end, and open at the other. Extending from the center of the rawhide, through the gourd and out the open end, is a long strip of waxed hair made from the tail of a horse. When the hair is rubbed or strummed, the rawhide vibrates with a sound amplified by the gourd. It can be heard for miles on a quiet night. For calling a puma, the call is altered to make a much higher-pitched sound.

Two calls are used by Indians in southern Mexico. A hollow piece of bamboo and a string are made to simulate the sounds of a hind or kid. This will attract the puma in to the hunter waiting in ambush. The other is a three-inch piece of cannon bone from the stag, with a thin film secured over one end of the tubular instrument. Sucking the open end produces a squeaking note to lure the animal.[9]

Predator calls are effective in all jungle areas of tropical America but are rarely employed where the open chase of the puma is possible. Calls have been used successfully on occasion for the animal in Arizona and New Mexico on what might be termed an experimental basis, but hunters in North America overwhelmingly prefer to seek the animal with dogs.

The regular method of jungle hunting along waterways must be abandoned in the Yucatán of Mexico because the rivers are underground. Underlying the entire peninsula is a porous limestone that accounts for the unique geological phenomenon. The conventional chase of the puma with trail hounds is also limited because of a tangled and matted jungle growth in the vast wilderness. Animals must instead be lured to the hunter whenever possible. Day hunting consists of soliciting reports in Indian villages of pumas in the vicinity and investigating the leads. The general method at night includes baiting with a burro, heifer, lamb, or other live decoy with the hunter stationed in a tree stand or platform above or in advance of the stakeouts. Two or more baits are sometimes tethered short distances apart so that their call to each other during the night will attract the predator. Some hunters prefer a hammock placed between trees nearby for their lonely vigil. It is more comfortable and less noisy than the sometimes adopted machan, a tree platform, as used in India for tiger hunting.

Hunting the puma in its southernmost habitat is not unlike the chase of the animal anywhere else in its wide geographic and climatic range.

The Argentine backcountry is a frontier of immense ranges and sparse population. Hunting is normally done gaucho style on horseback with a couple of spotters going out in advance to look for fresh tracks. Using a system of smoke signals, the advance men communicate with the other hunters. Intermittent signals mark the direction of travel. Two smoke puffs signify that trail sign has been found. Dogs are then put on the scent or track and the hunt begins in earnest.

Intersecting the parched ground of the vast Patagonian tableland are numerous ravines and dry washes. More often than not a puma will use the smooth floor of a ravine as a pathway to the rivers for water. Dry sediment in the

98

A rare hunting scene of the famous Pennsylvania hunter Conrad Sox [Sax] and his wife Mary killing three pumas in the Shades of Death, a great swamp between Wilkes-Barre and the Delaware River. Philadelphia illustrator John James Barralet portrayed all three as large spotted cats, a *characteristic of young animals, with long tails. If the artist, who came to America in 1795, had never seen an adult puma, he may have approximated the leopard, or Old World panther, a namesake of the Pennsylvania panther. (From Oliver Oldschool, ed.,* Port Folio (Dennie), *1812)*

bottom is highly sensitive to tracks and is a prime object for investigation by the hunters. If the puma does not travel the dry beds, it must cross the fine sand at some time or another. For pumas that live in the woods, the hunter must check for entrances that are regularly used by the animal going into the bush.

The first settlers in the Americas hunted primarily for food or fur and to exterminate prowling marauders. Few probably found time to hunt for the fun of it. From earliest times, the American lion has been considered a denizen of the forest. The first record of hunting the animal for sport is from Sir Walter Raleigh in

1595, who wrote of the common delights of hunting in Guyana for a variety of beasts including "Lyons."[10]

Acosta wrote in 1604 that Indians in Peru assembled in troops to hunt the animal, forming circles around the quarry and killing it with stones, staves, and other weapons. He added: "These lions use to climbe trees, where being mounted, the *Indians* kil them with launces and crossbowes, but more easily with harquebuzes."[11]

Hunting what he called the panther as vermin in Virginia furnished pleasure and profit to the sportsman as early as 1705, according to

99

Robert Beverly, who lived there.[12] In 1709 John Lawson recognized that the dog was important in Carolina in this type of hunting, stating that a cur would make the beast take a tree, whereupon the huntsman would then shoot it.[13]

The prowess of frontier hunters was greatly enhanced when they could boast of a personal encounter with the American lion. The more they embellished and fabricated the yarn, the more attentive and spellbound the listener and the more legendary the animal. The less adventuresome had difficulty in separating fact and fancy. Typical of the tales in frontier dialect is one from an 1839 *Crockett Almanac* of a Kentucky woodsman who fought two at one time:

> The hunter ketched hold of the catamount's tail and took a turn with it around a young sapling and tied a knot that held him fast for a while. He had to be pesky quick in doing this, for the cretur wouldn't hold still a minnit. Then the hunter went to help his dog, who had the other varmint by the lip, and held on upon it as if it had been a apron full of Jackson currency. The hunter loaded his rifle, and put it again the varmint's backside and fired. It was such a fire and brimstone glister as put him out of pain in a wonderful quick time — though he kicked and squirmed most beautiful at fust. By this time the other catamount had jerked out his tail, and the dog was just giving up the ghost, and the hunter thought it was quite unsartin what would happen. So he made a blow at the cretur with the breech of his rifle, and the varmint caught it in his teeth; the hunter let him get it away, as he knew the cretur wouldn't know how to use it arter he got it. He left his rifle with the catamount, and put down his legs one arter the other, for home, as fast as if a Yankee pedler was drinking up his whiskey and chewing the barrell.[14]

Hunting the puma by natives of South America began centuries ago. Their main implement was the bola or *boleadora*, a three-thonged entangling snare that was hurled at the legs of

"Desperate Fight with two Catamounts." (From Crockett Almanac, *vol. 2, 1839)*

A Tehuelche Indian killing a puma with the bolas on the Argentine pampas. (From George C. Musters, At Home with the Patagonians, *1871)*

running animals to hobble them and render them incapable of further flight. Hunting was practiced in this manner from southern Brazil and Uruguay, and from Peru southward to the Straits of Magellan, reaching its perfection with the Tehuelche Indians of Patagonia. Gauchos adopted both the weapon and the method.[15]

The chase of the puma was a favorite, though rare and dangerous sport of the natives at the time of the visit of Benjamin Franklin Bourne in the mid-nineteenth century.[16] Charles Darwin reported that in a three-month period near Tandil, south of La Plata, one hundred pumas were "first entangled with the bolas, then lazoed, then dragged along the ground till rendered insensible."[17]

A California vaquero, master of the reata, has sport with a lion in the Santa Inez Valley in this sketch by Frederic Remington. (From E.P. Roe, "Some stories about 'The California lion,'" in St. Nicholas, *vol. 15 [September 1888])*

Bolas consist of three plaited sinews, seven or eight feet in length, made from guanaco or mare hides. At the end of each thong is attached a heavy globular stone or hardwood sphere, grooved for binding, and wrapped tightly in rawhide. The other ends are united. Indians held the set by the shortest of the three *sogas*, or thongs, and swung it around and around over the head while in a full gallop on horseback and propelled it toward the legs of the quarry. The weapon left the hand in an area diameter of fourteen to sixteen feet, whiplashing and binding the animal securely on contact. The encumbered victim was then killed with a quick blow to the head by the hunter using a single bola.

Pushing back the frontier and extending the raising of domestic livestock into new lands, increased the possibility of depredations on herds by American lions. Hunting and eliminating what frontiersmen considered a menace proceeded with methodical determination and became an established routine of the cowboy, the vaquero, the gaucho, and their Chilean coun-

terpart, the *hauso*. Its pursuit offered a sportful diversion from the normal chores of these colorful herdsmen. Theodore Roosevelt wrote: "If cowboys come across a cougar in open ground they invariably chase and try to rope it — as indeed they do any wild animal." Before the beast could turn on the assailant, it would be dragged to death.[18]

Roping and capturing an American lion alive became a mark of distinction among cowboys. A folk hero of their kind, High Chin Bob, was created in 1908 in a poem written by Charles Badger Clark. It has since become a classic ballad of the Southwest with the immortal subject still riding "the glory trail" because of his daring exploit. He reflected on the feat he hoped to accomplish:

No man has looped a lion's head
And lived to drag the bugger dead.[19]

Instead of looping the head, the cowboy "bellyroped" the beast and failed in his attempt to lay it low. But, as the song says, he never has turned the animal loose. Legend has Bob astride his top horse, forever scampering silently

101

by moonlight through the Mogollon Mountains of Arizona and New Mexico with his chin held high and the lion trailing peacefully along behind.

The mountain lion of the American West is one of the few beasts that rates a role in the superhuman exploits of Pecos Bill, greatest of all mythical cowboys.[20]

In the later nineteenth century, settlers in the Patagonian frontier of Argentina were compelled to hunt the puma because of its destruction to their sheep flocks. Seventy-three pumas were killed by two pioneers in one winter. Elsewhere, fourteen were killed during the winter of 1900 on one farm at Bahia Camerones.[21]

Andreas Madsen, a Danish globetrotter, arrived in Patagonia in 1900 and established his ranch on the north shore of Lago Viedma in the shadows of Mount Fitzroy. He became renowned for his skill and bravery in hunting pumas for the protection of sheep and equally known for his stories of hunting experiences.[22]

Sportsmen in North America became interested in the American lion as a game animal chiefly through the writings of Theodore Roosevelt and Zane Grey. These two outdoorsmen probably did more to popularize lion hunting as a sport than anyone else.

Roosevelt discussed the cougar, as he called the animal, in a number of his writings. His

Andreas Madsen, pioneer Argentine rancher, with a family of five pumas killed in 1930 in the high glacier country of southwestern Patagonia near Lago Viedma.

firsthand knowledge, however, was gained during a five-week lion hunt near Meeker, Colorado, with guide John B. Goff in 1901, the year Roosevelt assumed the presidency of the United States. His subsequent writings of the hunt and of the animal became valuable materials for sportsmen and naturalists. Of the fourteen cougars taken on the hunt, Roosevelt killed all but two. His last one, a male weighing 227 pounds and 8 feet in length, was taken near Juniper Mountain on 14 February, the last day of the hunt. Data on the last animal in particular were important contributions to science, and the specimen stood for forty-three years as the largest North American trophy in the Boone and Crockett Club record files. This largest kill at the eleventh hour and the unique hazard involved resulted in a thrilling climax to the successful hunting expedition. Roosevelt described the kill of the big tom:

> He stood in such an awkward position that I could not get a fair shot at the beast, but a bullet broke his back well forward, and the dogs seized him as he struck the ground. There was still any amount of fight in him and I ran as fast as possible, jumping and slipping over the rocks and the bushes as the cougar and the dogs rolled and slid down the steep mountain-side — for, of course, every minute's delay meant the chance for a dog being killed or crippled. It was a day of misfortune for Jim, who was knocked completely out of the fight by a single blow. The cougar was too big for the dogs to master, even crippled as he was; but when I came up close Turk ran in and got the great beast by one ear, stretching out the cougar's head, while he kept his own forelegs tucked way back so that the cougar could not get hold of them. This gave me my chance and I drove the knife home, leaping back before the creature could get round me.[23]

In July 1913, Roosevelt again chased cougars. This time, accompanied by a son and a nephew, he hunted the northern rim of the Grand Canyon with game warden Uncle Jimmy

102

Owens acting as guide. Members of the party bagged one lion each.[24]

In 1906 a struggling young dentist-writer, Zane Grey, attended a lecture given in New York by Charles Jesse Jones, popularly known as Buffalo Jones, a preserver of the American bison. His vivid stories of capturing wild animals alive with a rope caught the imagination of Grey, who longed to travel west and write about similar adventures. Following an appeal by Grey, the old plainsman agreed to take him to Arizona to hunt mountain lions with a lasso. One Grey biographer wrote of their chance meeting: "It is still quite possible that Zane Grey would eventually have returned to dental practice — or even to professional baseball — had he not chanced to meet Buffalo Jones."[25]

Uncle Jimmy Owens in the Grand Canyon as guide for Theodore Roosevelt's July 1913 cougar hunt. (Courtesy Nicholas Roosevelt) ➤

Zane Grey and John, the brown-and-white hound that Buffalo Jones considered his living talisman of good luck. The dog hunted with Jones in the Yellowstone, Grand Canyon, and finally in Europe, Asia, and Africa. Photograph made in 1907 while Grey and Jones were hunting mountain lions on the North Rim of the Grand Canyon. ➤

John B. Goff, hunter-guide, and Theodore Roosevelt with Roosevelt's first cougar. The six-foot, eighty-pound female was killed near Meeker, Colorado, 14 January 1901. (Philip B. Stewart photo, courtesy Pioneers Museum of Colorado Springs) ▼

Early in 1908, Grey took part in the chase and capture of numerous mountain lions on Buckskin Mountain, the vast tableland forming a part of the northern rim of the Grand Canyon. True to his word, Buffalo Jones lassoed the magnificent wild beasts and brought them back to camp alive. Accompanying the hunters was Uncle Jimmy Owens. Grey took photographs, wrote stories and books about Jones and the hunt, and returned the next year for another adventure.[26] These hunting trips were the outstart of a series of novels that eventually made Zane Grey the most prolific and the most popular early writer on the American cowboy.

By the 1930s the U.S. Biological Survey had more than two hundred professional lion hunters in its employ to protect livestock and other game animals from this predator. In some states trappers were paid a salary, plus a bounty supplemented by individual stockmen and their associations. As a result, the animal became scarce or disappeared completely in many of its last strongholds in the western United States.

The cost of individual kills rose to more than $500 in some areas. Kills in California at one time cost the taxpayers as much as $629 per animal. Game departments and conservation clubs finally began to realize that lion bounties were not economical, could be harmful to other phases of wildlife management, and that sportsmen could eliminate any troublesome predators or those that had become a nuisance.

The cost of a hunt is necessarily high, but Americans came close to paying a much higher price, that of destroying yet another vital link in the wonderful scheme of nature.

Because of better ecological understanding and more reliable conservation practices, this truly American sport will probably be available to sportsmen in the future. It has no equal.

Buffalo Jones roping a mountain lion in a ponderosa pine on the North Rim of the Grand Canyon in 1907. (Photo by Zane Grey) ➤

Buffalo Jones with hunting dogs Sounder and Ranger in camp during a mountain lion hunt on the North Rim of the Grand Canyon, Arizona, in 1907. (Photo by Zane Grey) ▼

Mountain lion in a dead juniper on the rim of the Grand Canyon in 1907. (Photo by Zane Grey)

12
Boone & Crockett Club Records

The Boone and Crockett Club was conceived in 1887 by Theodore Roosevelt as a fraternity for big game hunters interested in travel and exploration, natural history, and the improvement of hunting arms. Among its many activities and accomplishments, the club is probably best known today as the arbiter of North American big game trophy records. Trophy statistics and classifications in order of merit have been an activity of the club since 1932, and its first committee to create an official scoring system was formed in 1949. Unfortunately, no similar type organization exists in Central and South America, so the competition in the cougar class is restrictive in coverage, and the current records cannot be honored as world records.

The Rowland Ward records of the puma were based on the overall lengths before the animals were skinned, but this is not a reliable basis for scoring.[1] Field measurements are often not accurate or possible and a dry skin can be stretched considerably. Weights, too, are many times impossible in the field; they are often delayed and they vary greatly according to length. A short cougar that has just eaten might be heavier than a much longer one. In addition to invalidating length, this also eliminates weight as a basis for rating.

A mathematical formula of skull measurements is more suited for an index and has been adopted by the Boone and Crockett Club as the official scoring system in the rating of North American cougars. Records are now classified on the sum total of the greatest overall length of the skull plus its width across the zygomatic arches.

In January and February 1901 Theodore Roosevelt and his hunting party collected fourteen cougars in northwest Colorado. Twelve of the specimens, personally taken by the colonel, were presented later in the year to the U.S. Biological Survey, accompanied by precise data giving the color, measurements, and weight of each animal. The series was of unusual value because it afforded a study of the nature of the differences resulting from sex and age, the individual variations, and a comparison with other subspecific members of the group. One of the skulls was that of a large male, taken by Roosevelt on the last day of the hunt, whose measurements surpassed any known specimen up to that time. It became the first North American record of the Boone and Crockett Club and alone retained the domination until 1955. The overall length in the flesh from tip of nose to tip of tail was 8 feet, and the animal weighed 227 pounds. The skull, Catalogue No. 108681, is presently housed in the Bird and Mammal Laboratory collection of the U.S. Museum in Washington, D.C.

The record male cougar taken by Roosevelt on 14 February 1901 near Meeker, Colorado, had a total skull measurement of 15-12/16 inches, 9-5/16 length without lower jaw, and 6-7/16 greatest width.

Ed Burton of Claresholm, Alberta, Canada, hunted cougars for a long time and believes that he threw away many big game heads that were in the record class before he became trophy conscious. His Airdales and blueticks on 22 February 1954 treed a cougar on Dutch Creek in Alberta that tied the Roosevelt record and would have exceeded it had not a part of the skull been removed with a stroke of an ax. Boone and Crockett records show that approximately two-sixteenths, or one-eighth of an inch was removed from the skull by the ax. The length of the dry hide was 9 feet 1 inch and the big male weighed 195 pounds.

In 1965 J. Scott Jarvie, taxidermist of Sandy, Utah, measured a number of cougar skulls in his possession that belonged to lion hunter Garth Roberts from the southern part of the state. He found that one exceeded the North American record. The skull was measured and scored by judges of the Boone and Crockett Club and officially declared the new record in 1966. The animal was not killed in Wayne County as originally claimed by Jarvie but in neighboring Garfield County.

The big male trophy animal was difficult to get because it would not take to a tree readily. But Garth Roberts, who has taken some three hundred cougars as best he can remember, was persistent. In January 1964 Roberts chased the big cat for the first time with two dogs, but was

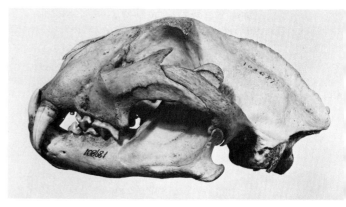

Skull of the record cougar taken by Theodore Roosevelt in Colorado in 1901. The length is 9 5/6 inches, and width is 6 3/8 inches. (Courtesy Smithsonian Institution)

Cougar killed by Ed Burton near Dutch Creek, Alberta, Canada, on 22 February 1954. This large male tied the North American record killed by Theodore Roosevelt in 1901 in Colorado. (Courtesy Ed Burton)

unsuccessful. He tried again the next day with four dogs, but again the cougar eluded him. A week later Roberts hit the track again and followed the animal for fifteen miles. In one place he found a large five-point buck killed by the cougar. After he struck the trail nearby, the animal finally took refuge in a tree, abandoned it, and went up another tree, only to leave it also. Finally, in a third tree, on the rim of Picture Canyon, a fork of Antimony Canyon, Roberts got his prize. The animal measured 8 feet 8 inches in length. Although it was not weighed, Roberts said the animal would go two hundred pounds. The official score tabulated and recorded by the Boone and Crockett Club totaled sixteen points.

A cougar taken by Douglas E. Schuk near Tatlayoko Lake, British Columbia, on 12 February 1979, raised the top score for its category to 16-4/16 total points. The day was overcast when Schuk killed his record cougar, with the temperature ten degrees Fahrenheit, and thirty-two inches of snow in some places. This is his story of the kill:

I trailed the cougar for about 5 miles from where I came upon its tracks while running my trap line. My youngest brother was along. The cougar had caught a rabbit the first mile, made several runs on deer, but missed them all. Finally, my brother got a glimpse of him as he left a rock bluff; so I turned my dog loose and in about 5 minutes he was baying. It took us about 15 minutes to get to the tree. The cat had to climb a fir tree that was growing at an angle; he was old, which is common for old cats to pick leaners. The first look I got at him he was snarling at my brother, who had gotten there first because he ran the ridge and I stayed on the trail which was through thigh deep snow, a habit I got into when running animals with dogs. My brother was only packing a .22 and it looked like the cat was going to jump onto the bluff or on my brother Len. He was about 30 feet back from the tree and about 12 feet lower than old tom. The cat was mad, which I've not seen any other cougars do towards humans. I drew a quick but sure bead on his shoulder and fired. My .308 Winchester 180-grain bullet didn't come out the far side. It was already getting dark, so we quickly skinned it out and then had a long trip home. I sold the pelt to the local taxidermist for $200.00. I needed the money because that's how I make my living. I didn't know till later it was a record cat.

With less pressure in the hunting field from predator hunters, more cougars could attain record-class size and more sportsmen share the record competition once dominated by professional hunters.

Wilburn Roberts with the record North American cougar killed by his son, Garth Roberts, in 1964 near Antimony, Utah. The head measurement had a Boone and Crockett Club score total of 16. (Courtesy Wilburn Roberts)

Trophies of a cougar hunt taken by Theodore Roosevelt in January-February 1901 near Meeker, Colorado. The cougar in the center was recognized by the Boone and Crockett Club as the North American record. It was tied in 1954. (From Scribner's Magazine, *1901)*

Photo by Ervin and Peggy Bauer, Teton Village, Wyoming

13
Ancestry and Species

ANCESTRY

Both modern and extinct pumas were present in the Americas in the Age of Mammals, along with the lynx and two extinct Felidae, the *Smilodon*, or saber-toothed "tiger," and *Felis atrox*, the great true cat, or "lion." The latter two did not survive.

Two pumas of the Pleistocene epoch are recognized as specifically distinct from the modern type. Other specimens of jaws cannot be distinguished readily from the modern species and the name *Felis concolor* is retained in the list of cats from the Pleistocene for the present.

Naturalist William Berry Scott believes that the Felidae of America were immigrants from Asia, supported by the fact that *F. atrox* is present in the Pleistocene of Alaska. "There had been previous arrivals of *Felis* in the Pliocene, which, when better known, may prove to be the ancestors of the puma (*Felis concolor*)," he says.[1]

Two species of pumas have been named from the Pleistocene mammals of the asphalt deposits of Rancho La Brea in Los Angeles, California. Closely related in size and structural characters to the modern puma is the *Felis bituminosa*, named from the skull and scattered skeletal elements.[2] Probably exceeding in size

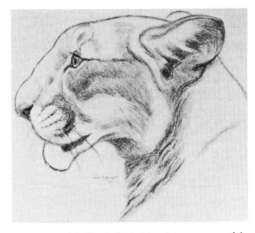

Restoration of the head of Felis bituminosa, *a puma of the Pleistocene fauna. (From John C. Merriam and Chester Stock, "The Felidae of Rancho La Brea," 1932)*

the largest pumas of today was *Felis daggeti*, named from the Rancho La Brea. Also, the massiveness of the cheek teeth and several other cranial characters differ noticeably from *F. concolor*.[3]

SPECIES AND SUBSPECIES

Proposed Genera and Subgenera
Felis Linnaeus, 1771[4]
Puma Jardine, 1834[5]
Panthera Severtzow, 1858[6]
Leopardus, Gray, 1867[7]
Uncia Cope, 1889[8]
Pristinofelis Spillman, 1931[9]
Profelis Sanderson, 1961[10]

Following the Linnaeus description and naming of *Felis concolor* in 1771, various authors proposed other names to identify presumed species from different regions.

Charles B. Cory of the Field Museum of Natural History in Chicago gave the Florida puma subspecific rank with his *Felis concolor floridana* in 1896,[11] and was followed by Oldfield Thomas of the Royal Society of London in 1901 with *Felis concolor pearsoni* from Patagonia.[12] Since then, subspecies have been named from various localities throughout the Western Hemisphere.

The first revision of the pumas was in 1901 by Clinton Hart Merriam, the American naturalist. Although skulls of all members of the group show strong resemblance to one another, Merriam pointed out that they differ in the degree of elevation or depression of the face and frontal region, massive skulls with heavy underjaws contrasting strongly with light ones having small jaws, and those having huge canines and carnassials strikingly different from the slender teeth of others. Merriam listed eleven forms of the puma under six species.[13]

In 1929 Edward William Nelson and Edward A. Goldman, both of the U.S. Biological Survey, listed nineteen geographic races or subspecies and assigned all of them to one nominal species, *Felis concolor*.[14]

The thirty subspecies recognized by Stanley P. Young and Edward A. Goldman in *The Puma: Mysterious American Cat* "are based on combinations of characters, including size, color, and details of cranial and dental structure

that prevail in areas over which environmental conditions tend to be uniform."[15]

Not everyone recognizes each of the following as a subspecies because the original proposers indicated various levels of relationships from species to subspecies. Some believe that an exact separation of subspecies cannot always be verified because the puma is an indefatigable traveler that respects only bigger physiographic obstacles and basic ecological changes. In addition, most mammalogists do not recognize separate common names for subspecies.

Felis concolor concolor Linneaus, 1771
Brazilian puma, Cayenne puma

The Carolus Linnaeus description of *F. concolor* in 1771 is based primarily on the 1648 Brazilian *cuguacuarana* of Georg Marcgrave, with references to other early writers.[16] In the first information about the animal in literature, Marcgrave compared it in size and shape to the jaguar [*jaguara*] with a likeness in color to the wild roebuck.[17] Because Marcgrave stayed in Loritzstadt, now Recife, with few limited excursions during his time in Brazil, it has been suggested that the type locality should be restricted to the region of Pernambuco.[18]

Felis concolor discolor Schreber, 1775
Guyanan puma

Even though the original *F. discolor* of Johann Christian Daniel Schreber is pictured in 1775 as a black animal with references to the black *ounce* from Guyana of Desmarchais and the *black tiger* of Pennant,[19] Schreber described the animal three years later as an animal with short, shiny, dark brown hair.[20] Some later writers have applied the name to the puma of Guyana.

Felis concolor couguar Kerr, 1792
Pennsylvania cougar, Adirondack cougar, Eastern panther

Comte de Buffon figured *le cougar de Pensilvanie* in 1776, an animal he said resembled the *couguar* of Cayenne, except for shorter limbs and lengthier body.[21] Robert Kerr, of the Royal Physical Society and the Royal Society of Surgeons, named it *F. couguar* and stated that it inhabited the mountains of Pennsylvania, Virginia, Carolina, and Georgia. The animal was described as having a remarkably thin and long body, reddish tawny above and whitish on the underparts.[22]

Felis concolor puma Molina, 1782
Chilean puma, Andean puma

The *pagi* of the Araucanian Indians of Chile was described by Juan Ignacio Molina, an early historian of Chile, and named *F. puma*. He said the Spanish called the animal a lion, which it resembled in its shape and roaring, though it was wholly destitute of a mane.[23] British naturalist and explorer Hesketh Prichard restricted the type to the silver-gray variety common in Patagonia.[24] Argentine scientist Dr. Angel Cabrera gives the range of the animal in the high cordillera from extreme southern Peru to the thirty-eighth degree of latitude north.[25]

Felis concolor oregonensis Rafinesque, 1832
Oregon cougar, Cascade mountain puma

Constantine Samuel Rafinesque, French naturalist who traveled extensively in the United States, wrote of a different variety of *couguar* of the western wilds of the Oregon mountains that was large and ferocious. He said it was dark brown, nearly black on the back, and had a white belly. He asked if it were not a peculiar species and suggested the name *Felix* [sic] *oregonensis*.[26]

Felis concolor californica [May], 1896
California lion

The Southern Pacific Company published numerous booklets during the last quarter of the nineteenth century in an extensive campaign to attract settlers to California. One, written in 1896 by W.B. May, was designed to appeal to sportsmen. It contained a halftone illustration of a mounted California lion captioned *Felis californica*. On another page is the statement that the mountain district of Kern County furnished ideal haunts for the animal.[27]

Felis concolor hippolestes Merriam, 1897
Rocky Mountain cougar, mountain lion

One of the pumas from the northwestern United States, described by C. Hart Merriam in 1897, was *F. hippolestes* ["horsekiller"] from the Wind River Mountains of Wyoming. This enormous size type with large and massive teeth is still regarded as one of the largest of all subspecies.[28]

Felis concolor olympus Merriam, 1897
Pacific Coast cougar

The second 1897 puma described by Merriam from the northwestern United States was *F. hippolestes olympus*, with the type specimen from Lake Cushman in the Olympic Mountains of Washington. It was described as similar to *F. hippolestes* but smaller and darker in color.[29]

Felis concolor coryi Bangs, 1896
Florida panther

American ornithologist Charles B. Cory killed a number of panthers in the Florida Everglades between Lake Worth and Biscayne Bay in 1895. He recognized them as a subspecies, *Felis concolor floridana*, with small feet, long tail, and bright yellowish bay color.[30] Because of the preoccupation of *floridana* the type was renamed *Felis coryi* in honor of the original collector.[31]

Felis concolor pearsoni Thomas, 1901
Patagonian puma, Santa Cruz coast puma

Oldfield Thomas, of the British Museum of Natural History, named *F.c. pearsoni* in 1901 from the skin of a puma from Santa Cruz, Patagonia. The specimen had been purchased from Indians by Hasketh Prichard and presented to the museum by the magazine publisher and explorer Cyril Arthur Pearson, following an expedition to Argentina. The skin was distinguished from the "drab-gray" of the extablished *F.c. puma* by a different "brownish clay-colour." It had a proportionately shorter tail, lighter colored ear backs, and an absence of dark markings around the digital pads.[32]

Felis concolor azteca Merriam, 1901
Mexican cougar, Sierra Madre puma

This is one of the three subspecies named by C. Hart Merriam in his 1901 revision of the pumas. His original name, *Felis hippolestes aztecus*, was later revised. Merriam wrote that three skulls at his disposal from Colonia García, Chihuahua, Mexico, showed enough variation in the size of the auditory bullae to characterize a distinct species as it normally would in other mammals.[33]

Felis concolor bangsi Merriam, 1901
North Andean puma, Colombian puma

Based on two skulls and skins from the Santa Marta Mountains in Colombia, collected by Outram Bangs, of the Museum of Comparative Zoology at Cambridge, Merriam described the species *F. bangsi* in 1901. Smaller cranial characters than those of other known species were noted.[34]

Felis concolor costaricensis Merriam, 1901
Central American puma

Also in 1901, Merriam considered two skins and skulls from Costa Rica to represent a subspecies of *F. bangsi* because of color and minor cranial differences.[35]

Felis concolor patagonica Merriam, 1901
South Andean puma

This subspecies was named in 1901 by Merriam from a skull and dry skin from the east base of the Andes Mountains in Patagonia. It was a large puma, gray colored, with distinct dental characters.[36]

Felis concolor browni Merriam, 1903
Colorado Desert puma

In 1903 Merriam named a puma presented by Herbert Brown to the U.S. Biological Survey, *Felis aztecus browni*. The specimen from the desert region of the Colorado River south of Yuma, Arizona, was said to have small bullae and small lateral teeth.[37]

Felis concolor arundivaga Hollister, 1911
Louisiana puma, Canebrake panther

Ned Hollister, American zoologist, hunted the canebrakes of eastern Louisiana for panthers in 1904 with Ben V. Lilly, but was unsuccessful. Lilly collected a specimen the following year that was described and named in 1911 by Hollister. He admitted the animal was closely related to the Florida variety but had marked color differences sufficient to regard it as a distinct species, *Felis arundivaga*.[38] Young and Goldman disagreed in 1946, and considered the type a part of the Florida race, *F.c. coryi*.[39]

Felis concolor improcera Phillips, 1912
Baja California puma

A new species of the puma from Calmalli, Baja California, was named *F. improcera* in 1912, from an adult male skin and skull, by American naturalist John Charles Phillips. The skull was described as very small, rounder, and less elongate than that of its relatives of closest proximity.[40]

Felis concolor soderstromii Lönnberg, 1913
Ecuadorean puma

This puma type, from high elevations in Ecuador, was named in 1913 by Einar Lönnberg, of the University of Uppsala in Sweden, from a specimen collected near Nono on the northwestern slope of Pichincha, the mountain on which Quito is located. He stated that the very dark, medium-sized animal occurred up to heights of twelve thousand feet.[41] Dr. Lönnberg made zoological collections in Ecuador in the early twentieth century.

Felis concolor incarum Nelson & Goldman, 1929
Inca puma

In 1929 Edward W. Nelson and Edward A. Goldman, of the U.S. Biological Survey, described three new pumas that initiated a series of eight subspecies named by them over a five-year period. The Inca puma of the high mountains near Cuzco, Peru, was a medium-sized, dark-colored, well-furred animal.[42]

Felis concolor osgoodi Nelson & Goldman, 1929
Bolivian puma

Differences in cranial details were said to warrant a separate recognition by name of this rich-red, short-haired puma from Bolivia by Nelson and Goldman in 1929. The type was named for Dr. Wilfred H. Osgood, curator of zoology at the Field Museum of Natural History.[43]

Felis concolor mayensis Nelson & Goldman, 1929
Guatemalan puma

The third subspecies named and described in 1929 by Nelson and Goldman was from the Department of Petén, Guatemala, and was said to be the smallest of its closest geographic relatives. Its color was tawnish or reddish, and it differed in cranial details from the Costa Rican puma in the form of the nasals and postorbital processes.[44]

Felis concolor kaibabensis Nelson & Goldman, 1931
Kaibab mountain lion

Nelson and Goldman named this geographic race in 1931 from a specimen taken on Powell Plateau, a part of the northern rim of the Grand Canyon, by J.T. ("Uncle Jimmy") Owens. It had comparatively slight differences from the neighboring Rocky Mountain form.[45]

Felis concolor anthonyi Nelson & Goldman, 1931
Venezuelan puma

From a single specimen from the upper Orinoco River, Nelson and Goldman named this large, rusty-red specimen with short hair, the Venezuelan puma in 1931, honoring H.E. Anthony, a curator of mammals at the American Museum of Natural History.[46]

Felis concolor greeni Nelson & Goldman, 1931
East Brazilian puma

Named in honor of Edward C. Green, a collaborator of the U.S. Biological Survey, was this puma from Rio Grande do Norte in extreme eastern Brazil. Nelson and Goldman described it in 1931 as a small, short-haired, rusty-red subspecies with remarkably small teeth.[47]

Felis concolor vancouverensis Nelson & Goldman, 1932
Vancouver Island mountain lion

In 1932 Nelson and Goldman named a distinctive form of the puma that occupied Vancouver Island, British Columbia, Canada. From a total of fifteen specimens examined, they described the subspecies as a very large and dark form with a skull deeply arched in the frontal region and deep fronto-nasal pits.[48]

Felis concolor borbensis Nelson & Goldman, 1933
Amazon puma

Nelson and Goldman described this new puma from Brazil in 1933 and said the type inhabited the vast lowlands of the Amazon River drainage. The type specimen from Borba on the Rio Madeira was rich rufescent in color and had a decidedly narrow skull.[49]

Felis concolor stanleyana Goldman, 1938
Texas mountain lion, Texas puma

E.A. Goldman alone described the Texas puma in 1936 from specimens collected in Webb County by his colleague, Stanley P. Young, and named the subspecies F.c. youngi. The colors varied from gray to tawny and the skulls and dentations were heavier than other types in close proximity.[50] Two years later, Goldman substituted stanleyana for youngi because of the preoccupation of the latter name by a fossil species.[51]

Felis concolor cabrerae Pocock, 1940
Argentine puma

Enough distinctive features from other established pumas from Argentina caused R.I. Pocock, of the British Museum of Natural History, to name a new race from the northern part of the country. It was characterized by a flat chin as well as other distinctive cranial features. The new subspecies was named for Dr. Angel Cabrera in acknowledgment of his intelligent and informative papers on the Chilean and Argentine pumas.[52]

Felis concolor araucanus Osgood, 1943
Chilean forest puma

In his article, "Mammals of Chile," Wilfred H. Osgood, of the Chicago Natural History Museum, described the forest puma from the Nahuelbuta Mountains in the Province of Malleco in 1943, and said the type inhabited the humid forests of south-central Chile. The principal distinction was the dark color in keeping with the climatic conditions of its habitat.[53]

Felis concolor missoulensis Goldman, 1943
Northern Rocky Mountain puma, Montana puma

Edward A. Goldman believed cranial details were distinctive enough in 1943 to name a new subspecies from near Missoula, Montana. It differed from hippolestes, also from the Rockies, in having a shorter and rounder skull with widely spreading zygomata.[54]

Felis concolor acrocodia Goldman, 1943
Matto Grosso puma

In 1943 Goldman named this medium-sized puma with a slender skull and narrow braincase. Its distribution was said to be in the lowlands of the upper part of the Paraguay River in southwestern Brazil, and in eastern Bolivia.[55]

Felis concolor capricornensis Goldman, 1946
Sao Paulo puma

The only new subspecies in the 1946 review of thirty types by Young and Goldman is this one from the state of Sao Paulo in southeastern Brazil. It was said to be similar in size to the Matto Grosso puma, but differed in having a broader braincase and frontal region and deep V-shaped nasals.[56]

Felis concolor punensis Housse, 1950
Tarapacá puna puma

R.P. Raffael Housse, a member of the Academia Chilena de Ciencias Naturales, suggested a subspecies after he described the puma from the high Tarapacá puna in northern Chile in 1950 as differing from the typical Chilean puma by brown hair and big teeth.[57] Writing about the mammals of the Tarapacá, Guillermo Mann had earlier stated that these features of the variety indicated a certain kinship with forms from Bolivia and Peru.[58]

Felis concolor schorgeri Jackson, 1955
Wisconsin puma

Following an evaluation of measurements and characteristics of old specimens from Kansas, Minnesota, and Wisconsin pumas in the University of Wisconsin Zoological Collection, Hartlet H.T. Jackson believed that an undescribed subspecies had once inhabited the upper Mississippi River Valley and Western Great Lakes region, and named this subspecies in 1955. Large skulls, posteriorly relatively narrow, differed in comparison with other subspecies from the central United States.[59]

Felis concolor hudsoni Cabrera, 1957
Argentine pampean puma

Dr. Angel Cabrera, of the Museo Nacional de La Plata, named the puma of the vast pampean plain and small sierras of the Argentine province of Buenos Aires in 1957 because of the minor differences in it and its closest relatives. He said the type was noticeably smaller, the skull less robust, and the nasals narrower.[60] The subspecies was named for Argentine naturalist W.H. Hudson.

Probably appropriate at this time would be a revision of the current list of names proposed for various populations of the puma throughout the Americas. Its wide distribution and scarcity would make the revision a task of major proportions, however. The disappearance of the animal in one zone should not mean the extinction of the respective subspecies, if admitted as such, for it often reappears suddenly after a long time in regions when it has already been considered gone forever.

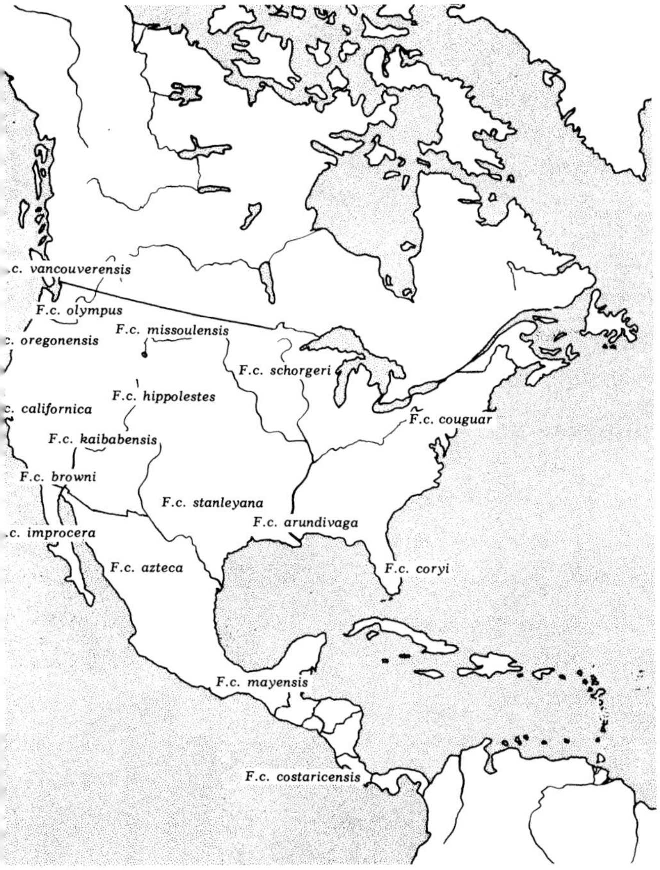

.c. vancouverensis
F.c. olympus
F.c. missoulensis
c. oregonensis
F.c. schorgeri
F.c. hippolestes
c. californica
F.c. couguar
F.c. kaibabensis
F.c. browni
F.c. stanleyana
F.c. arundivaga
.c. improcera
F.c. azteca
F.c. coryi
F.c. mayensis
F.c. costaricensis

Distribution of past and present subspecies of Felis concolor *from North America and Central America.*

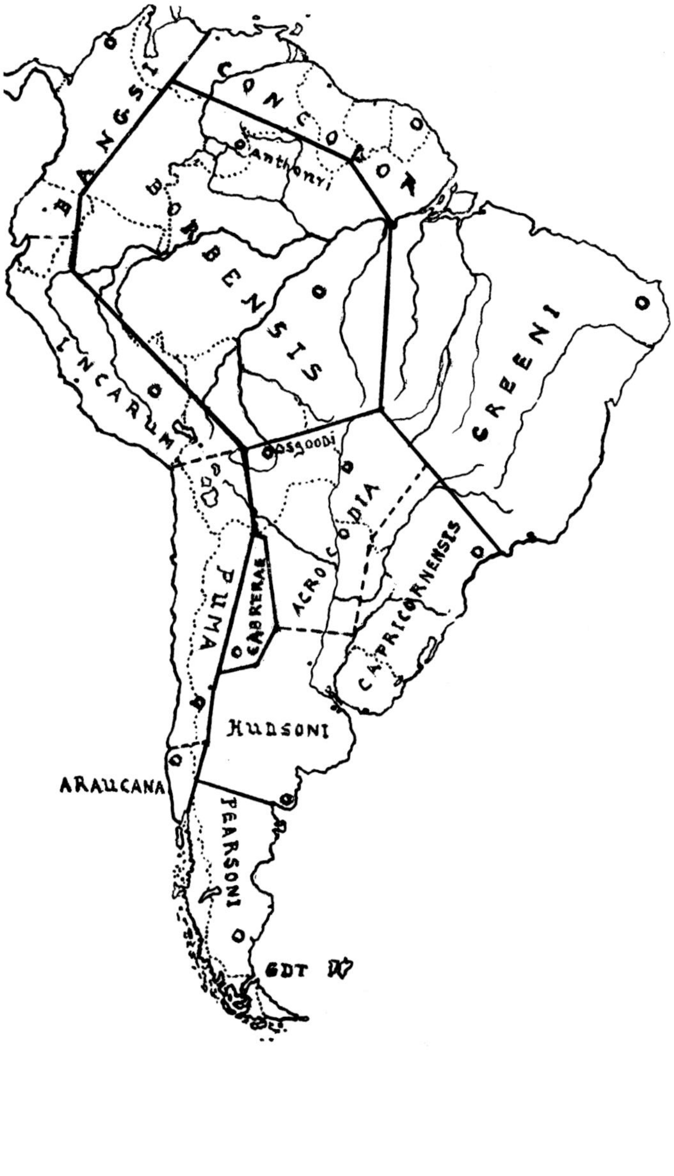

BANGSI
CONCOLOR
Anthonyi
BORBENSIS
INCARUM
OSGOODI
GREENI
ACRO
CODIA
CAPRICORNENSIS
PUMA
CABRERAE
HUDSONI
ARAUCANA
PEARSONI
GDT

Zoogeogramma of the South American pumas by Dr. Georges Dennler de La Tour of the Sociedad Cientifica Argentina. Circles show the type localities of the appertinent subspecies.

Notes

Chapter 1: A New Lease on Life

1. Edwin A. Barber, "Rock inscriptions," 716-25.
2. Richard Schomburgk, *Reisen in Britisch-Guiana*, 64-70.
3. Francois Javier Clavijero, *Storia della California*, 100-101.
4. Glover M. Allen, "Extinct and vanishing mammals," 233-52.
5. Thomas Cooper, *The Statutes at large*, 108-10, 179-80.
6. Henry M. Burt, *The first century*, 2:348.
7. Frederic Remington, "Mountain lions," 12-14.
8. Ferris Weddle, "The cougar in our national parks," 4-7.
9. George M. Wright and Ben H. Thompson, "Fauna of the national parks," 45-55.
10. Ferris Weddle, "A cougar is killed," 13-15.
11. R.H. Lambeth, "A uniform bounty system," 63-64.
12. Jim Zumbo, "The great cougar comeback," 61-63, 97.
13. Floyd E. Potter to Jim Bob Tinsley, 1 April 1985.
14. U.S. Congress, P.L. 93-205, 979-1002.
15. U.S. Congress, P.L. 89-669, 1095-1101.
16. Stewart Udall, "Native fish," 4001.
17. Committee on Rare and Endangered Wildlife Species, "Rare and endangered fish," I:viii.
18. U.S. Congress, P.L. 93-205, 979-1002.
19. Spencer H. Smith, "Amendments to lists," 14678.
20. Lynn A. Greenwalt, "Endangered status," 24062-67.
21. Florida Game and Fresh Water Fish Commission, "Hunting season in 1950-51," 18.
22. Florida Game and Fresh Water Fish Commission, "Back on the protected list," 27.
23. Florida Game and Fresh Water Fish Commission, "Panther — state animal," 46.
24. Morrie Naggiar, "The Florida panther," 17-20.
25. George Leposky, "Panther's progress," 2-5.

Chapter 2: Still a Puma by Any Name

1. Claude T. Barnes, *The cougar or mountain lion*, 10-12.
2. Victor Cahalane, "King of cats," 217-59.
3. Christopher Columbus, *Select letters*, 193.
4. Garcilasso de la Vega, *First part of the Royal commentaries*, 2:238.
5. Adriaen van der Donck, "A description," 1:167.
6. Georges Frederic Cuvier and Edward Griffin, *The animal kingdom*, 2:334-40.
7. William T. Hornaday, "The cat family," 409-16.
8. Pedro de Castañeda de Nágera, *Relación de la jornada*, pt. 2, chap. 3.
9. Alfred Edmund Brehm, *Brehms tierleben*, 381-82.
10. Konrad Guenther, *A naturalist in Brazil*, 127-28.
11. Stanley P. Young and Edward A. Goldman, *The puma*, 4.
12. Félix de Azara, *Apuntamientos para la historia natural*, 1:120-32.
13. Adolph Murie, "Mammals from Guatemala," 1-30.
14. Hornaday, "The cat family," 409-16.
15. William Byrd, *The Westover manuscripts*, 56.
16. Robert E. Marshall, *The onza*, 71.
17. Georges Louis Leclerc comte de Buffon, *Natural history*, 197-205.
18. Thomas Ash, *Carolina*, 20-21.
19. Charles Marie de La Condamine, *A succinct abridgment*, 81.
20. Thomas Pennant, *Synopsis of quadrupeds*, 179-81.
21. Works Progress Administration, *Palmetto place names*, 105-6.
22. Pierre Francois Xavier de Charlevoix, *Histoire et description*, 1:272.
23. Pennant, *Synopsis of quadrupeds*, 179-81.
24. Vincent Roth, *Notes and observations*, 150-53.
25. Cornelius Pauw, *Recherches philosophiques*, 7-8.
26. Dr. [Oliver] Goldsmith, *The deserted village*, 19-20.
27. Francis Harper, "The mammals of the Okefinokee Swamp," 317-20.
28. Ned Buntline [Edward Z.C. Judson], "My first cougar," 994.
29. Prof. J.P. Kirtland, "Report on the zoology of Ohio," 176.
30. Willem Piso, *Historia natvralis Brasiliae*, 234-36.
31. Piso, *Gulielmi Pisonis*, 103-5.
32. Buffon, *Histoire naturelle*, 9:216-30.
33. Henry Walter Bates, *The naturalist*, 1:176-77.
34. Elliott Coues, "The quadrupeds of Arizona," 281-92.
35. Spencer F. Baird, "Mammals of the boundary," pt. 2, 5-6.
36. Theodore Roosevelt, "With the cougar hounds," pt. 1, 417-35.
37. Frederick Marryat, *The travels and adventures*, 350.
38. Theodore H. Hittell, *The adventures of James Copen Adams*, 254-59.
39. William Penn, *A letter from William Penn*, 4.
40. Henry W. Shoemaker, *The Pennsylvania lion*, 18.
41. Robert Beverly, *The history of the present state*, pt. 2, 37-38, 73.
42. John Lawson, *A new voyage to Carolina*, 117-18.
43. William Bartram, *Travels*, 6, 46.
44. James Fenimore Cooper, *The pioneers*, 2:171-72.
45. James Whitcomb Riley, *The complete works*, 4:166-78.
46. William Gilmore Simms, "How Sharp Snaffles got his capital," 667-87.
47. Charlevoix, *Histoire et description*, 2:129.
48. Samuel Williams, *The natural and civil history*, 86-87.
49. [John Neal], *Brother Jonathan*, 1:109-10.
50. Oliver Wendell Holmes, *The complete poetical works*, 30-31.
51. Phillip Ashton Rollins, *The cowboy*, 184-85.
52. James P. McMullen, *Cry of the panther*, 373.
53. R.D. Lawrence, *The ghost walker*, 76.
54. Abraham Gesner, *New Brunswick*, 261.
55. [Henry David Thoreau], "Chesuncook," 309.
56. William D. Williamson, *The history of the state of Maine*, 1:134-35.
57. W.H. Hudson, *The naturalist in La Plata*, 31-58.
58. Frank Hamilton Cushing, "Zuñi fetishes," 9-45.
59. Frederick W. True, "The puma," 591-608.
60. Bruce S. Wright, "The cougar in New Brunswick," 108-19.
61. Elliott S. Barker, *When the dogs bark*.
62. Henry W. Shoemaker, *Extinct Pennsylvania animals*, pt. 1, 9.
63. Herbert Ravenel Sass, "The panther prowls," 31, 133-34, 136.
64. Edward A. Preble, "A biological investigation," 208-9.

65. William Duncan Strong, "Indian records," 59-60.
66. Ernest Ingersoll, *Wild neighbors*, 38-58.
67. Francois Javier Clavijero, *Storia della California*, 100-101.
68. Hans Gadow, *Through southern Mexico*, 371-72.
69. C.S. Rafinesque, "On the Zapotecas," 51-56.
70. Murie, "Mammals from Guatemala," 1-30.
71. Rev. W.H. Brett, *Mission work*, 138-40.
72. Sir Robert Schomburgk, "Information," 324-27.
73. Stanley E. Brock, *Leemo*, 38.

74. Félix de Azara, *Apuntamientos*, 120-32.
75. Angel Cabrera and José Yepes, *Historia natural*, 168-72.
76. True, "The puma," 591-608.
77. J.R. Rengger, *Naturgeschichte*, 181-91.
78. Cabrera and Yepes, *Historia natural*, 168-72.
79. Barnes, *The cougar or mountain lion*, 17.
80. Alberto Vuletin, *Zoonomia andina*, 132-33.
81. Juan Ignacio Molina, *Saggio sulla storia naturale*, 295-300.
82. R.P. Rafael Housse, "Los pumas o cuguardos," 33-46.

Chapter 3: Description

1. Ogden Nash, *Many long years ago*, 210.
2. *Boston Weekly News-Letter*, ["Notice of a cattamount"], [2].
3. Carl von Linné [Carolus Linnaeus], "Regni animalis," 522.
4. Police News, "Here, there and everywhere," 11.
5. "Rambler," *Guide to Florida*, 133-34.
6. Stanley P. Young and Edward A. Goldman, *The puma*, 54.
7. Leon T. Mott, "Stalking the giant puma," 102-7.
8. Robert Eaton to Jim Bob Tinsley, 8 October 1967.
9. Ivan T. Sanderson, *Living mammals of the world*, 160-68.
10. Stanley E. Brock, *Leemo*, 37.
11. Frank Dufresne, "Predators and pests," 267-76.
12. L.J. Bates, "Old Strategy," 342-47.
13. Theodore Roosevelt, "With the cougar hounds," pt. 1, 545-64.
14. Angel Cabrera, "Los félidos vivientes," 161-247.
15. Roosevelt, "With the cougar hounds," pt. 1, 435.
16. Angel Cabrera and José Yepes, *Historia natural*, 168-72.

17. [Martín de la Cruz], *The Badianus manuscript*, 324.
18. Xil Yorris, "The white panther," 110-11.
19. Nicholas Rowe, ed., "White mountain lions," 201.
20. Thomas Heron McKee, "'Uncle Jim' Owen," 50-51, 172-74.
21. Garcilasso de la Vega, *First part of the Royal commentaries*, 1:231-32; 2:30, 238-41, 341, 385.
22. Charles Darwin, *The descent of man*, 528.
23. Ferris Weddle, "The cougar," 180-91.
24. Robert Barrett and Katherine Barrett, *A yankee in Patagonia*, 68-69, 205, 220, 229-46.
25. Ernest Thompson Seton, *Lives of game animals*, 1:35-136.
26. Robert C. Belden, "Florida panther recovery plan," 18-20.
27. Charles Livingston Bull, "The puma," 112-13.
28. Willis Peterson, "The Mogollon Rim," 2-5, 8-12, 29-33, 38.
29. Disney Productions, *Walt Disney's worlds of nature*, 62.

Chapter 4: Role in Amerind Cultures

1. Charles E. Humberger to Jim Bob Tinsley, 17 August 1965.
2. Will C. Barnes, "The Bandelier National Monument," 563-74.
3. William C. Mills, *Certain mounds and village sites*, 2:149-51.
4. Frank Hamilton Cushing, "Exploration of ancient key dwellers," 329-453.
5. C.S. Rafinesque, "On the Zapotecas," 51-56.
6. William Burnet Stevenson, *Historical and descriptive narrative*, 2:80-81.
7. Antonio Vazques de Espinosa, "Compendium and description," 550.
8. Garcilasso de la Vega, *First part of the Royal commentaries*, 1:232; 2:30, 238-39, 341.
9. Ibid.

10. Simon Clark, The puma's claw, 15.
11. Francisco Javier Clavijero, *Storia della California*, 100-101.
12. Ibid.
13. John H. Seger, trans., *Tradition of the Cheyenne Indians*, 1-12.
14. Franc Johnson Newcomb, et al., "A study of Navajo symbolism," 31-32.
15. Stanley P. Young and Edward A. Goldman, *The puma*, 7.
16. [Martín de la Cruz], *The Badianus manuscript*, 324.
17. Frank Hamilton Cushing, "Zuñi fetishes," 9-43.
18. Ibid.
19. Ibid.
20. Joseph Blethen, "The fire cat," 314-21.
21. Ibid.

Chapter 5: Early Chroniclers

1. Christopher Columbus, *Select letters*, 193.
2. Bernal Díaz del Castillo, *Historia verdadera*, 46-47.
3. Bernardino de Sahagún, *Historia general*, 322-23.
4. Alvar Núñez Cabeza de Vaca, *La relacion que dio*, chap. 7.
5. Hernando de Soto, *Relacam verdadeira trabalhos*, chaps. 23, 44.
6. Pedro de Castañeda, *Relación de la jornada*, chap. 3.
7. René Goulaine de Laudonnière, *L'Histoire notable de la Floride*, 3.
8. John Sparke (the younger), *The voyage made by Iohn Hawkins*, 59.
9. Francisco Hernández, *Rervm medicarvm novae hispaniae*, 3-4.
10. Thomas Hariot, *A brief and true report*, [28].
11. Sir W. Raleigh, *The discoverie*, 94.
12. M. John Brereton, *A briefe and true relation*, 12-13, 37-44.
13. Garcilasso de la Vega, *First part of the Royal commentaries*, 2:385.

14. José de Acosta, *The natvrall and morall historie*, 69-70, 303.
15. Antonio Vazques de Espinosa, "Compendium and description," 550, 663.
16. Henry Spelman, *Relation of Virginia*, 28.
17. Captaine John Smith, *The General Historie of Virginia*, 27.
18. William Wood, *New Englands prospect*, 16-17.
19. John Josselyn, *New-Englands rarities discovered*, 21-22.
20. Willem Piso, *Historia natvralis Brasiliae*, 234-36.
21. Piso, *Gulielmi Pisonis*, 103-5.
22. Adriaen van der Donck, "A description of the New-Netherlands," 167.
23. Francois Coreal, *Voyages de Francois Coreal*, 1:28-29, 108-98; 2:352.
24. John Lederer, *The discoveries of John Lederer*, 4-8.
25. Samuel Clarke, *A true and faithful account*, 32.
26. Zénobe Membré, "Narrative of La Salle's voyage," 179-80.

27. Thomas Ash, *Carolina*, 20-21.

28. William Penn, *A letter from William Penn*, 4.

29. John Ray, *Synopsis methodica animalium*, 168-70.

30. Robert Beverly, *The history and present state*, 37-38, 73.

31. John Lawson, *A new voyage to Carolina*, 117-18.

32. John Brickell, *The natural history*, 115-16.

33. Woodes Rogers, *A cruising voyage round the world*, 95, 335, 342.

34. Antoine Simon Le Page du Pratz, *The history of Louisiana*, 2:63-64.

35. Pierre Barrère, *Essai sur l'histoire naturelle*, 166.

36. Mark Catesby, *The natural history*, 2:xxix-xxv.

37. Charles Marie de La Condamine, *A succinct abridgment*, 81.

38. Mathurin Jacques Brisson, *Regnum animale*, 270-72.

39. George Louis Leclerc comte de Buffon, *Histoire naturelle*, 9:270-72.

40. Buffon, *Histoire naturelle*, supp. 3:222-23.

41. Major Robert Rogers, *A concise account of North America*, 191, 261.

42. Carl von Linné [Carolus Linnaeus], "Regni animalis," 522.

Chapter 6: Range and Population

1. Herbert Ravenel Sass, "The panther prowls," 31, 133-34, 136.

2. Einer Lönnberg, "Mammals from Ecuador," 2-5.

3. Edward Whymper, *Travels amongst the great Andes*, 229.

4. Oliver P. Pearson, "Mammals in the highlands," 136-37.

5. Victor Cahalane, *A preliminary study*, 1-22.

6. Lt. Ronald M. Nowak, *The cougar in the United States*, 6-7.

7. Jim Zumbo, "The great cougar comeback," 61-63.

8. Bruce S. Wright, "The cougar in eastern Canada," 144-48.

9. George Jennings Gale, "Cougars in Alaska," 4.

10. Bob Housholder, "Arizona's reigning predator," 18-20.

11. Christopher Columbus, *Select letters*, 193.

12. Alfred K. Moe, "Honduras," 19.

13. William Henry Burt and Ruben A. Stirton, "The mammals of El Salvador," 49-50.

14. Miguel Ruiz Herrero, "Nicaragua, paraiso de cazadores," 18-25.

15. Wilfred H. Osgood, "Mammals from western Venezuela," 6, 33-66.

16. Stanley E. Brock to Jim Bob Tinsley, 7 March 1966.

17. Frederic Walter Miller, "Notes on some mammals," 15-16.

18. Pearson, "Mammals in the highlands," 136-37.

19. Federico E. Ahlfeld, *Geografia de Bolivia*, 92.

20. Georg Ludwig Hartwig, *The tropical world*, 28, 614-16.

21. E.W. Nelson and E.A. Goldman, "List of pumas," 345-50.

22. Leon T. Mott, "Stalking the giant puma," 102-7.

23. Juan H. Figueira, "Contribución al conocemento," 207-8.

24. Andreas Madsen, *Cazando pumas*.

25. John Byron, *The narrative of the Honourable John Byron*, 54-56.

26. Andrew Murray, *The geographical distribution*, 100.

Chapter 7: Life Story

1. R.P. Rafael Housse, "Los pumas o cuguardos," 69-88.

2. Jay C. Bruce, "The problem of mountain lion control," 1-17.

3. Robert Baudy, "Observation of first complete mating," 1-2.

4. Devereau Fuller, "[Report on the period]," 62.

5. J.A. Allen, "On mammals collected," 47-80.

6. John James Audubon and Rev. John Buchman, *The quadrupeds of North America*, 2:305-13.

7. Housse, "Los pumas o cuguardos," 69-88.

8. Jay C. Bruce, "Lioness tracked to lair," 152-53.

9. Franklin Welles Calkins, "About the cougar," 448-55.

10. Enos A. Mills, *Wild animal homesteads*, 17-19.

11. Stanley P. Young and Edward A. Goldman, *The puma*, 112-14.

12. Edward J. Connolly, Jr., "The food habits," 117-18.

13. Ben V. Lilly, *Mountain lions of New Mexico*, 2.

14. Theodore H. Hittell, *The adventures of James Copen Adams*, 78-79, 119-20, 204, 231-33, 254-66, 314-18.

15. Claude T. Barnes, *The cougar or mountain lion*, 136.

16. Robert Easton and Mackenzie Brown, *Lord of beasts*, 153-59, 266-67.

17. M.E. Musgrave, "Some habits," 282-85.

18. Stanley P. Young, "Mountain lion," 158-60.

19. John Fannin, "The panther in British Columbia," 184.

20. Young and Goldman, *The puma*, 115.

21. Barnes, *The cougar or mountain lion*, 139.

22. W. Leslie Robinette, et al., "Notes on cougar productivity," 204-17.

23. Jay C. Bruce, "The why and how of mountain lion hunting, 108-14.

24. John A. Morris, "California lion pets," 400-402.

25. Theodore Roosevelt, "With the cougar hounds," pt. 2, 548-49.

26. O.O. S[mith], "Story of a cougar skin," 768-71.

27. James Fullerton, "Is nature faking just?" 215-17.

28. Hittell, *The adventures of James Copen Adams*, 78-79, 119-20, 204, 231-33, 254-66, 314-18.

29. Young and Goldman, *The puma*, 109-11.

30. California Division of Fish and Game, *Outdoor California*, 1.

31. Robinette, et al., "Notes on cougar productivity," 204-17.

32. C. Hart Merriam, "The vertebrates of the Adirondack region," 29-39.

33. Roosevelt, "With the cougar hounds," pt. 1, 435.

34. S.E. Jorgensen and L. David Mech, *Proceedings of a symposium*, 60-64.

35. William L. Finley and Irene Finley, "Baby panthers," 5-7, 35.

36. Morris, "California lion pets," 400-402.

37. Charles B. Cory, *Hunting and fishing in Florida*, 41-49, 109-10.

38. Barnes, *The cougar or mountain lion*, 56.

39. Robert A. McCabe, "The scream of the mountain lion," 305-6.

40. Paul Fountain, *The great mountains and forests*, 74-80.

41. Barnes, *The cougar or mountain lion*, 57.

42. Ivan T. Sanderson, *Living mammals of the world*, 160-68.

43. Stanley E. Brock, *More about Leemo*, 32-35.

44. Dave Hancock, "Picnic with a cougar," 26-27.

45. Howard H. Smith, "My lions," 121-22.

46. Stanley E. Brock, *Leemo*, 26-27.

47. Maurice Hornocker, "Stalking the mountain lion," 638-55.

48. Young and Goldman, *The puma*, 81-83.

49. A. Starker Leopold, *Wildlife of Mexico*, 478-82.

50. Christen Wemmer and Kate Scow, "Communication in the Felidae," 749-66.

51. J. Frank Dobie, "Lion markers," 9-10, 111-15.

52. Charles Darwin, *Journal of researches*, 116-17, 136, 183, 269-70.

53. Harley G. Shaw, "A mountain lion field guide," 1-27.

54. Hornocker, "Stalking the mountain lion," 638-55.

55. John C. Seidensticker IV, et al., "Mountain lion social organization," 1-60.

56. Maurice Hornocker, "Cougars up close," 42-47.

57. Lewis R. Freeman, "The California lion," 119-31.

58. Henry G. Tinsley, "Western mountain lions," 691-98.

59. Roosevelt, "With the cougar hounds," pt. 2, 562.

60. Charles J. Lisle, "An Idaho cougar hunt," 931-33.

61. Georges Louis Leclerc comte de Buffon, *Natural history*, 222-23.

62. J.C. Hughes, "The American panther," 103.

63. Jack Morley, "A sea-going cougar," 25-26.

64. Hancock, "Picnic with a cougar," 26-27.

65. Ernest G. Holt, "Swimming cats," 72-73.

66. Ned Buntline [Edward Z.C. Judson], "My first cougar," 994.

67. *Florida Star*, "Local items," [8].

68. William T. Hornaday, "The cat family," 409-16.

69. J.R. Rengger, *Naturgeschichte der säugethiere*, 181-91.

70. James C. McKee, et al., "Mountain lions climb trees," 308; "Panthers climb trees," 350.

71. Brock, *More about Leemo*, 88-94.

72. Ibid.

73. Tinsley, "Western mountain lions," 691-98.

74. Livingston Stone, "Habits of the panther," 1188-90.

75. Merriam, "The vertebrates of the Adirondack region," 29-39.

76. Lisle, "An Idaho cougar hunt," 931-33.

77. Dobie, "Lion markers," 9-10, 111-15.

78. Connolly, *The food habits*, 129-31.

79. Carl B. Koford, "A California mountain lion," 274-75.

80. W.E. Round, "When nature fails," 25, 71-73.

81. Housse, "Los pumas o cuguardos," 69-88.

82. Ibid.

83. Connolly, *The food habits*, 23.

84. Brock, *More about Leemo*, 43-44, 73-74.

85. Connolly, *The food habits*, 11.

86. Harlen G. Johnson, "Mountain lion bags," 2, 11.

87. Housse, "Los pumas o cuguardos," 69-88.

88. Robert Barrett and Katherine Barrett, *A yankee in Patagonia*, 68-69, 205, 220, 229-46.

89. Enos A. Mills, *Watched by wild animals*, 189-204.

90. U.S. Forest Service, "Wilderness conflict," 1.

91. Richard H. Manville, "Report of deer attacking cougar," 476-78.

92. Jay S. Gashwiler and W. Leslie Robinette, "Accidental fatalities," 123-26.

93. Frank C. Hibben, "The mountain lion and ecology," 584-86.

94. W. Leslie Robinette, et al., "Food habits of the cougar," 261-73.

95. Hornocker, "A study of the ecology," 1-23.

96. John Lesowski, "The silent hunter," 44-47, 104-8.

97. Connolly, *The food habits*, 73.

98. Vernon Bailey, "The mammals and life zones," 261-65.

99. Leopold, *Wildlife of Mexico*, 478-82.

100. F.P. Cronemiller, "Mountain lion preys," 68.

101. O. Earle Frye, "The disappearing panther," 8-9, 31-32.

102. Housse, "Los pumas o cuguardos," 69-88.

103. Mills, *Watched by wild animals*, 189-204.

104. Timothy Flint, *Biographical memoir of Daniel Boone*, 21, 45-47, 75-76.

105. Young and Goldman, *The puma*, 137.

106. J.A. Allen, "On a collection of mammals," 253-54.

107. Young, "Mountain lion," 158-60.

108. Lesowski, "Two observations," 586.

109. Bruce B. Ackerman, et al., "Cougar food habits," 147-55.

110. Robinette, et al., "Food habits of the cougar," 261-73.

111. Jay C. Bruce, "The problem of mountain lion control," 1-17.

112. Connolly, *The food habits*, 70-71.

113. Hesketh Prichard, "Field notes," 273-75.

114. Connolly, *The food habits*, 65.

115. Young and Goldman, *The puma*, 141-43.

116. Robert J. Eaton to Jim Bob Tinsley, 8 October 1967.

117. Hugh M. Halliday, *Wildlife trails across Canada*, 152-64.

118. H. Russell Suminski, "Mountain lion predation," 62-66.

119. Kenneth R. Dixon, "Evaluation of the effects of mountain lion predation," 141-64.

120. Larry W. Sitton, et al., "Mountain lion predation," 174-86.

121. Zénobe Membré, "Narrative of La Salle's voyage," 179-80.

122. Félix de Azara, *Apuntamientos para la historia natural*, 120-30.

123. Stewart Pearce, *Annals of Luzerne County*, 488-500.

124. Dr. W.J. McKnight, "'Bill Long', king of hunters," 40-42.

125. Henry Bannon, "A prehistoric Indian naturalist," 164-65, 187-88.

126. J. Frank Dobie, "Panther covered sleeping man," 20.

127. Frederick Gerstäcker, *Wild sports in the Far West*, 99, 159-60, 253-60, 300-33.

128. James Pike, *The scout and ranger*, 28-29.

129. Alwin Frache, "Buried by a cougar," xxix.

130. Freeman, "The California lion," 119-31.

131. Sir Robert Schomburgk, "Information respecting botanical travellers," 324-27.

132. Zadock Thompson, *The natural history of Vermont*, 37.

133. Will F. Evans, "The super-strength of the mountain lion," 344-45.

134. Musgrave, "Some habits," 282-85.

135. W.H. Hudson, *The naturalist in La Plata*, 31-58.

136. Victor Gonzales K. to Jim Bob Tinsley, 26 November 1966.

137. John C. Cremony, *Life among the Apaches*, 225-26.

138. Tracy I. Storer, "Rabies in a mountain lion," 45-48.

139. Halliday, *Wildlife trails across Canada*, 152-64.

140. Jorgensen and Mech, eds., *Proceedings of a symposium*, 60-64.

141. Einer Lönnberg, "Mammals from Ecuador," 2-5.

142. Housse, "Los pumas o cuguardos," 69-88.

143. Rui Díaz de Guzmán, *La Argentina*, 77-82.

144. J. Frank Dobie, "Tales of the panther," 22-27, 57, 60-61.

145. Charles John Cornish, *Animal artisans*, 199-200.

146. Park DeVane, "Taming a Florida panther."

147. W.A. Perry, "The cougar," 405-27.

148. Hudson, *The naturalist in La Plata*, 31-58.

149. Calkins, "About the cougar," 448-55.

150. Charles Livingston Bull, "The puma," 112-13.

151. Perry, "The cougar," 405-27.

152. P.A. Parsons, "[Do cougars attack and kill humans?]" 4.

153. Hancock, "Picnic with a cougar," 26-27.

154. Azara, *Apuntamientos para la historia natural*, 120-30.

155. Hesketh Prichard, *Through the heart of Patagonia*, 242-44.

156. Barnes, *The cougar or mountain lion*, 162.

157. Frederick W. True, "The puma, or American lion," 591-608.

158. Young and Goldman, *The puma*, 58-60.

159. Ibid.

160. Zane Grey, "Lassoing lions in the Siwash," 776-85.

161. Bruce, "The problem of mountain lion control," 1-17.

162. Thomas Heron McKee, "'Uncle Jim' Owen and his dogs," 50-51, 172-74.

163. Christoval de Molina, *An account of the fables and rites*, 44-45.

164. Philip Ainsworth Means, *Ancient civilizations of the Andes*, 348.

165. John Brickell, *The natural history of North-Carolina*, 115-16.

Chapter 8: Conflicting Accounts

1. John Spargo, *The catamount in Vermont*.

2. Harold Lambert, *"There ain't no 'painters' in West Virginia,"* 10-12.

3. Bill Walsh, *"Panthers are popular,"* 4-10.

4. Robert P. Crawford, *"Romantic days on the Missouri,"* 3-4, 48, 51-52.

5. Frank Heath, ed., [Editorial], 1.

6. Gerald T. Bue and Milton H. Stenlund, *"Are there mountain lions in Minnesota?"* 32-37.

7. Henry W. Shoemaker, *"The panther in Pennsylvania,"* 7, 28, 32.

8. Bruce S. Wright, *"The return of the cougar,"* 262-65, 292-96.

9. Bruce S. Wright, *The eastern panther*, vii-x.

10. B.F. [Beebe] Johnson, *American lions and cats*, 148-51.

11. Herbert Ravenel Sass, "The panther prowls," 31, 133-34, 136.

12. National Wildlife Federation, "Slowing down," 1.

13. David M. Newell, "Panther!" 10-11, 70-72.

14. J. Fred Thornton, "Mountain lion comeback," 30-31.

15. Lyle S. St. Amant, *Louisiana wildlife inventory*, 180-82.

16. John A. Sealander, "Mountain lion in Arkansas," 34.

17. Glenn Harris, "Stranger on the river," 7.

18. Theodore Roosevelt, *The wilderness hunter*, 335-47.

19. Vernon Bailey, "The mammals and life zones," 261-65.

20. J.H. Batty, "The Felis concolor, or panther," 51-52.

21. Casper W. Whitney, "The cougar," 238-54.

22. John H. Logan, *A history of the upper country of South Carolina*, 53-66.

23. William A. Baillie-Grohman, *Camps in the Rockies*, 83-84.

24. Marjorie Kinnan Rawlings, *Cross Creek*, 157-59.

25. Ap-wa-cun-na, "Hunting in Montana," 204-5.

26. Batty, "The Felis concolor," 51-52.

27. J.R. Mead, "Felis concolor," 278-79.

28. Franklin Welles Calkins, "About the cougar," 448-55.

29. Don Dedera, "Calling Ford bird," 13.

30. H.S. Garfield, "About the puma," 7-12.

31. Walter Lee Davis, "I heard a cougar scream," 39, 63, 73.

32. Stanley P. Young, "Our wild lyric soprano," 26-27, 51-54.

33. Dedera, "Calling Ford bird," 13.

34. Stanley P. Young and Edward A. Goldman, *The puma*, 92-93.

35. Dorothy M. Ferrell, *Bear tales and panther tracks*, 15.

36. [Beebe] Johnson, *American lions and cats*, 123.

37. L.D. Rubin, "Pride of lions," 4.

38. George Louis Leclerc comte de Buffon, *Natural history*, 5:197-205.

39. Félix de Azara, *Apuntamientos para la historia natural*, 1:120-32.

40. Thomas Stewart Traill, "Remarks on some of the American animals," 464-74.

41. John Frost, *History of the state of California*, 283-84.

42. John James Audubon and Rev. John Bachman, *The quadrupeds of North America*, 2:305-13.

43. Maj. S.W. Atkison, *Oklahoma Bill, hunter and trapper*, [2].

44. C. Hart Merriam, "The vertebrates of the Adirondack region," 29-39.

45. Monroe H. Goode, "The real cougar," 26-27, 70-72.

46. W.H. Hudson, "The puma," 553-64.

47. Goode, "The real cougar," 26-27, 70-72.

48. Amadeo Bilo (younger), "El león del Colorado," 26-27, 29-32, 65.

49. Calkins, "About the cougar," 448-55.

50. Charles Waymen Hogue, "The feline terror of the Ozarks," 14-15.

51. William Gilmore Simms, "Personal and literary memorials," 109-33.

52. Simms, "The cub of the panther," 571-83.

53. Davey Gnann Volkhardt, "When Florida was panther country," 44-45.

54. William H.G. Kingston, *The western world*, 392-95.

55. Theodore Roosevelt, *Hunting trips of a ranchman*, 32-33.

56. Ben V. Lilly, *Mountain lions of New Mexico*, 30-36.

57. S.E. Jorgensen and L. David Mech, eds., *Proceedings of a symposium*, 60-64.

58. *New York Herald*, "Boy and girl get medal," 2.

59. Charles Bombardier, "Mountain lion attack," 16-17.

60. John Lesowski, "The silent hunter," 44-47, 104-8.

61. *Arizona Champion*, "[Mountain lion killed]," [2].

62. Charles Darwin, *Journal of researches*, 116-17, 136, 183, 269-70.

63. R.P. Rafael Housse, "Los pumas o cuguardos," 33-46.

64. Henry W. Shoemaker, "Panthers kill 9 persons," 14.

65. Bill Hall, "Work of unknown tombstone maker," 1.

66. *Clarke County Register*, "Killed by a cougar," 3.

67. *Siskiyou Telegraph*, "A horrible death," [3].

68. *Spokane Chronicle*, "Spokane boy killed by cougar," 1.

69. F.S. Hall, "Killing of a boy by a mountain lion," 33-37.

70. *West Coast Advocate*, "Youngster dead," 1.

71. *Merritt Herald*, "Son of former residents killed," 1.

72. Richard Everett, "Boy killed by mountain lion," 1.

73. Michael Bernard, "Cougar kills girl," 1-2.

74. Ibid.

Chapter 9: Black Panther Controversy

1. Willem Piso, *Historia natvralis Brasiliae*, 234-36.

2. Jean Labat, *Voyage du Chevalier des Marchais en Guinée*, 283-85.

3. Mathurin Jacques Brisson, *Regnum animale*, 270-72.

4. Thomas Pennant, *Synopsis of quadrupeds*, 179-81.

5. Johann Christian Daniel Schreber, *Die säugethiere in abbildungen nach der natur*, 2:pl. 104, 104B.

6. Robert Kerr, *The animal kingdom*, 150-51.

7. George Louis Leclerc comte de Buffon, *Natural history*, 197-205.

8. Sr. William Jardine, *The natural history of the felinae*, 124-34.

9. Pablo Lévy, *Notas geográficas y económicas*, 197.

10. William Thomson, *Great cats I have met*, 19-32, 73-85.

11. Frederick Boyle, "A puma rug," 342-52.

12. Miguel Ruiz Herrero, "Nicaragua, paraiso de cazadores," 18-25.

13. Leon T. Mott to Jim Bob Tinsley, 14 March 1966.

14. Neal Griffith Smith to Jim Bob Tinsley, 22 June 1967.

15. Eleuterio F. Tiscornia, *"Martín Fierro" comentado y anotado*, 158-60.

16. William D. Williamson, *The history of the state of Maine*, 134-35.
17. Bruce S. Wright, "The cougar in New Brunswick," 111-13.
18. Bill Walsh, "Panthers are popular," 4-10.
19. Thomas Barbour, *That vanishing Eden*, 143-44.
20. David H. Johnson to E. Milby Burton, 9 October 1958.

21. Don Richie, "'Naturalized' citizens without citizenship papers," 6-7.
22. Wilfred T. Neill, "On the trail of the jaguarondi," 10-13.
23. John Paradiso, "Melanism in Florida bobcats," 215-16.
24. Fred A. Ulmer, Jr., "Melanism in the Felidae," 285-88.
25. Percy Brown, "Willie's black panther," 46-53.

Chapter 10: The Mysterious Onza

1. Bernal Díaz del Castillo, *Historia verdadera de la conquista*, 46-47.
2. Bernardino de Sahagún, *Historia general*, 66-68, 126-28.
3. Francisco Hernández, *Rervm medicarvm novae hispaniae*, 3-4.
4. Woodes Rogers, *A cruising voyage round the world*, 95, 335, 342.

5. Ignaz Pfefferkorn, *Beschreibung der landschaft Sonora*, 1:258-61.
6. *Arizona Daily Star*, "'Those Lee boys,'" 9.
7. Robert E. Marshall, *The onza*, 191.
8. A. Starker Leopold, *Wildlife of Mexico*, 478-82.

Chapter 11: Hunting the American Lion

1. Warren Page, "Lion hunters are nuts," 64-65.
2. Stephen Trumbull, "Hunting for panthers in Florida," 1-B.
3. Frank C. Hibben, "The cougar," 33-35, 81-82.
4. David Crockett, *Col. Crockett's exploits and adventures*, 152-55.
5. J. Frank Dobie, *The Ben Lilly legend*, 91.
6. William L. Kent, "Lion hunting," 6-9.
7. Jay C. Bruce, "The why and how of mountain lion hunting," 108-14.
8. S. Omar Barker, "Old cap cougar," 62-63, 136-39.
9. Hans Gadow, *Through southern Mexico*, 371-72.
10. Sir W. Raleigh, *The discoverie*, 94.
11. José de Acosta, *The natvrall and morall historie*, 69-70, 303, 341.
12. Robert Beverly, *The history and present state of Virginia*, 37-38, 73.
13. John Lawson, *A new voyage to Carolina*, 117-18.

14. Crockett Almanac, *"Go ahead!!" Containing adventures*, 9-11.
15. Col. George Earl Church, *Aborigines of South America*, 293-95.
16. Benjamin Franklin Bourne, *The captive in Patagonia*, 53.
17. Charles Darwin, *Journal of researches*, 116-17, 136, 183, 269-70.
18. Theodore Roosevelt, *The wilderness hunter*, 335-47.
19. Charles Badger Clark, Jr., "The glory trail," 355-56.
20. Edward O'Reilly, "The saga of Pecos Bill," 826-33.
21. Hesketh Prichard, "Field-notes upon some of the larger mammals," 273-75.
22. Andreas Madsen, *Cazando pumas en la Patagonia*, 153.
23. Theodore Roosevelt, "With the cougar hounds," pt. 2, 562-64.
24. Roosevelt, "A cougar hunt," 259-66.
25. Jean Karr, *Zane Grey: man of the West*, 33.
26. Zane Grey, *The last of the plainsmen*, 314.

Chapter 12: Boone and Crockett Club Records

1. Rowland Ward, *Rowland Ward's records of big game*, 488-89.

Chapter 13: Ancestry and Species

1. William Berryman Scott, *A history of land mammals*, 601-4.
2. John C. Merriam and Chester Stock, "The Felidae of Rancho La Brea," 199-216.
3. John C. Merriam, "New puma-like cat," 535-37.
4. Carl von Linné [Carolus Linnaeus], "Regni animalis," 522.
5. Sir William Jardine, *The natural history of the felinae*, 124-34.
6. M.N. Severtzow, "Notice sur la classification multisériale des carnivores," 385-93.
7. Dr. J.E. Gray, "Notes on the skulls of cats," 258-77.
8. E.D. Cope, "On the mammalia obtained by the naturalist exploring expedition," 128-50.
9. Franz Spillman, *Die säugetiere Ecuadors im wandel der zeit*, 53-56.
10. Ivan T. Sanderson, *Living mammals of the world*, 160-68.
11. Charles B. Cory, *Hunting and fishing in Florida*, 41-49, 109-10.
12. Oldfield Thomas, "On a new form of puma," 188-89.
13. C. Hart Merriam, "Preliminary revision of the pumas," 577-600.
14. E.W. Nelson and E.A. Goldman, "List of pumas," 345-50.
15. Stanley P. Young and Edward A. Goldman, *The puma*, 183-86.
16. Linné, "Regni animalis," 522.
17. Willem Piso, *Historia natvralis Brasiliae*, 234-36.
18. Philip Hershkovitz, "The type locality of *Felis concolor concolor* Linnaeus," 97-100.

19. Johann Christian Daniel Schreber, *Die säugethiere in abbildungen nach der natur*, 2:pl. 104, 104B.
20. Ibid.
21. Georges Louis Leclerc comte de Buffon, *Histoire naturelle*, 222-23.
22. Robert Kerr, *The animal kingdom*, 150-51.
23. Juan Ignacio Molina, *Saggio sulla storia naturale*, 295-300.
24. Hesketh Prichard, *Through the heart of Patagonia*, 251-52.
25. Angel Cabrera, "Los félidos vivientes," 161-247.
26. C.F. Rafinesque, "Cougars of Oregon," 62-63.
27. [W.B. May], *California game "marked down*," 21-22.
28. C. Hart Merriam, "Description of two new pumas," 219-20.
29. Ibid.
30. Cory, *Hunting and fishing in Florida*, 109-10.
31. Outram Bangs, "The land mammals of peninsula Florida," 157-235 [234-35].
32. Thomas, "On a new form of puma," 188-89.
33. Merriam, "Preliminary revision," 577-600.
34. Ibid.
35. Ibid.
36. Ibid.
37. C. Hart Merriam, "Eight new mammals from the United States," 73-78.

38. N. Hollister, "The Louisiana puma," 175-78.
39. Young and Goldman, *The puma*, 234-37.
40. J.C. Phillips, "A new puma from Lower California," 85-86.
41. Einer Lönnberg, "Mammals from Ecuador," 2-5.
42. Nelson and Goldman, "List of pumas," 345-50.
43. Ibid.
44. Ibid.
45. Nelson and Goldman, "Three new pumas," 209-12.
46. Ibid.
47. Ibid.
48. Nelson and Goldman, "A new mountain lion from Vancouver Island," 105-7.

49. Nelson and Goldman, "A new puma from Brazil," 523-25.
50. E.A. Goldman, "A new puma from Texas," 137-38.
51. Goldman, "A substitute name," 63.
52. R.I. Pocock, "Description of a new race of puma," 307-13.
53. Wilfred H. Osgood, "The mammals of Chile," 75-79.
54. Goldman, "Two new races of the puma," 228-31.
55. Ibid.
56. Young and Goldman, *The puma*, 246-48.
57. R.P. Rafael Housse, "Los pumas o cuguardos," 69-88.
58. Guillermo Mann, "Mamíferos de Tarapacá," 65-66.
59. Hartley H.T. Jackson, "The Wisconsin puma," 149-50.
60. Angel Cabrera, "Dos félidos argentinos inéditos," 70-72.

Selected Bibliography

BOOKS/ARTICLES

Ackerman, Bruce B., Frederick G. Lindzey, and Thomas Hemker. "Cougar food habits in southern Utah." *Journal of Wildlife Management* 48 (January 1984).

Acosta, José de. *The natvrall and morall historie of the East and West Indies.* Vol. 1. London: 1604.

Ahlfeld, Federico E. *Geografia de Bolivia.* La Paz: Editorial, Los Amigos del Libro, 1969.

Allen, Glover M. "Extinct and vanishing mammals of the Western Hemisphere with the marine species of all the oceans." *Special Publication of the American Committee on International Protection* 11 (1942).

Allen, J.A. "On a collection of mammals from Arizona and Mexico, made by W.W. Price, with field notes by the collector." *Bulletin of the American Museum of Natural History* 7 (29 June 1895).

_____. "On mammals collected in Bexar County and vicinity, Texas, by Mr. H.P. Atwater, with field notes by the collector." *Bulletin of the American Museum of Natural History* 8 (1896).

Annabel, Russell. "Trophy hunt in mañana land." *Sports Afield* 140 (July 1950).

_____. "The mysterious onca." *Sports Afield* 143 (April 1960).

_____. "Death of an onza." *Sports Afield* 145 (March 1961).

Ap-wa-cun-na. "Hunting in Montana." *Forest and Stream* 15 (14 October 1880).

Arizona Champion (Flagstaff). "[Mountain lion killed in whose stomach was found a gold finger ring and several pantaloon buttons.]" 12 July 1884.

Arizona Daily Star (Tucson). "'Those Lee boys' bring out specimen of legendary cat." 1 October 1938.

Ash, Thomas (supposed author). *Carolina: or a description of the present state of that country, and the natural excellences thereof.* London: 1682.

Atkinson, Maj. S.W. *Oklahoma Bill, hunter and trapper.* New York: Dick's Publishing House, (189?).

Audubon, John James. "Hunting the cougar, or American lion; and deer hunting." *Edinburgh New Philosophical Journal,* n.s., 11 (April 1831).

_____ and Rev. John Bachman. *The quadrupeds of North America.* Vol. 2. New York: V.G. Audubon, 1854.

Azara, Félix de. *Apuntamientos para la historia natural de los quadrúpedos del Paragüay y Río de la Plata.* Vol. 1. Madrid: 1802.

_____. *Voyages dans l'Amérique Méridionale, par Don Félix de Azara, commissaire et commandant des limites Espagnoles dans la Paraguay depuis 1781 jusqu'en 1801.* Vol. 1. Paris: Dentu, 1809.

Bailey, Vernon. "The mammals and life zones of Oregon." *North American Fauna* 55 (June 1936).

Baillie-Grohman, William A. *Camps in the Rockies, being a narrative of life on the frontier, and sport in the Rocky Mountains, with an account of the cattle ranches of the West.* London: S. Low, Marston, Searle, & Rivington, 1882.

Baird, Spencer F. "Mammals of the boundary." In *Report on the United States and Mexican boundary survey, made under the direction of the secretary of the interior, by William H. Emory, major, First Cavalry, and the United States commissioner.* Pt. 2. Washington: C. Wendell, 1859.

Bangs, Outram. "The land mammals of peninsula Florida and the coast region of Georgia." *Proceedings of the Boston Society of Natural History* 28 (1898).

_____. "The Florida puma." *Proceedings of the Biological Society of Washington* 13 (31 January 1899).

Bannon, Henry. "A prehistoric Indian naturalist." *Forest and Stream* 91 (April 1921).

Barber, Edwin A. "Rock-inscriptions of the 'ancient pueblos' of Colorado, Utah, New Mexico, and Arizona." *American Naturalist* 10 (1876).

Barbour, Thomas. *That vanishing Eden: a naturalist's Florida.* Boston: Little, Brown & Co., 1944.

Barker, Elliott S. *When the dogs bark 'treed': a year on the trail of the longtails.* Albuquerque: University of New Mexico Press, 1946.

Barker, S. Omar. "Horses to hunt on." *The Cattleman* 31 (September 1944).

_____. "Old cap cougar." *Sports Afield* 119 (April 1948).

Barnes, Claude T. "The terror of the range." *St. Nicholas* 50 (November 1922).

_____. *The cougar or mountain lion.* Salt Lake City: Ralton Co., 1960.

Barnes, Will C. "The Bandelier National Monument." *American Forestry* 27 (September 1921).

_____. "Does the mountain lion scream?" *American Forests* 34 (June 1928).

Barrère, Pierre. *Essai sur l'histoire naturelle de la France Equinoxiale.* Paris: Chez Pibet, 1741.

Barrett, Robert, and Katherine Barrett. *A yankee in Patagonia, Edward Chase.* Boston and New York: Houghton Mifflin Co., 1931.

Bartram, William. *Travels through North and South Carolina, Georgia, East and West Florida, the Cherokee country, the extensive territories of the Muscogules or Creek confederacy, and the country of the Chactaws.* Philadelphia: James & Johnson, 1791.

Bates, Henry Walter. *The naturalist on the River Amazons, a record of adventures, habits of animals, sketches of Brazilian and Indian life and aspects of nature under the Equator during eleven years of travel.* Vol. 1. London: J. Murray, 1863.

Bates, L.J. "Old Strategy." *St. Nicholas* 29 (February 1902).

Batty, J.H. "The Felis concolor, or panther." *American Sportsman,* n.s., 30 (25 April 1874).

Baudy, Robert. "Observation of first complete mating of Florida panthers at the Rare Feline Breeding Compound." *Report to the Florida Panther Recovery Team.* (Bushnell, Fla.: September 1978).

[Beebe] Johnson, B.F. *American lions and cats.* New York: D. McKay Co., 1963.

Belden, Robert C. "If you see a panther." *Florida Wildlife* 31 (September-October 1977).

_____. "Florida panther recovery plan implementation." *Progress Report to the Florida Panther Recovery Team.* Gainesville: Florida Game and Fresh Water Fish Commission, 29 September 1982.

Bernard, Michael. "Cougar kills girl." *Campbell River Courier* (Campbell River, B.C.) 16 July 1976.

Beverly, Fred [F.A. Ober]. "The Florida panther." *Forest and Stream* 3 (December 1874).

Beverly, Robert. *The history and present state of Virginia, in four parts.* Pt. 2. London: 1705.

Bilo, Amadeo (younger). "El león del Colorado." *Diana* (Buenos Aires) 28 (January-April 1967).

Blethen, Joseph. "The fire cat." *St. Nicholas* 30 (February 1903.)

Blonk, H.L. "Einige bemerkungen über das fellmuster bei einem Surinam-Puma, *Puma concolor discolor* (Schreber 1775)." *Säugetierkundliche Mitteilungen,* Stuttgart, 13 (April 1965).

Bombardier, Charles, as told to Bob Housholder. "Mountain lion attack." *Arizona Wildlife and Travelogue* 34 (September 1963).

Boston Weekly News-Letter. "[Notice of a cattamount on exhibition in Roxbury]." 9-16 April 1741.

Bourne, Benjamin Franklin. *The captive in Patagonia; or, life among the giants.* Boston: Gould and Lincoln, 1853.

Boyle, Frederick. "A puma rug." *Belgravia Magazine* 49 (January 1883).

Brehm, Alfred Edmund. *Brehms tierleben, allgemeine kunde des tier-reichs. Die säugethiere.* Vol. 1. Leipzig: 1876.

Brereton, M. John. *A briefe and true relation of the discoverie of the North Part of Virginia.* London: 1602.

Brett, Rev. W.H. *Mission work among the Indian tribes in the forests of Guiana.* London and New York: E. & J.B. Young & Co., [1881].

Brickell, John. *The natural history of North-Carolina, with an account of the trade, manners, and customs of the Christian and Indian inhabitants.* Dublin: James Carson, 1737.

Brisson, Mathurin Jacques. *Regnum animale in classes IX distributum.* Paris: 1756.

Brock, Stanley E. *Leemo: a true story of a man's friendship with a mountain lion.* London: Robert Hale, 1966.

_____. *More about Leemo: the adventures of a puma.* New York: Taplinger Pub. Co., 1967.

Brown, Percy. "Willie's black panther." *Outdoor Life* 105 (June 1950).

Browning, Meshach. *Forty-four years of the life of a hunter; being the reminiscences of Meshach Browning a Maryland hunter.* Philadelphia: J.B. Lippincott & Co., 1860.

Bruce, Jay C. "Lioness tracked to lair." *California Fish and Game* 4 (July 1918).

_____. "The why and how of mountain lion hunting in California." *California Fish and Game* 8 (April 1922).

_____. "The problem of mountain lion control in California." *California Fish and Game* 11 (January 1925).

Bue, Gerald T., and Milton H. Stenlund. "Are there mountain lions in Minnesota?" *Conservation Volunteer* 15 (September-October 1952).

Buffon, Georges Louis Leclerc comte de. *Histoire naturelle, générale et particulière.* Vol. 9. Paris: De l'Imprimerie royale, 1761.

_____. *Histoire naturelle, générale et particulière.* Supp. Vol. 3. Paris: De l'Imprimerie royale, 1776.

_____. *Natural history, general and particular, translated into English.* Vol. 5. London: 1781.

Bull, Charles Livingston. "The puma." *Century Magazine* 87 (November 1913).

Buntline, Ned [Edward Z.C. Judson]. "My first cougar." *Forest and Stream* 13 (15 January 1880).

Burt, Henry M. *The first century of the history of Springfield; the official records.* Vol. 2. Springfield, Mass.: H.M. Burt, 1898-99.

Burt, William Henry, and Ruben A. Stirton. "The mammals of El Salvador." *Miscellaneous Publications of the Museum of Zoology, University of Michigan,* Ann Arbor 117 (22 September 1961).

Byrd, William. *The Westover manuscripts: containing the history of the dividing line betwixt Virginia and North Carolina; a journey to the land of Eden, A.D. 1733; and a progress to the mines.* Petersburg, Va.: E. & J.C. Ruffin, 1841.

Byron, John. *The narrative of the Honourable John Byron containing an account of the great distresses, suffered by himself and his companions on the coast of Patagonia, from the year 1740, til their arrival in England.* London: S. Baker [etc.], 1768.

Cabrera, Angel. "Notas sobre los pumas de la América austral." *Revista Chilena de Historia Natural* 33 (1929).

_____. "Dos félidos argentinos inéditos (Mammalia, Carnivora)." *Neotropica* (Buenos Aires) 3 (1957).

_____. "Los félidos vivientes de la República Argentina." *Revista del Museo Argentino de Ciencias Naturales "Bernardino Rivadavia," Instituto Nacional de Investigación de las Ciencias Naturales* (Buenos Aires) 6 (1961).

_____ and José Yepes. *Historia natural ediar. Mamíferos Sud-Americanos.* Buenos Aires: Compañía Argentina de Editores, 1940.

Cahalane, Victor. "King of cats and his court." *National Geographic Magazine* 83 (February 1943).

_____. *A preliminary study of distribution and numbers of cougar, grizzly and wolf in North America.* Bronx, N.Y.: New York Zoological Society, September 1964.

California Division of Fish and Game. *Outdoor California* 3 (4 January 1943).

Calkins, Franklin Welles. "About the cougar." *Outing* 40 (July 1902).

Castañeda, Pedro de. *Relación de la jornada de Cíbola conquesta por Pedro de Castañeda de Niçera. Donde se trata de todos aquellos poblados y ritos, y costumbres, la qual fué el Año de 1540.* Seville: N.p., n.d., Pt. 2, Chap. 3.

Catesby, Mark. *The natural history of Carolina, Florida, and the Bahama Islands.* Vol. 2. London: 1743.

Charlevoix, Pierre Francois Xavier de. *Histoire et description générale de la Nouvelle France, avec le Journal historique d'un voyage fait par ordre du roi dans l'Amérique Septentrionnale.* Vols. 1-3. Paris: Nylon fils, 1744.

Christensen, G.C., and R.J. Fischer. *Transactions of the Mountain Lion Workshop.* Nuggett Sparks, Nevada: U.S. Fish and Wildlife Service and Nevada Fish and Game Department, 1976.

Church, Col. George Earl. *Aborigines of South America.* London: Chapman & Hall, 1912.

Clark, Charles Badger, Jr. "The glory trail." *Pacific Monthly* 25 (April 1911).

Clark, Simon. *The puma's claw.* Boston: Little, Brown & Co. 1959.

Clarke, Samuel. *A true and faithful account of the four chiefest plantations of the English in America, to wit, of Virginia, New-England, Bermudus, Barbados.* London: 1670.

Clarke County Register (Vancouver, Washington Terr.). "Killed by a cougar." 30 March 1882.

Clavijero, Francisco Javier. *Storia della California opera postuma del nob. sig. abate D. Francesco Saverio Clavigero.* Venice: M. Frenzo, 1789.

Columbus [Colombo], Christopher. *Select letters of Christopher Columbus, with other original documents, relating to his four voyages to the New World.* Translated and edited by R.H. Major. London: Hakluyt Society, 1847.

Committee on Rare and Endangered Wildlife Species. "Rare and endangered fish and wildlife of the United States." *Resource Publication.* Vol. 34, Iv, M-17. Bureau of Sport Fisheries and Wildlife, U.S. Department of the Interior, Washington, D.C., July 1966.

128

_____. "Rare and endangered fish and wildlife of the United States." *Revised Resource Publication.* Vol. 34, lviii. Bureau of Sport Fisheries and Wildlife, U.S. Department of the Interior, Washington, D.C., December 1968.

Connolly, Edward J. "The food habits and life history of the mountain lion (*Felis concolor hippolestes*)." Master's thesis, University of Utah, 1949.

Cooper, James Fenimore. *The pioneers, or, the sources of the Susquehanna; a descriptive tale.* Vol. 2. Philadelphia: 1832.

Cooper, Thomas. *The statutes at large of South Carolina; edited, under the authority of the legislature.* Vol. 2. Columbia: 1837.

Cope, E.D. "On the mammalia obtained by the naturalist exploring expedition to southern Brazil." *American Naturalist* 23 (February 1889).

Coreal, Francois. *Voyages de François Coreal aux Indes Occidentales contenant ce qu'il y a vû de plus remarquable pendant son séjour depuis 1666 jusqu'en 1697.* Vols. 1-2. Amsterdam: 1722.

Cornish, Charles John. *Animal artisans and other studies of birds and beasts.* London and New York: Longmans, Green & Co., 1907.

Cory, Charles B. *Hunting and fishing in Florida, including a key to the water birds known to occur in the State.* Boston: 1896.

Coues, Elliott. "The quadrupeds of Arizona." *American Naturalist* 1 (August 1867).

Cramond, Michael. "The killer cougars." *True* 34 (October 1954).

Crawford, Robert P. "Romantic days on the Missouri; the old fur and gold route awakens at a new call to duty." *Country Gentleman* 93 (March 1928).

Cremony, John C. *Life among the Apaches.* New York: A. Roman & Co., 1868.

Crockett Almanac. *"Go Ahead!!" Containing adventures, exploits, sprees & scrapes in the West, & life and manners in the backwoods.* Vol. 2. Nashville, Tenn.: 1839.

Crockett, David. *Col. Crockett's exploits and adventures in Texas.... [A pseudo-autobiography generally ascribed to Richard Penn Smith (1799-1854)].* Philadelphia: T.K. & P.G. Collins, 1836.

Cronemiller, F.P. "Mountain lion preys on bighorn." *Journal of Mammalogy* 29 (February 1948).

[Cruz, Martín de la]. *The Badianus manuscript.* Codex Barberini, Latin 241, Vatican library; an Aztec herbal of 1552. Baltimore: Johns Hopkins Press, 1940.

Cushing, Frank Hamilton. "Zuñi fetishes." *Report of the Bureau of American Ethnology* 2 (1883).

_____. "Exploration of ancient key dwellers remains on the Gulf Coast of Florida." *Proceedings of the American Philosophical Society* 35 (December 1896).

Cuvier, Georges Frédéric, Baron. *The animal kingdom arranged in conformity with its organization, by the Baron Cuvier.* Translated by H. M'Murtrie. Vol. 1. New York: G. & C. & H. Carvill, 1831.

_____ and Edward Griffin. *The animal kingdom.* Vol. 2. London: G.B. Whittaker, 1827.

Dahne, Bob. "The truth about black panthers." *Florida Wildlife* 12 (November 1958).

Darwin, Charles. *Journal of researches into the natural history and geology of the countries visited during the voyage of H.M.S. Beagle round the world, under the command of Capt. Fitz Roy, R.N.* New York: A. Appleton & Co., 1871.

_____. *The descent of man, and selection in relation to sex.* New York: A.L. Burt, 1874.

Davis, Walter Lee. "I heard a cougar scream." *Outdoor Life* 75 (April 1935).

Dedera, Don. "Calling Ford bird; his lion is busy." *Outdoor Arizona* 45 (February 1973).

Dennler de La Tour, Georges. "Cazando pumas en la Patagonia." *Diana* (Buenos Aires) 19 (October 1958).

DeVane, Park. "Taming a Florida panther." In *DeVane's early Florida history.* Vol. 2. Sebring, Fla.: Sebring Historical Society, 1979.

Díaz de Guzmán, Ruy. *La Argentina, historia del descubrimiento, población y conquista de las provincias del Río la Plata.* Buenos Aires: Espasacalpe Argentina, 1945.

Díaz del Castillo, Bernal. *Historia verdadera de la conquista de la Nueva-España.* Madrid: 1632.

Disney (Walt) Productions. *Walt Disney's worlds of nature.* New York: Simon & Schuster, 1957.

Dixon, Kenneth R. "Evaluation of the effects of mountain lion predation." *Job Completion Report, Colorado Department of Game, Fish and Parks,* Fort Collins, W-38-R-21 (1967).

Dobie, J. Frank. "Lion markers." *Country Gentleman* 93 (May 1928).

_____. "Tales of the panther." *Saturday Evening Post* 216 (11 December 1943).

_____. *The Ben Lilly legend.* Boston: Little, Brown & Co., 1950.

_____. "Panther covered sleeping man with leaves, to keep him for supper." *Fort Worth Star-Telegram,* Fort Worth, Texas, 25 January 1953.

Donck, Adriaen van der. "A description of the New- Netherlands." *Collections of the New York Historical Society* 1 (1841).

Doughty, J. and T. (eds.) "The cougar — Felis concolor." *Cabinet of Natural History and American Rural Sports* 2 (1832).

Downing, Robert L. "How to differentiate between tracks of dogs and cougars." *Eastern Cougar Newsletter (Supplement)* [2] (1979).

_____ and Virginia L. Fifield. "Differences between tracks of dogs and cougars." Massachusetts Eastern Cougar Survey Team, Worcester Science Center, Worcester, Mass. (1978).

Dufresne, Frank. "Predators and pests." In *The Great Outdoors,* edited by Joe Godfrey, Jr., and Frank Dufresne. New York and Toronto: Whittlesey House, 1947.

Easton, Robert, and Mackenzie Brown. *Lord of beasts — the saga of Buffalo Jones.* Tucson: University of Arizona Press, 1961.

Erxleben, Johann Christian Polykarp. *Systema regni animalis per classes, ordines, genera, species, varietates, cum synonymia et historia animalium.* Leipsig: 1777.

Evans, G.W. ("Dub"). *Slash Ranch Hounds.* Albuquerque: University of New Mexico Press, 1951.

Evans, Will F. "A mountain quartet." *Sports Afield* 67 (July 1921).

_____. "The super-strength of the mountain lion." *Outdoor Life* 49 (May 1922).

Everett, Richard. "Boy killed by mountain lion." *The New Mexican,* Santa Fe, N.Mex., 21 January 1974.

_____. "Killer-beast not rabid." *The New Mexican,* 22 January 1974.

Fannin, John. "The Panther in British Columbia." *Forest and Stream* 48 (6 March 1897).

Ferrell, Dorothy M. *Bear tales and panther tracks.* Atlanta, Ga.: Appalachian Publisher, 1965.

Figueira, Juan H. "Contribución al conocemento de la fauna Uruguaya. Enumeración de mamíferos." *Anales del Museo de historia natural de Montevideo* 2 (October 1894).

Finley, William L. "Cougar kills a boy." *Journal of Mammalogy* 6 (August 1925).

_____ and Irene Finley. "Baby panthers for playmates." *Nature Magazine* 4 (July 1924).

129

Finsterbusch, Carlos A. "El leon." *Caza y Pesca* (Santiago) 5 (December 1950).

Fitzroy, Robert. *Narrative of the surveying voyages of His Majesty's ships Adventure and Beagle, between the years 1826 and 1836, describing their examination of the southern shores of South America, and the Beagle's circumnavigation of the globe.* Vol. 3. London: H. Colburn, 1839.

Flint, Timothy. *Biographical memoir of Daniel Boone, the first settler of Kentucky: interspersed with incidents in the early annals of the country.* Cincinnati: N. & G. Guilford, 1833.

Florida Game and Fresh Water Fish Commission. "Hunting season in 1950-51 to have no staggered days." *Florida Wildlife* 4 (August 1950).

————. "Back on the protected list." *Florida Wildlife* 12 (September 1958).

————. "Panther — state animal." *Florida Wildlife* 36 (May-June 1982).

Florida Star (Titusville). "Local items." 20 December 1883.

Fosburgh, P.W. "Panther." *New York State Conservationist* 5 (June-July 1951).

Fountain, Paul. *The great mountains and forests of South America.* London and New York: Longmans, Green & Co., 1902.

Frache, Alwin. "Buried by a cougar." *Recreation* 17 (September 1902).

Freeman, Lewis R. "The California lion." *Western Field* 4 (March 1904).

Friends of the Middle Border. "High Chin Bob and the mountain lion's ghost." *Middle Border Bulletin* 6 (September 1946).

Frost, John. *History of the state of California.* Auburn, N.Y.: Derby, Orton, & Mulligan, 1853.

Frye, O. Earle, with Bill and Les Piper. "The disappearing panther." *Florida Wildlife* 5 (October 1950).

Fuller, Devereau. "[Report on the period of gestation of the puma, *Felis concolor*]." *Proceedings of the Zoological Society of London* 2 (10 April 1832).

Fullerton, James. "Is nature faking just?" *Sports Afield* 51 (September 1913).

Gadow, Hans. *Through southern Mexico, being an account of the travels of a naturalist.* London: Witherby & Co., 1908.

Gale, George Jennings. "Cougars in Alaska." *Outdoor Life* 116 (November 1955).

Garcilasso de la Vega (el Inca). *La Florida del Ynca.* Pt. 1. Lisbon: 1605.

————. *First part of the Royal commentaries of the Yncas.* Edited by Clements R. Markham. Vols. 1-2. London: Hakluyt Society, 1869.

Garfield, H.S. "About the puma, his cry, his prey." *Sports Afield* 32 (January 1904).

Gashwiler, Jay S., and W. Leslie Robinette. "Accidental fatalities of the Utah cougar." *Journal of Mammalogy* 38 (February 1957).

Gerstäcker, Frederick. *Wild sports in the Far West.* London: George Routledge & Co., 1854.

Gesner, Abraham. *New Brunswick: with notes for emigrants.* London: Simmonds & Ward, 1847.

Goldman, E.A. "Mountain lion, puma or cougar." In *Records of North American Big Game.* Edited by Prentis N. Gray. New York: Derrydale Press, 1932.

————. "A new puma from Texas." *Proceedings of the Biological Society of Washington* 49 (1936).

————. "A substitute name for *Felis concolor youngi*." *Proceedings of the Biological Society of Washington* 51 (1938).

————. "The puma, description and distribution." In *North American Big Game*, edited by Alfred Ely, H.E. Anthony, and R.R.M. Carpenter. New York and London: Charles Scribner's Sons, 1939.

————. "Two new races of the puma." *Journal of Mammalogy* 24 (June 1943).

Goldsmith, Dr. [Oliver]. *The deserted village, a poem.* London: 1770.

Goode, Monroe H. "The scourge of the livestock country." *Cattleman* 28 (December 1941).

————. "Man-killing mountain lions." *Sports Afield* 119 (January 1948).

Gray, Dr. J.E. "Notes on the skulls of cats (*Felidae*)." *Proceedings of the Zoological Society of London* (1867).

Greenwalt, Lynn A. "Endangered status of 159 taxa of animals." *Federal Register* 41 (14 June 1976).

Gregg, John. "Those accidental summers." *Western Fish and Wildlife* 9(January 1974).

Grey, Zane. "Tige's lion." *Field and Stream* 13 (June 1908).

————. "Lassoing lions in the Siwash." *Everybody's Magazine* 18 (June 1908).

————. *The last of the plainsmen.* New York: Outing Pub. Co., 1908.

————. "Roping lions in the Grand Canyon." *Field and Stream* 13-14 (January-August 1909).

Grinnell, Joseph, and Joseph Dixon. "The systematic status of the mountain lion of California." *University of California Publications in Zoology* 21 (1923).

Guenther, Konrad. *A naturalist in Brazil.* Boston and New York: Houghton Mifflin Co., 1931.

Haley, Charles. "Killer cougar." *Field and Stream* 57 (March 1953).

Hall, Bill. "Work of unknown tombstone maker in southern Chester County is unearthed." *Daily Local News* (West Chester, Pa.), 8 October 1956.

Hall, F.S. "Killing of a boy by a mountain lion (*Felis oregonensis oregonensis*)." *Murrelet* 6 (May 1925).

Halliday, Hugh M. *Wildlife trails across Canada.* Toronto: T. Allen, 1956.

Haltenorth, Dr. Theodor. "Weisse pumas-schwarze panther." *Freunde des Kölner Zoo* 7 (December 1964).

Hancock, Dave. "Picnic with a cougar." *Weekend Magazine, Sunday Sun* (Vancouver, B.C.), 14 July 1968.

Hariot, Thomas. *A brief and true report of the new found land of Virginia.* London: N.p., 1588.

Harper, Francis. "The mammals of the Okefinokee Swamp region of Georgia." *Proceedings: Boston Society of Natural History* 38 (1927).

Harris, Glenn. "Stranger on the river." *NEBRASKAland* 45 (July 1967).

Hartwig, Georg Ludwig. *The tropical world.* London: Longmans, Green & Co., 1873.

Heath, Frank, ed. "[Editorial]." *Frontier Palladium* (Malone, N.Y.), 1 August 1850.

Henning, Bob, ed. "[Reports of cougars in Alaska]." *Alaska Sportsman* 34 (April, August 1968).

Hernández, Francisco. *Rervm medicarvm Novae Hispaniae thesavrvs sev plantarvm animalivm mineralivm Mexicanorvm. Historiae animalivm.* Rome: 1651.

Hershkovitz, Philip. "The type locality of *Felis concolor concolor Linnaeus*." *Proceedings of the Biological Society of Washington* 72 (24 July 1959).

Hewitt, J.N.B. "Erie." In "Handbook of American Indians north of Mexico," edited by Frederick Webb Hodge. *Bureau of American Ethnology Bulletin* 30 (1907.)

Hibben, Frank C. "A preliminary study of the mountain lion (Felis oregonensis sp.)." *University of New Mexico Bulletin* 5 (15 December 1937).

_____. "The mountain lion and ecology." *Ecology* 20 (October 1939).

_____. *Hunting American lions*. New York: Thomas Y. Crowell Co., 1948.

_____. "The cougar — our greatest game animal." *Sports Afield* 156 (December 1966).

Hittell, Theodore H. *The adventures of James Copen Adams, mountaineer and grizzly bear hunter, of California*. San Francisco: Towne & Bacon, 1860.

Hogue, Charles Waymen. "The feline terror of the Ozarks." *New York Herald Tribune Magazine*, 17 May 1931.

Holesch, Ditha. *Manso, der puma; roman*. Berlin: Im Duetschen Verlag, 1939.

Hollister, N. "The Louisiana puma." *Proceedings of the Biological Society of Washington* 24 (16 June 1911).

Holmes, Oliver Wendell. *The complete poetical works of Oliver Wendell Holmes*. Boston and New York: Houghton, Mifflin Co., 1895.

Holt, Ernest G. "Swimming cats." *Journal of Mammalogy* 13 (February 1932).

Hornaday, William T. "The cat family in our country." *St. Nicholas* 21 (March 1894).

Hornocker, Maurice G. "A study of the ecology of the mountain lion." *First Annual Report, Department of Zoology*, University of British Columbia, Vancouver (1965).

_____. "Stalking the mountain lion — to save him." *National Geographic Magazine* 136 (November 1969).

_____. "Cougars up close." *National Wildlife* 14 (October-November 1976).

Horsford, B. "The panther's leap." *Forest and Stream* 20 (17 May 1883).

Housholder, Bob. "The mountain lion." *Arizona Wildlife-Sportsman* 31 (March 1960).

_____. "Arizona's reigning predator." *Arizona Wildlife-Sportsman* 31 (March 1960).

_____., et al. "Information pertinent to H.B. 10." Arizona Game Protective Association (January 1967).

Housse, R.P. Rafael. "Los pumas o cuguardos." *Anales de la Academia chilena de ciencias naturales* (Santiago) 15 (1950).

Howard, Charles B. "An instance of a mountain lion's attack upon a boy." *Outdoor Life* 36 (August 1915).

Hudson, W.H. "The puma." *Longman's Magazine* 8 (September 1886).

_____. *The naturalist in La Plata*. London: J.M. Dent & Co., 1903.

Huestes, W.A. "Man has scared puma out of his screams." *Hunting and Fishing* 24 (February 1947).

Hughes, J.C. "The American panther." *Forest and Stream* 21 (6 September 1883).

Ingersoll, Ernest. *Wild neighbors, out-door studies in the United States*. London and New York: Macmillan & Co., 1897.

Jackson, Hartlet H.T. "The Wisconsin puma." *Proceedings of the Biological Society of Washington* 68 (31 October 1955).

Jardine, Sir William. *The natural history of the felinae*. Edinburgh: W.H. Lizers, 1834.

Johnson, Harlen G. "Mountain lion bags new Kaibab record." *Arizona Wildlife and Sportsman* 4 (25 March 1942).

[Johnson, L.]. *History of the Delaware and Iroquois Indians formerly inhabiting the middle states, with various anecdotes, illustrating their manners and customs*. Philadelphia: 1832.

Jones, Hathaway. "Cougar attacks eight year old girl." *Oregon Sportsman* 4 (January 1916).

Jorgensen, S.E., and L. David Mech, eds. *Proceedings of a symposium on the native cats of North America, their status and management*. Bureau of Sports Fisheries and Wildlife, Region 3, Twin Cities, Minn., 1971.

Josselyn, John. *New-Englands rarities discovered*. London: 1672.

Karr, Jean. *Zane Grey: man of the West*. New York: Greenburg, 1949.

Kent, William L. "Lion hunting: ace of sports." *Colorado Outdoors* 6 (January-February 1957).

Kerr, Robert. *The animal kingdom; or, Zoological system, of the celebrated Sir Charles Linnaeus*. London: 1792.

Kingston, William H.G. *The western world, picturesque sketches of nature and natural history in North and South America*. London: T. Nelson & Sons, 1874.

Kirtland, Prof. J.P. "Report on the zoology of Ohio." In *Second Annual Report on the Geological Survey of the State of Ohio*, edited by W.W. Mather. Columbus: 1838.

Koford, Carl B. "A California mountain lion observed stalking." *Journal of Mammalogy* 27 (August 1946).

Labat, Jean. *Voyage du Chevalier des Marchais en Guinée, isles voisines, et à Cayenne, fait en 1725, 1726, 1727*. Vol. 3. Amsterdam: 1731.

La Condamine, Charles Marie de. *A succinct abridgment of a voyage made within the inland parts of South-America*. London: 1747.

Lambert, Harold. "There ain't no 'painters' in West Virginia." *West Virginia Conservation* 19 (March 1955).

Lambeth, R.H. "A uniform bounty system for mountain lion." *Proceedings of the Annual Conference of Western Association of State Game and Fish Commissioners* 31 (30 April-2 May 1951).

Laudonnière, René Goulaine de. *L'Histoire notable de la Floride*. Paris: 1586.

Lawrence, R.D. *The ghost walker*. New York: Holt, Rinehart & Winston, 1983.

Lawson, John. *A new voyage to Carolina; containing the exact description and natural history of that country*. London: 1709.

Layne, James M., and Mindy N. McCauley. "Biological overview of the Florida panther." *Proceedings of the Florida Panther Conference*, Florida Audubon Society, Maitland, Fla., 1976.

Lederer, John. *The discoveries of John Lederer, in three several marches from Virginia, to the west of Carolina, and other parts of the continent: begun in March 1669, and ended in September 1670*. Collected and translated by Sir William Talbot. London: 1672.

Leopold, A. Starker. *Wildlife of Mexico*. Berkeley and Los Angeles: University of California Press, 1959.

Le Page du Pratz, Antoine Simon. *Histoire de la Louisiane, contenant la découverte de ce vaste pays*. Vol. 2. Paris: 1758.

_____. *The history of Louisiana, or of the western parts of Virginia and Carolina*. Vol. 2. London: 1763.

Leposky, George. "Panther's progress." *Florida Wildlife* 29 (August 1975).

Lesowski, John. "Two observations of cougar cannibalism." *Journal of Mammalogy* 44 (November 1963).

_____. "The silent hunter." *Outdoor Life* 140 (July 1967).

Lesson, René Primevère. *Nouveau tableau du règne animal. Mammifères*. Paris: A. Bertrand, 1842.

Lévy, Pablo. *Notas geográficas y económicas sobre la República de Nicaragua*. Paris: E. Denné Schmidt, 1873.

Lilly, Ben V. *Mountain lions of New Mexico*. Archives Collection, University of Texas Library, Austin. 1940.

Link, Heinrich F. *Beyträge zur naturgeschichte*. Vol. 2. Rostock and Leipzig: K.C. Stiller, 1795.

Linné, Carl von [Carolus Linnaeus]. "Regni animalis." In *Mantissa plantarum generum editionis VI et specierum editionis II.* Stockholm: 1771.

Lisle, Charles J. "An Idaho cougar hunt." *Field and Stream* 19 (January 1915).

Locherty, Lorraine. "Cougar killed near Gold River." *Campbell River Courier* (Campbell River, B.C.) 30 July 1976.

Logan, John H. *A history of the upper country of South Carolina, from the earliest periods to the close of the War of Independence.* Vol. 1. Charleston: S.G. Courtenay & Co. 1859.

Lönnberg, Einer. "Mammals from Ecuador and related forms." *Arkiv För Zoologie* (Uppsala) 8 (28 April 1913).

————. "A second contribution to the mammalogy of Ecuador with some remarks on Caenolestes." *Arkiv För Zoologie* (Uppsala) 14 (23 February 1921).

McCabe, Robert A. "The scream of the mountain lion." *Journal of Mammalogy* 30 (August 1949).

McKee, James C., et al. "Mountain lions climb trees." *Forest and Stream* 30 (10 May 1888).

————. "Panthers climb trees." *Forest and Stream* 30 (24 May, 14 June 1888).

McKee, Thomas Heron. "'Uncle Jim' Owen and his dogs have killed 1500 cougars." *American Magazine* 97 (April 1927).

McKnight, Dr. W.J. *Pioneer outline history of northwestern Pennsylvania.* Philadelphia: J.B. Lippincott Co., 1905.

————. "'Bill Long,' king of hunters." *Forest and Stream* 82 (3 and 10 January 1914).

McMullen, James P. *Cry of the panther: quest of a species.* Englewood, Fla.: Pineapple Press, Inc., 1984.

Madsen, Andreas, with Carlos A. Bertomeu. *Cazando pumas en la Patagonia.* Buenos Aires: Impresora oeste, 1956.

Mann, Guillermo. "Mamíferos de Tarapacá." *Biológica* (Santiago) 2 (July 1945).

Manville, Richard H.. "Report of deer attacking cougar." *Journal of Mammalogy* 36 (August 1955).

Marryat, Frederick. *The travels and adventures of Monsieur Violet in California, Sonora, and western Texas.* London: D. Bryce, 1843.

Marshall, Robert E. *The onza: the story of the search for the mysterious cat of the Mexican highlands.* New York: Exposition Press, 1961.

[May, W.B.]. *California game "marked down"; scenic mountain woodland coverts, and tide-marsh resorts for game.* San Francisco: Southern Pacific Co., 1896.

Mead, Charles W. "Conventional figures in ancient Peruvian art." *Anthropological Papers of the American Museum of Natural History* 12 (1916).

Mead, J.R. "Felis concolor." *Transactions of the Kansas Academy of Science* 16 (June 1899).

Means, Philip Ainsworth. *Ancient civilizations of the Andes.* New York and London: C. Scribner's Sons, 1931.

Membré, Zénobe. "Narrative of La Salle's voyage down the Mississippi, by Father Zenobius Membré, Recollect." In *Discovery and exploration of the Mississippi Valley,* edited by John Gilmary Shea. New York: Redfield, 1853.

Merriam, C. Hart. "The vertebrates of the Adirondack region, northeastern New York." *Transactions of the Linnaean Society of New York* 1 (1882).

————. "Description of two new pumas from the northwestern United States." *Proceedings of the Biological Society of Washington* 11 (1897).

————. "Preliminary revision of the pumas (Felis concolor group)." *Proceedings of the Washington Academy of Sciences* 3 (11 December 1901).

————. "Eight new mammals from the United States." *Proceedings of the Biological Society of Washington* 16 (1903).

Merriam, John C. "Recent discoveries of carnivora in the Pleistocene of Rancho La Brea." *Bulletin of the Department of Geology (University of California)* 7 (12 September 1912).

————. "New puma-like cat from Rancho La Brea." *Bulletin of the Department of Geology (University of California)* 10 (20 April 1918).

———— and Chester Stock. "Occurrence of Pleistocene vertebrates in an asphalt deposit near McKittrick, California." *Science,* n.s. 54 (9 December 1921).

———— ————. "The Felidae of Rancho La Brea." *Publications, Carnegie Institute of Washington* (December 1932).

Merritt Herald (Merritt, B.C.). "Son of former residents killed by cougar in Lytton." 6 January 1971.

Miller, Frederic Walter. "Notes on some mammals of southern Matto Grosso, Brazil." *Journal of Mammalogy* 11 (February 1930).

Mills, Enos A. "The mountain lion." *Saturday Evening Post* 190 (23 March 1918).

————. *Watched by wild animals.* Garden City, N.Y., and London: Doubleday, Page & Co., 1922.

————. *Wild animal homesteads.* New York: Doubleday, Page & Co., 1923.

Mills, William C. *Certain mounds and village sites in Ohio.* Vol. 2. Columbus: F.J. Heer, 1916.

Moe, Alfred K. "Honduras." *House of Representatives Document.* U.S. Congress. House. 58th Cong., 3d sess., 1904, pt. 4.

Molina, Christoval de. *An account of the fables and rites of the Yncas.* Edited by Clements R. Markham. London: Hakluyt Society 48 (1873).

Molina, Juan Ignacio. *Saggio sulla storia naturale del Chili, del signor abate Giovanni Ignazio Molina.* Bologna: 1782.

Morley, Jack. "A sea-going cougar." *Outdoorsman* 86 (November-December 1944).

Morris, John A. "California lion pets." *Sports Afield* 17 (December 1896).

Mott, Leon T., as told to Junius Armfield. "Stalking the giant puma." *Sports Afield Hunting Annual* (1963).

Murie, Adolph. "Mammals from Guatemala and British Honduras." *Miscellaneous Publications of the Museum of Zoology, University of Michigan* 26 (July 1935).

Murray, Andrew. *The geographical distribution of mammals.* London: Day & Son, 1866.

Musgrave, M.E. "Some habits of mountain lions in Arizona." *Journal of Mammalogy* 7 (November 1926).

Naggiar, Morrie. "The Florida panther." *Florida Wildlife* 36 (September-October 1982).

Nash, Ogden. *Many long years ago.* Boston: Little, Brown & Co., 1945.

National Wildlife Federation. "Slowing down and yielding to the Florida panther." *Conservation News and Features* 2 (December 1984).

[Neal, John]. *Brother Jonathan; or, the New Englander.* Vol. 1. Edinburgh: W. Blackwood, 1825.

Neill, Wilfred T. "On the trail of the jaguarondi, Florida's black cat of mystery." *Florida Wildlife* 15 (July 1961).

Nelson, E.W., and E.A. Goldman. "List of pumas, with three described as new." *Journal of Mammalogy* 10 (November 1929).

———— ————. "Three new pumas." *Journal of the Washington Academy of Science* 21 (1931).

132

_____ _____. "A new mountain lion from Vancouver Island." *Proceedings of the Biological Society of Washington* 45 (15 July 1932).

_____ _____. "A new puma from Brazil." *Journal of the Washington Academy of Science* 23 (15 November 1933).

Nessmuk [George W. Sears]. "Hemlock sketches No. VI." *Porter's Spirit of the Times* 8 (31 March 1860).

New York Herald. "Boy and girl get medal for heroic fight with panther." 15 August 1917.

Newcomb, Franc Johnson, Stanley Fishler, and Mary C. Wheelright. "A study of Navajo symbolism." *Papers of the Peabody Museum of American Archeology & Ethnography* 32 (1956).

Newell, David M. *Cougars & cowboys.* New York and London: Century Co., 1927.

_____. "Panther!" *Saturday Evening Post* 208 (13 July 1935).

Nowak, Lt. Ronald M. "Panther killed in Louisiana." *Defenders of Wildlife* 41 (April-May-June 1966).

_____. "Louisiana protects wolf, cougar, and all birds of prey." *Defenders of Wildlife* 46 (Fall 1971).

_____. *The cougar in the United States and Canada.* U.S. Department of the Interior, Fish and Wildlife Service, Washington, D.C., and the New York Zoological Society, New York (1976).

Núñez Cabeza de Vaca, Alvar. *La relacion que dio Alvar Núñez Cabeça de Vaca de lo acaescido en las Indias en la armada donde yua por gouernador Pãphilo de Narbaez.* Zamora: 1542.

Office of Endangered Species and International Activities. "Threatened wildlife of the United States." *Resource Publication* 114. Bureau of Sport Fisheries and Wildlife, U.S. Department of the Interior, Washington, D.C. (1973).

Oldschool, Oliver, ed. "American scenery — for the Port Folio." *Port Folio (Dennie),* n.s., 8 (December 1812).

O'Reilly, Edward. "The saga of Pecos Bill." *Century Magazine* 106 (October 1923).

Osgood, Wilfred H. "Mammals from western Venezuela and eastern Colombia." *Publications. Field Museum of Natural History, Zoological Series* 10 (10 January 1912).

_____. "The mammals of Chile." *Fieldiania: Zoology* 30 (1943).

Page, Warren. "Lion hunters are nuts." *Field and Stream* 71 (November 1966).

Paradiso, John. "Melanism in Florida bobcats." *Florida Scientist* 36 (Spring, Summer, Fall 1973).

Parsons, P.A. "[Do cougars attack and kill humans?]." *Outdoor Life* 100 (August 1947).

Pauw, Cornelius. *Recherches philosophiques sur les Américains, ou Mémoires intéressants pour servir à l'histoire de l'espèce humaine.* London: 1771.

Pearce, Stewart. *Annals of Luzerne County* [Pennsylvania]; *a record of interesting events, traditions, and anecdotes.* Philadelphia: J.B. Lippincott & Co., 1860.

Pearson, Oliver P. "Mammals in the highlands of southern Peru." *Bulletin of the Museum of Comparative Zoology at Harvard College* 106 (June 1951).

Penn, William. *A letter from William Penn proprietary and governour of Pennsylvania in America, to the committee of the Free Society of Traders of that Province, residing in London.* London: 1683.

Pennant, Thomas. *Synopsis of quadrupeds.* Chester: J. Monk, 1771.

_____. *History of quadrupeds.* London: 1793.

Peregrinus [Dr. Robert H. Rose]. "A panther hunt in Pennsylvania." *Port Folio (Dennie)* 17 (June 1824).

Perry, W.A. "The cougar." In *The big game of North America.* Edited by G.O. Shields. Chicago and New York: Rand, McNally & Co., 1890.

Peterson, Willis. "The Mogollon Rim." *Arizona Highways* 43 (October 1967).

Pfefferkorn, Ignaz. *Beschreibung der landschaft Sonora.* Cologne: 1794.

Phillips, J.C. "A new puma from lower California." *Proceedings of the Biological Society of Washington* 25 (4 May 1912).

Pike, James. *The scout and ranger: being the personal adventures of Corporal Pike.* Cincinnati and New York: J.R. Hawley & Co., 1865.

Piso, Willem. *Historia natvralis Brasiliae.* [Posthumous description of Georg Marcgrave]. Amsterdam: 1648.

_____. *Gulielmi Pisonis ... De Indiae utriusque re naturali et medica libri qvatvordecim.* Amsterdam: 1658.

Pocock, R.I. "Description of a new race of puma (*Puma concolor*), with a note on an abnormal tooth in the genus." *Annals and Magazine of Natural History.* London 6 (September 1940).

Police News. "Here, there and everywhere." *Illustrated Police News, Law Courts and Weekly Record* (Boston) 17 December 1874.

Preble, Edward A. "A biological investigation of the Athabaska-Mackenzie region." *North American Fauna* 27 (26 October 1908).

Prichard, Hesketh. "Field-notes upon some of the larger mammals of Patagonia, made between September 1900 and June 1901." *Proceedings of the Zoological Society of London* 1 (15 April 1902).

_____. *Through the heart of Patagonia.* New York: D. Appleton & Co., 1902.

Rafinesque, C.S. "Extracts from the journal of Mr. Charles Le Raye, relating to some new quadrupeds of the Missouri region, with notes by C.S.R." *American Monthly Magazine and Critical Review* 1 (1817).

_____. "On the North American couguars." *Atlantic Journal and Friend of Knowledge* 1 (1832).

_____. "Couguars of Oregon." *Atlantic Journal and Friend of Knowledge* 1 (1832).

_____. "On the Zapotecas and other tribes of the state of Oaxaca." *Atlantic Journal and Friends of Knowledge* 1 (1832).

Raleigh, Sir W. *The discoverie of the large, rich, and bevvifvl empire of Gviana, with a relation of the great and golden citie of Manoa (which the Spanyards call El Dorado) and the prouinces of Emeria, Arromaia, Amapaia and other countries, with their riuers, adjoyning.* London: Robert Robinson, 1596.

[Rambler]. *Guide to Florida.* New York: American News Co., 1875.

Rawlings, Marjorie Kinnan. *Cross Creek.* New York: C. Scribner's Sons, 1942.

Ray, John. *Synopsis methodica animalium quadrupedum et serpentini generis.* London: S. Smith & B. Walford Society, 1693.

Raymond, Henry J., ed. "The lion and its kind." *Harper's New Monthly Magazine* 10 (May 1855).

Remington, Frederic. "Mountain lions in Yellowstone Park." *Collier's Weekly* 24 (17 March 1900).

Rengger, J.R. *Naturgeschichte der säugethiere von Paraguay.* Basel: 1830.

_____. *Reise nach Paraguay in den jahren 1818 bis 1826.* Aarau: H.E. Saeurlaender, 1835.

Richie, Don. "'Naturalized' citizens without citizenship papers." *All Florida Magazine* 9 (15 January 1961).

Riley, James Whitcomb. *The complete works of James Whitcomb Riley.* Vol. 4. Indianapolis: Bobbs-Merrill Co., 1913.

Robinette, W. Leslie, Jay S. Gashwiler, and Owen W. Morris. "Food habits of the cougar in Utah and Nevada." *Journal of Wildlife Management* 23 (July 1959).

————. "Notes on cougar productivity and life history." *Journal of Mammalogy* 42 (May 1961).

Rogers, Maj. Robert. *A concise account of North America.* London: 1765.

Rogers, Woodes. *A cruising voyage round the world: first to the South-Seas, thence to the East-Indies, and homewards by the Cape of Good Hope.* London: 1712.

Rollins, Philip Ashton. *The cowboy.* New York: Charles Scribner's Sons, 1936.

Roosevelt, Theodore. *Hunting trips of a ranchman: sketches of sport on the northern cattle plains.* New York and London: G.P. Putnam's Sons, 1885.

————. *The wilderness hunter.* New York: G.P. Putnam's Sons, 1893.

————. "With the cougar hounds." *Scribner's Magazine*, pts. 1 and 2, 30 (October-November 1901).

————. "A cougar hunt on the rim of the Grand Canyon." *Outlook* 105 (4 October 1913).

Roth, Vincent. *Notes and observations on animal life in British Guiana, 1907-1941; a popular guide to colonial mammalia.* Georgetown: Daily Chronicle, 1941.

Round, W.E. "When nature fails." *Field and Stream* 42 (April 1938).

Rowe, Nicholas, ed. "White mountain lions." *American Field*, 20 (1 September 1883).

Rubin, L.D. "Pride of lions." *Field and Stream* 70 (November 1965).

Ruiz Herrero, Miguel. "Nicaragua, paraiso de cazadores." *Revista Conservadora* (Managua) 7 (September 1963).

Sahagún, Bernardino de. *Historia general de las cosas de Nueva España.* Vol. 2. Mexico: A. Valdés, 1829.

St. Amant, Lyle S. *Louisiana wildlife inventory and management plan.* New Orleans: Louisiana Wild Life and Fisheries Commission, 1959.

Sanderson, Ivan T. *Living mammals of the world.* Garden City, N.Y: Hanover House, 1961.

Sass, Herbert Ravenel. "The cat of the Cherokees." *Collier's* 77 (5 June 1926).

————. "The panther prowls the East again!" *Saturday Evening Post* 226 (13 March 1954).

Schomburgk, Richard. *Reisen in Britisch-Guiana in den jahren 1840-1844.* Leipzig: J.J. Webber, 1848.

Schomburgk, Sir Robert. "Information respecting botanical travellers." *Annals and Magazine of Natural History*, London 4 (1840).

Schreber, Johann Christian Daniel. *Die säugethiere in abbildungen nach der natur.* Vols. 2, 3. Erlangen: 1775, 1778.

Schueren, Arnold C. *Foxy's lion tales.* Chicago: N.p., 1943.

————. "Utah lion hunt." *Field and Stream* 50 (September 1945).

Scott Valley News (Fort Jones, Calif.). "Killed by a panther." 28 June 1890.

Scott, William Berryman. *A history of land mammals in the Western Hemisphere.* New York: Macmillan Co., 1937.

Sealander, John A. "Mountain lion in Arkansas." *Journal of Mammalogy* 32 (August 1951).

Seger, John H., trans. *Tradition of the Cheyenne Indians.* Colony, Okla.: Arapaho Bee Print, 1905.

Seidensticker, John C., IV, Maurice G. Hornocker, Wilber V. Wiles, and John P. Messick. "Mountain lion social organization in the Idaho Primitive Area." *Wildlife Monographs, Wildlife Society* 35 (December 1973).

Seton, Ernest Thompson. *Lives of game animals.* Vol. 1. New York: Doubleday, Doran & Co., 1929.

Severtzow, M.N. "Notice sur la classification multisériale des carnivores, spécialement des Félidés, et les études de zoologie générale qui s'y rattachent." *Revue et magasin de zoologie pure et appliquée* 10 (1858).

Shaw, Harley G. "A mountain lion field guide." *Special Report, Arizona Game and Fish Department* 9 (December 1979).

Shoemaker, Henry W. "The panther cry." *Altoona Tribune* (Altoona, Pa.). 12 January 1914.

————. *The Pennsylvania lion or panther, a narrative of our grandest game animal.* Altoona: Altoona Tribune Co., 1914.

————. *Extinct Pennsylvania animals.* Pt. 1. Altoona, Pa.: Altoona Tribune Publishing Co., 1917.

————. "The panther in Pennsylvania." *Pennsylvania Game News* 13 (February 1943).

————. "Panthers kill 9 persons in Pennsylvania." *Altoona Mirror* (Altoona, Pa.). 5 November 1951.

Simms, William Gilmore. "Personal and literary memorials." In "An edition of William Gilmore Simm's 'The Cub of the Panther.'" Ph.D. diss. by Mariam Jones Shillingsburg, University of South Carolina, Columbia, 1969.

————. "The cub of the panther; a mountain legend." *The Old Guard* 7 (August 1869).

————. "How Sharp Snaffles got his capital and wife." *Harper's New Monthly Magazine* 41 (October 1870).

Siskiyou Telegraph (Yreka, Calif.). "A horrible death — a little boy killed and partly devoured by panthers." 28 June 1890.

Sitton, Larry W., Susan Sitton, and Dick Weaver. "Mountain lion predation on livestock in California." *California-Nevada Wildlife* (1978).

Smith, Howard H. "My lions." *American Sportsman* 2 (Spring 1969).

Smith, Captaine John. *The General Historie of Virginia, New-England, and the Summer Isles with the names of the Adventurers, Planters and Governours from their first beginning, Ano: 1584 to this present 1624.* London: 1624.

S[mith], O.O. "Story of a cougar skin." *Forest and Stream* 71 (14 November 1908).

Smith, Samuel. *The history of the colony of Nova-Caesaria, or New-Jersey.* Burlington, N.J.: James Parker, 1765.

Smith, Spencer H. "Amendments to lists of endangered fish and wildlife." *Federal Register* 38 (4 June 1973).

Society for the Investigation of the Unexplained. "Black pumas." *Pursuit* (Columbia, N.J.) 5 (January 1972).

Soto, Hernando de. *Relaçam verdadeira dos trabalhos q̃ ho gouernador dõ Fernãdo d'Souto.* Evora, Portugal: A. de Burgos, 1557.

Spargo, John. *The catamount in Vermont.* Bennington, Vt.: N.p., 1950.

Sparke (the younger), John. *The voyage made by Iohn Hawkins Esquire.* In Richard Hakluyt *The principal navigations, voyages, traffiques and discoveries of the English nation.* Glasgow: 1565.

Spears, John Randolph. *The gold diggings of Cape Horn: a study of life in Tierra del Fuego and Patagonia.* New York: G.P. Putnam's Sons, 1895.

Spelman, Henry. *Relation of Virginia by Henry Spelman, 1609.* London: Claiswick Press, 1872.

Spillman, Franz. *Die säugethiere Ecuadors im wandel der zeit.* Quito: Universidad central, 1931.

Spokane Chronicle (Spokane, Wash.). "Spokane boy killed by cougar." 18 December 1924.

Spokesman-Review (Spokane, Wash.). "Cougar killed boy in battle." 19 December 1924.

Stevenson, William Burnet. *Historical and descriptive narrative of twenty years' residence in South America.* Vol. 2. London: Longman, Rees, Orma, Brown & Green, 1829.

Stone, Livingston. "Habits of the panther in California." *American Naturalist* 17 (November 1883).

Storer, Tracy I. "Rabies in a mountain lion," *California Fish and Game* 9 (April 1923).

Strong, William Duncan. "Indian records of California carnivores." *Journal of Mammalogy* 7 (1926).

Suminski, H. Russell. "Mountain lion predation on domestic livestock in Nevada." *Proceedings of the Tenth Vertebrate Pest Conference.* University of California, Davis. (June 1982).

Thomas, Oldfield. "On a new form of puma from Patagonia." *Annals and Magazine of Natural History.* London. 7 (September 1901).

Thompson, Zadock. *The natural history of Vermont, and an appendix.* Burlington, Vt.: N.p., 1853.

Thomson, William. *Great cats I have met, adventures in two hemispheres.* Boston: Alpha Publishing Co., 1896.

[Thoreau, Henry David]. "Chesuncook." *Atlantic Monthly* 2 (August 1858).

Thornton, J. Fred. "Mountain lion comeback in Alabama." *Alabama Conservation* 25 (March-April 1954).

Tinsley, Henry G. "Western mountain lions." *Century* 100 (September 1920).

Tinsley, Jim Bob. *The Florida panther.* St. Petersburg, Fla.: Great Outdoors Publishing Co., 1970.

_____. "Reprieve and recovery of the Florida panther." *Central Florida Outdoors* 1 (April-May 1971).

Tioga Eagle (Wellsboro, Pa.). "A man killed by a panther." 10 February 1847.

Tiscornia, Eleuterio F. *"Martín Fierro" comentado y anotado.* Vol. 1. Buenos Aires: Coni, 1925.

Tozzer, Alfred M., and Glover M. Allen. "Animal figures in the Mayan codices." *Papers of the Peabody Museum of American Archaeology and Ethnography* 4 (1910).

Traill, Thomas Stewart. "Description of a new species of Felis from Guyana." *Memoirs of the Wernerian Natural History Society.* Edinburgh 3 (1819).

_____. "Remarks on some of the American animals of the genus *Felis,* particularly on the jaguar, *Felis onca,* Linn." *Memoirs of the Wernerian Natural History Society.* Edinburgh 4 (1823).

True, Frederick W. "The puma, or American lion: Felis concolor of Linnaeus." *Report of the U.S. National Museum.* Miscellaneous Document 224 (1889).

Trumbull, Stephen. "Hunting for panthers in Florida isn't all it's cracked up to be." *Miami Herald.* 29 April 1946.

_____. "Florida panther hunt." *Florida Sportsman* 2 (July 1946).

Udall, Stewart L. "Native fish and wildlife endangered species." *Federal Register* 32 (11 March 1967).

Ulmer, Fred A., Jr. "Melanism in the Felidae, with special reference to the genus Lynx." *Journal of Mammalogy* 22 (14 August 1941).

U.S. Congress. "Endangered Species Protection Act." *Public Law 89-669.* Laws of the 89th Cong., 2d sess. (15 October 1966). 80 Stat. 926.

_____. "Endangered Species Conservation Act of 1969." *Public Law 91-135.* Laws of the 91st Cong., 1st sess. (5 December 1969). 83 Stat. 275.

_____. "Endangered Species Act of 1973." *Public Law 93-205.* Laws of the 93d Cong., 1st sess. (1973). 87 Stat. 884.

U.S. Forest Service. "Wilderness conflict." *Administrative Bulletin, Intermountain Region, U.S. Forest Service* 17 (13 May 1949).

Vazques de Espinosa, Antonio. "Compendium and description of the West Indies." Translated by Charles Upton Clark. *Smithsonian Miscellaneous Collections.* (Washington) 102 (1942).

Volkhardt, Davey Gnann. "When Florida was panther country." *Guide to North Florida Living* 2 (March-April 1982).

Vuletin, Alberto. *Zoonomia andina (nomenclature zoológico).* Santiago del Estero, Argentina: Folklore y Arqueología Publicaciones, 1960.

Wallace, Ralph. "Them reckless Lees of Tucson." *True* 28 (April 1951).

Walsh, Bill. "Panthers are popular." *Pennsylvania Game News* 27 (January 1956).

Ward, Rowland. *Rowland Ward's records of big game.* 9th ed. London: R. Ward, 1928.

Weddle, Ferris. "On the cougar's secretive trail." *Defenders of Wildlife News* 40 (January 1965).

_____. "A cougar is killed — a deer is saved." *Sierra Club Bulletin* 50 (September 1965).

_____. "The cougar: prince of wilderness country." *Defenders of Wildlife News* 41 (April-May-June 1966).

_____. "The cougar in our national parks and monuments." *National Parks Magazine* 40 (May 1966).

Wemmer, Christen and Kate Scow. "Communication in the Felidae with emphasis on scent markings and contact patterns." In *How animals communicate.* Edited by Thomas A. Seabok. Bloomington, Ind.: 1977.

West Coast Advocate (Port Alberni, B.C.). "Youngster dead after attack by loco cougar." 23 June 1949.

_____. "Jury holds death of child accidental." 30 June 1949.

White, Helen A. "Bare hands vs. fangs." *Western Sportsman* 12 (January-February 1952).

Whitney, Casper W. "The cougar." in *Hunting in many lands.* Edited by Theodore Roosevelt and George Bird Grinnell. New York: Forest and Stream Publishing Co., 1895.

Whymper, Edward. *Travels amongst the great Andes of the Equator.* New York: C. Scribner's Sons, 1892.

Williams, Samuel. *The natural and civil history of Vermont.* Walpole, N.H.: I. Thomas & D. Carlisle, 1794.

Williamson, William D. *The history of the state of Maine: from its first discovery, A.D. 1602, to the separation, A.D. 1820, inclusive.* Vol. 1. Hallowell, Maine: Glazier, Masters & Co., 1832.

Wilson, Alexander. "The foresters; a poem: descriptive of a pedestrian journey to the falls of Niagara, in the autumn of 1803." *Port Folio (Dennie)* 2 (July 1809).

Wood, William. *New Englands prospect: A true lively, experimental description of that part of America, commonly called New England.* London: 1639.

Works Progress Administration. *Palmetto place names.* Columbia, S.C.: Sloan Printing Co., 1941.

Wright, Bruce S. "The Fundy lions." *Field and Stream* 53 (September 1948).

_____. *The ghost of North America: the story of the eastern panther.* New York, Washington, Hollywood: Vantage Press, 1959.

_____. "The return of the cougar." *Audubon Magazine* 62 (November-December 1960).

_____. "The cougar in eastern Canada." *Canadian Audubon* 27 (November-December 1965).

_____. *The eastern panther: a question of survival.* Toronto and Vancouver: Clarke, Irwin & Co., 1972.

————. "The cougar in New Brunswick," in S.E. Jorgensen and David Mech, eds. *Proceedings of a symposium on the native cats of North America, their status and management*, Bureau of Sport Fisheries and Wildlife, Region 3, Twin Cities, Minn., 1971.

Wright, George M., and Ben H. Thompson. "Fauna of the national parks of the United States." *Contributions of the Wildlife Division, U.S. Department of the Interior.* Faunal Ser. 2 (July 1934).

Yorris, Xil. "The white panther." *Forest and Stream* 17 (8 September 1881).

Young, Stanley P. "Mountain lion eats its kitten." *Journal of Mammalogy* 8 (May 1927).

————. "Our wild lyric soprano." *American Forests* 73 (August 1967).

———— and Edward A. Goldman. *The puma: mysterious American cat.* Washington: American Wildlife Institute, 1946.

Zumbo, Jim. "The great cougar comeback." *Outdoor Life* 171 (February 1984).

Index

138

139

142